Richard Halliburton (1900–1939) was America's greatest adventurer and one of the most successful adventure travel writers of the twentieth century. Through a life spent chasing horizons and concocting ever more daring schemes – from swimming the length of the Panama Canal to flying around the world in an open cockpit plane or crossing the Alps on an elephant – Halliburton dazzled the Western world. His final adventure, sailing a junk across the Pacific, was also his last. Halliburton disappeared in March 1939 and was never seen again. A great and original traveller, his wild adventures live on in the books that have captivated millions of readers and inspired generations of writers.

'From the Jazz Age through the Great Depression to the eve of World War II, he thrilled an entire generation of readers. Clever, resourceful, undaunted, cheerful in the face of dreadful odds, ever-optimistic about the world and the people around him, always scheming about his next adventure... a spokesman for the youth of a generation.'

James O'Reilly

Tauris Parke Paperbacks is an imprint of I.B.Tauris. It is dedicated to publishing books in accessible paperback editions for the serious general reader within a wide range of categories, including biography, history, travel, art and the ancient world. The list includes select, critically acclaimed works of top quality writing by distinguished authors that continue to challenge, to inform and to inspire. These are books that possess those subtle but intrinsic elements that mark them out as something exceptional.

The Colophon of Tauris Parke Paperbacks is a representation of the ancient Egyptian ibis, sacred to the god Thoth, who was himself often depicted in the form of this most elegant of birds. Thoth was credited in antiquity as the scribe of the ancient Egyptian gods and as the inventor of writing and was associated with many aspects of wisdom and learning.

THE FLYING CARPET

Adventures in a Biplane from Timbuktu to Everest and Beyond

Richard Halliburton

Foreword by Tahir Shah

TPP

TAURIS PARKE
PAPERBACKS

New paperback edition published in 2012 by Tauris Parke Paperbacks
An imprint of I.B.Tauris and Co Ltd
6 Salem Road, London W2 4BU
175 Fifth Avenue, New York NY 10010
www.ibtauris.com

Distributed in the United States and Canada Exclusively by Palgrave Macmillan
175 Fifth Avenue, New York NY 10010

First published in 1933 by Geoffrey Bles Ltd

Foreword copyright © Tahir Shah, 2012

Cover image: © Mary Evans Picture Library / Onslow Auctions Limited

ISBN: 978 1 84885 914 2

A full CIP record for this book is available from the British Library
A full CIP record is available from the Library of Congress

Library of Congress Catalog Card Number: available

Printed and bound in Sweden by ScandBook AB

CONTENTS

Maps showing the route of the Flying Carpet are on pages 24–5 and 184–5

FOREWORD

Great travel writing is all about evoking an atmosphere of adventure. But more than that, it's about storytelling, plain and simple. Far too many works of travel slip into obscurity because the writing is lacklustre, dated, or downright dull. Trawl the shelves of the London Library and you'll find miles and miles of books that are all but forgotten. And many of them deserve to be left there – deep underground. Yet from time to time you come across an author whose work is a beacon of originality.

The American adventurer, Richard Halliburton, whose life was snuffed out at far too early an age, was one such writer. Although his work has a small but devoted following, his books warrant a far greater readership – and are the kind of travel literature that have withstood the test of time, and continue to inspire the youth to achieve.

Born in 1900, in Brownsville, Tennessee, Halliburton was always destined for great things. His family were wealthy enough to send him to Princeton, a springboard into the Ivy League lifestyle so fêted in the rip-roaring Twenties. A contemporary of Hemingway, the young Halliburton had none of the melancholy and all of the passion. Brimming with charm, good looks and natural charisma, he was the kind of man to whom both men and women were drawn. While others were languishing on the terrors of the Great War, Halliburton was setting about making a name for himself by criss-crossing crumbling empires by any means possible. Making use of the media with impressive foresight, one can only imagine the heights he would have soared to given the technologies we all take for granted today.

To grasp Halliburton's celebrity, it helps to understand the time in which he lived. His playground was the world caught in a no-man's-land between the Wars. The British Empire still ruled the seas, ferocious tribes inhabited the endless African plains and the seething jungles of the Amazon and Borneo; and motor cars were a jeu du jour for tin-pot dictators, Maharajahs, and for anyone else with the means to afford them. But most of all, it was a time in which great marvels were still to be found, and in which new technologies suddenly put great holy grails of worldwide travel within reach. And, there was no piece of machinery more revolutionary in the arena of modern exploration than the aeroplane. A pioneer, a trailblazer, not to mention a media junkie, Halliburton understood the power of making a splash. In the vein of *Ripley's Believe It or Not*, he tantalized his readers with jaw-dropping accounts of intrigue, exploration and awe.

Of the handful of books he published, there is one that stands out as a monument to the time in which he lived, as much as it is a chronicle of everything Halliburton stood for. *The Flying Carpet* is a rare and enthusing tale of *Boy's Own* bravado. It's one of those books that stays with you, not so much because of the intoxicating roll call of adventure, but because of the frantic sizzle of the tale.

Halliburton may have been thirty but he was gripped as ever by the raw enthusiasm of a twelve-year-old. Longing to once again be, as he put it, a 'footloose vagabond', he searched for an aeroplane capable of crossing deserts and jungles, oceans and seas. Without hardly any preparation, and almost no background knowledge of flight, he bought one on the spur of the moment – a Stearman biplane. Shiny and small, with an open cockpit, he christened it 'The Flying Carpet'. The only thing needed now was a pilot.

By a stroke of luck he was introduced to a young Stanford graduate named Moye Stephens, who was employed to fly passengers over the Rockies. Sharing the same lust for daredevil adventure, Stephens readily agreed to pilot them both on a circumnavigation of the globe – 'to all the outlandish places on earth'. He was promised no pay, but unlimited expenses. His only question was when they were to leave. 'In half an hour,' Halliburton replied casually. And, pulling him to the door, they did.

The journey was the kind of feat that people are drawn to recreate today, but with a rigid safety net of support. And yet the alluring thing about Halliburton and Stephens' epic flight, was the absolute lack of safety, and the child-like zigzagging of wonders of the old world. Flying by the seats of their pants, and with almost nothing in the way of preparation, the pair set off into the unknown.

Halliburton was dead set on visiting Timbuktu first.

Lured by the mystery of the name and by its seeming inaccessibility, all he knew was that it was somewhere in Africa. To reach it, they traversed the United States eastwards from California, headed south through Europe, and into the mysterious hinterland of Morocco. Soaring high above the Atlas, they climbed to fifteen thousand feet, to avoid pot shots from the tribesmen eager to bring down a shiny little plane like theirs. And, then, laden with extra fuel, they began the gruelling flight southwards, with the endless dunes of the Sahara laid out in an endless ocean beneath. Warned time and again about sand storms, but taking no notice, they flew headlong into one after the next, their faces and The Flying Carpet rasped raw.

Causing immense excitement as it came to land at Timbuktu, the little biplane assured the two Americans immediate celebrity. They were received by Père Yakouba, the so-called 'White Monk of Timbuktu' – the first of many intriguing locals they encountered.

Flying on eastwards, they reached the Algerian Sahara, where they were welcomed into the folds of the French Foreign Legion, at Colomb-Béchar. Amazing all they met with acrobatics and tall tales of their journey so far, they flew back up to Europe. In an era in which travel was far more leisurely an activity, they took off and landed where they liked, *when* they liked. Reaching Italy through the Simplon Pass, they made a beeline for Venice, where they spent a month. Then they wondered where next. Halliburton wrote:

> Once more we unrolled our world map. Moye suggested Berlin. I voted for Malta. We compromised on Constantinople. A few hours later The Flying Carpet and its crew were in the air. Our first stop was Vienna. Then to Budapest – to Belgrade – to Bucharest – through storms, across plains, over mountains – on to Constantinople and the Golden Horn.

On and on they flew – across Turkey, down through the Holy Land, to Cairo and the Pyramids, over the Nabatean ruins of Petra, and eastwards over the great basalt desert to Baghdad. The frequency with which they landed must have reflected the trying conditions of low altitude open-cockpit flight. Yet always gung-ho in style, Halliburton's writing brushes aside the air-sickness from what must have been rollercoaster flights. But their eagerness to land was inspired, too, by a genuine delight in witnessing new realms.

At a time when the globe was not yet homogenized by mass media and equally mass travel, Halliburton and Stephens observed first-hand the last vestiges of the old world order. And wherever they went, their celebrity status was enough for the doors of palaces, monasteries, and jungle longhouses to be flung open for them. No one, it seemed, wanted to be left out.

3

In Baghdad, they took the young Crown Prince Ghazi up for a ride; and, in Persia, they carried aloft the daughter of the Shah, Princess 'Flower-of-the-Morning'. While in Persia, they helped out the stricken German aviatrix, Elly Beinhorn, who was flying solo around the world, and had just arrived from Timbuktu. Aged just twenty-three, she was the same age as Stephens. She must have outlived all the other early pilots for whom longevity was at odds with their sport. She finally passed away aged 100, in 2007.

Halliburton was a great believer in wonders of the world. He understood that associating his expedition with great landmarks would guarantee the media exposure he so desired. Soaring over the Taj Mahal was a natural way to hit the headlines back home, as was the daring flight in the shadows of Mount Everest. A devoted aficionado of George Mallory, who had perished on that mountain seven years before, Halliburton was desperate to do a fly-by in some kind of tribute.

Risking life and limb, and freezing solid in the ultra-thin air, they managed, with Halliburton, to take the first aerial shots of the mountain with his camera. The episode is Halliburton's description at its best. He wrote:

> And then Everest itself, indescribably magnificent, taunting the heavens with its gleaming crown. Her precipice, her clinging glacier shield, her royal streamer forever flying eastward from the throne, her court of gods and demons, her hypnotic, deadly beauty… what incomparable glory crowns this Goddess Mother of all mountains!

Of all the characters and encounters, my very favourite comes a little further, once they had traversed Burma, Indochina, and arrived at the seething steaming jungles of Borneo. There, they found the fabulously eccentric English aristocrat the 'Ranee' Lady Sylvia Brooke, whose husband ruled Sarawak, a principality the size of Britain, peopled with Dyak headhunters. The author of a remarkable book herself (entitled *Queen of the Headhunters*), they took her up and did acrobatics over the jungles that were her home.

An astounding success, the Flying Carpet Expedition helped in making Halliburton a household name across the United States. The adventure supposedly cost him $50,000, but he recouped twice that in media deals – a huge amount for the time. The project's popularity came about because of the intoxicating cocktail it contained. There was adventure in great measure, humour and a smattering of history. But, more importantly, there was the overwhelming sense that just about

4

anyone could follow Halliburton's lead and embark on a madcap escapade just like him.

And, for me, that's the great attraction of all his work. A fresh young-faced layman with no technical experience, Richard Halliburton surfed a tidal wave of enthusiasm and good old get-up-and-go. He wasn't trying to impress with groundbreaking hypotheses, or by discovering far-flung lands. Rather, his writing was a sympathetic lens through which ordinary people could experience the extraordinary world in which they lived. But most of all, it was storytelling *par excellence*.

Tahir Shah

CHAPTER I

THE FLYING CARPET

TEN thousand feet above the California hills. The airplane sailed through the sky with the ease and grace of a sea-gull. It hurdled the clouds, soared over the mountain-tops, dived toward the sea, and skimmed the waves. Two sets of gleaming golden wings extended on either side of the scarlet body. The motor and cowling were shining black; the tail was as gold as the wings. And down each side of the body stretched a golden band, bearing in small black letters a name—*The Flying Carpet*.

In this ship, with fleet lines and flashing colours, I was setting forth once again on the royal road to romance.

Several years had passed since last I travelled on this road. But they had not diminished my love for it. Instead, they had allowed me ample time to comprehend, in retrospect, the freedom I had enjoyed during my wander-days about the world as a sailor and a vagabond, and taught me I could never be content leading a life less strenuous, less venturesome, than that.

During these intervening years I had tried to accept the routine of a fixed existence. It had not been a happy experiment.

Now, tired of being prudent, of being tethered, I was returning to the old life. Returning . . . but this time with a newer, less earth-bound means of travel than the cargo boats and hobnail boots that once had served me.

Wings! With a winged ship, I could still be a vagabond, but a vagabond with the clouds for my province, as well as the continents. Jungle and desert—Africa and Himalaya—Arabia and the islands of the sea . . . with wings, I need only speak these names to be carried, swiftly, back into the adventurous lands.

When I visited the airports in search of a plane that

would fit my purpose, the salesmen had shown me big planes and little planes, biplanes and monoplanes. At last I noticed a small biplane with especially graceful yet sturdy lines. The wings were gold, the tapering body lacquered red. It was love at first sight.

"Will this ship fly over the Alps—over the Matterhorn and Mont Blanc?" I asked the agent.

"Easily," he replied.

"Will it cross the Sahara and the China Sea?"

"Yes—with extra tanks."

"Will it fly upside down, and loop-the-loop, and slow-roll, and whip-stall?"

"Better than any ship we have."

"Sold!"

And so I had the Flying Carpet.

But who would pilot it? I might learn to fly easily enough—was indeed already learning—but the mechanics of the engine, for me, would always remain black magic. The Flying Carpet must have a pilot-engineer who would understand what made the wheels go round.

By a stroke of good fortune I soon found the flying companion I was looking for, in Moye Stephens, Jr., a young Stanford graduate living in Los Angeles. For three years he had been carrying an airline's passengers back and forth across the Rockies on daily schedule, with a flawless record. The moment we met, I was impressed by his self-possessed appearance and quiet capable manner; so I went straight to the point.

"Stephens, I've just given myself an airplane. I want to fly in it to all the outlandish places on earth. Will you be the captain?"

"Certainly. I'll go."

"All right—we're leaving in half an hour."

"I can't do that—not in half an hour. There's the transport company. My plane and passengers . . ."

"Oh, resign! Your plane is only a big passenger bus anyway. I tell you I've a *flying carpet*."

"Guess I can fly carpets, too. But where are we going?"

"We're going to Turkey and Pasadena and Persia and Jerusalem and the North Pole and—Paris," I said, leading him out the front door. "We're going to fly across deserts and over mountains and rescue imprisoned princesses and fight dragons"—pushing him into a taxicab.

8

"Well, for Heaven's sake," he remonstrated, "—wait till I get my *hat*, will you!"

And so it happened that when the Flying Carpet first took to the air, Moye Stephens was at the controls. With him as pilot, the Carpet flew superbly. He made it loop, tumble, tail-spin, waltz, ride a bicycle and smoke cigars. We flew upside down. We located my house on the hilltop and tried to take the top brick off the chimney.

Moye's enthusiasm mounted with my own. Our confidence began to soar. We must have the world. We *could* have the world.

But not all at once—some place had to be first. Where —with such limitless horizons before us—where should we begin?

We did not argue long. We were going streaking straight to Africa and fly to Timbuctoo. All my life I'd been wanting to go to Timbuctoo. We did not know exactly where to find this mythical city. We only knew it was in Africa, fabulously far away, somewhere beyond the rim of the world. Legend had made it a symbol of remoteness, a city that was rather a phrase than a fact. We knew that only a handful of white visitors had been there, and that these few had not dissipated to any great extent its shroud of mystery. But no matter how inaccessible, we could find it now. We had wings! We had the Flying Carpet. To-morrow morning we would bid farewell to California and depart for Timbuctoo.

And to-morrow morning, we *did*.

Across America the Flying Carpet sped, frightening cattle on the plains of Texas, dodging steeples in Tennessee, struggling through fogs in Pennsylvania, and reached New York. Here the little problem of the Atlantic faced us. Europe, which meant the route to Africa, lay three thousand miles away, and our cruising radius was not even one quarter of that. So we lifted the airplane aboard a liner, and, when again on land, spread our wings for Paris.

Even Paris could not arrest the ardour of our quest for Timbuctoo. So southward we flew, ever toward Africa, down the Rhone Valley with the Alpine barricade of ice gleaming in the east.

The Pyrenees faced us next. Storm clouds enveloped them. We could not go over, we must go round, and around meant going out to sea. So out to sea we sailed, and straight down the rocky, sun-scorched coast of Spain.

I knew it was coming, and strained my eyes to watch for it. The Rock of Gibraltar! We had come this way because I wanted to revisit the almighty Rock—and there it was just ahead, revealed in a burst of sunshine, imperious and provocative as ever.

We flew nearer and nearer to its thousand-foot precipices. What memories I had of that great fortress! Once before, on a juvenile vagabond tour of Spain, I had climbed to its utmost peak and beheld the two oceans, the two continents, and believed that *this*, surely, was the climax of adventure. Now here I was, back again, five thousand feet above the great symbol that had set bonfires aglow in me at twenty-one. Back again in the tracks of my first royal road to romance—but this time, I knew, would be even more enchanting than the first. In my wildest fancies I had never dreamed then, atop Gibraltar's pinnacles, of flying carpets some day flying me back above that eagle's nest and off to Timbuctoo.

Several times around the Rock we sailed. Then with a salute of wobbled wings to the old tyrant, we darted out over the Straits, and sped on toward Morocco—a gold and scarlet arrow gleaming in the sunshine, high above the indigo waters of the Mediterranean Sea.

CHAPTER II

FROM HERE TO TIMBUCTOO

WITH Fez behind we were in the air again; and never had the Flying Carpet flown so fast. But fast as we flew the storm gathered faster. Sand-spouts were whirling angrily about us, raising their heads like enraged cobras a hundred feet into the air and racing across the desert. Now they had mingled their smoke together in one vast pall blown furiously along by a steady blast. We struggled higher to escape it—and lost the earth completely. So we plunged back into the stratum of flying Sahara. We pitched and spun. The sand dug beneath our goggles, into our eyes, into our nostrils, mouths, lungs. There was no tiniest part of us or the motor where those frantic grains did not penetrate.

We were on our way to the oasis of Colomb Bechar—the jumping-off place for Timbuctoo.

Back in Fez, where we had come down to earth after our flight over the Straits of Gibraltar, we had made ready to face the difficulties ahead. We had found there were two ways to reach our goal. One was to fly down the western coast of Africa for eighteen hundred miles, and then, at Dakar, follow the Senegal and Niger Rivers inland a thousand miles more. The other way was over the Atlas Mountains into the Sahara and sixteen hundred miles straight through the heart of the vastest, hottest, cruellest desert in the world.

We chose the second route. It offered considerably more dangers and complications, but we felt that the saving in distance would compensate for these—and anyway, the idea of tackling the Sahara with our Flying Carpet greatly appealed to us.

We had to tackle the Atlas Mountains first. Two hundred miles beyond them lay Colomb Bechar, the first outpost of the vast sand ocean. Here we would fill our gas tanks to the brim, and say good-bye to the civilised world.

The moment we left Fez behind, the snowy summits of these mountains faced us. From the flying field there, at sunset the night before, we had watched the purple shadows fall across their barricades of ice. We blessed them, then, for their gleaming pure beauty, for their cold streams of water, for the protection they gave us against the furnace of the Sahara burning on the other side. But now that we must come to grips with them in the Flying Carpet, with their blasts and their cloud banks, they did not seem so amiable.

Nor were altitude and storms the only hazards. The Atlas Mountains were enjoying a lively war at the time between their bandit inhabitants and French troops. Airplanes were being used extensively to bomb the rebels, who in turn had the ill grace to shoot back at all airplanes. There were incredibly fine shots . . . and a gold and scarlet target such as the Flying Carpet would be an inspiration to their marksmen.

Their greatest hope was that the airplane crew could be brought to earth alive, for then they could enjoy sweet and slow revenge against the unassailable infidels who slaughtered their high mountain-top villages with bombs.

However, at fourteen thousand feet the Arab sharpshooters would probably miss us.

We climbed to fifteen thousand.

At this height, well above the highest peaks, we were almost torn to pieces by the wind. But our Flying Carpet was a strong little ship. We endured; we held together: and finally we struggled safely over without being annihilated by the blasts or shot down by the mountaineers.

On the north side of the Atlas the land had been deep in verdure, flowing with water, fragrant with Spring. On the south side stretched the wilderness of the great Sahara. Down close to it we flew to pick up our course leading to Colomb Bechar.

But to have escaped the mountain-tops and reached the desert proved to be only a leap from one difficulty into another. We had been warned in Fez against trying to fly the Sahara at this time, for the sand-storm season was at hand. If caught by such a storm, flying carpets, magic or otherwise, could only expect disaster. During April,

May and June, the scorching winds rush and rage across the unbroken wastes, churning the sand into a wild cloud and driving this cloud forward at incredible speed. No pilot can see fifty feet ahead, and no engine can function long, in such a stinging yellow fog.

But however great the risk, we must go now. To wait three months for the sand-storm season to end was out of the question. We would trust to luck—and pray.

Alas, our prayers were not answered.

It was immediately evident as we struck the flat desert country that the winds we had encountered on top the Atlas were not limited to the upper altitudes. They were blowing straight from the Sahara, and diminished not at all as we dived to lower levels to pick up the faint desert trail that was our only guide.

Moye and I noticed them at the same time—sand-spouts ahead. They should have warne dus. They *did* warn us, but it seemed so unreasonable—so like a story-book— for us to encounter a sand-storm the very first day, the very first moment, we saw the desert. Perhaps this wasn't the real article—just a feint, a mild sand shower. Anyway we knew we could not get back now—dared not go back, with our fuel so nearly spent—over that range of mountains. We must face whatever lay ahead.

But all doubts about the true nature of the storm were soon swept away, when, after a few moments more, the see-thing fog of sand grew so dense that the daylight was turned off and twilight encompassed us. Moye forced the engine to its utmost speed. We had about fifty miles to fly to reach the Colomb Bechar military landing field. Could we endure that long? . . . could we hold our course through the yellow darkness?

A dozen times we had been warned that if we struck a storm of sand we must come down and land at once. But we couldn't land; we were in a gullied valley strewn with boulders. I felt myself growing more and more taut from anxiety. The handkerchief tied over my mouth and nose helped not in the least to keep out those diabolic grains which the storm flung upon us in ever-increasing fury. But Moye had his jaws set, and continued to hurl us forward, grimly, relentlessly, at a hundred and twenty miles an hour. He had no intention whatsoever of landing, for landing on such ground would be no less dangerous than continuing to fly. . . . Only a few miles more should remain before we came to the oasis. We dropped still lower to watch for it—within a hundred feet of the ground—into the thick of things. . . . Where, oh, where, was Colomb Bechar? We had to look around the windshields now, for they were completely blanketed with sand caught there by the splattered oil. A blast of needles struck us in the face . . . but there, there, below, were palm trees bent over by the wind . . . and a fort. . . and a broad smooth field. Gasping and exhausted we brought the airplane down to earth. It took twenty soldiers to drag our Carpet through the onslaught of the storm into the military hangar.

For six days the sixteen hundred miles of unbroken yellow ocean that still separated us from Timbuctoo was tortured by the sand hurricanes. However, the day came when the desert was quiet once more, though for how long no one could say. We were able to start south again.

The question of fuel now had to be faced. Our capacity at best was only seven hundred miles. There was a military motor track we were supposed to follow, leading across the Sahara to the Niger River, thirteen hundred miles away. Once every fortnight from October till May a truck is driven along this track. To fuel the truck, automobile gasoline was on deposit at an oasis four hundred miles farther south, and again in a solitary unattended tank—the loneliest fuel station in the world—five hundred miles beyond that. This supply took one still another four hundred miles to a military post called Gao, on the Niger. The last three hundred miles were westward along the river to Timbuctoo.

So, provided we could follow the track from one deposit to another, we would have enough gasoline. To do this with an airplane is, under the best conditions, exceedingly difficult, so faintly is the trail marked upon the desert. But now that one million square miles of sand had been charging back and forth over the track for six days it was questionable whether there was any trail left whatsoever.

And yet one dare not lose it. For a thousand miles to either side there is absolutely and literally nothing but sand, sand, sand. At sea there is a chance for a floating wreck to be found by passing ships. But no ship ever passes here. The caravan route is hundreds of miles to the west. If our Flying Carpet lost the thread we had an area as large as all the United States east of the Mississippi to be lost in, and as barren and waterless as the moon.

If we were forced down *on* the trail, we had, at worst, fourteen days to wait for the truck, provided we could live that long with the thermometer at one hundred and twenty degrees eight hours each day.

There was the possibility of missing the tank of gasoline and running out of fuel.

Another cursed sand-storm was more than likely to attack us, for the season was now well advanced.

However, that was the situation and we simply had to face it. We were not in the least discouraged. In fact the very difficulties ahead gave us a certain elation. We had not expected to find the Sahara other than cruel and defiant. Had it been safe, had it been commonplace, there would have been no challenge to meet, no satisfaction in overcoming it. We felt sure the airplane could get safely across; we needed only confidence in ourselves.

I knew it would take all Moye's skill to get the Carpet off the ground, so heavy-laden was it with fuel and provisions —every tank overflowing, and food and water for two weeks. We found a hundred thousand square miles of flat desert adjoining the military field, and decided that if our plane wouldn't rise and fly to Timbuctoo, we'd taxi there on the ground.

But it rose, slowly, slowly, in the hot dry air, an inch at a time . . . turned . . . and faced the Sahara.

If the Sahara has a soul, that soul must have looked down, or up, with astonishment as the gold and scarlet Carpet, shining and alive, climbed into the copper sky, and sailed straight out across the infinity of sand.

Our great and immediate concern was the motor track below. Fortunately the track had not disappeared; that is, not entirely. For long stretches the sand had covered it over completely, but by climbing to five thousand feet we could pick it up ahead or behind, and thus orient ourselves again.

At a hundred miles an hour the Sahara was sliding by, hard, dead, petrified, burning our lungs with its heated winds and our eyes with its blazing glare. As the leagues upon leagues of nothingness rolled on we began hungrily to watch for relief from this monotony—monotony of topography, of colour, of sky, of horizon. So delighted were we, after two hundred miles of desert emptiness, to note ahead a cluster of tiny oases, watered by wells, that we circled low over their palm-tops to assure ourselves the trees were real, and not mirage.

Another hundred miles beyond, the wastes were broken by a vast island of soft yellow sand dunes, tossed into great troughs and ridges by the winds. Reaching out in desperation from the edges of this creeping sand juggernaut, appeared the strangled tops of palm trees—all that remained of an oasis which these relentless dunes had buried alive.

Four hundred miles from Colomb Bechar our disappearing-and-reappearing motor track led us to the oasis of Adrar, where another supply of truck fuel awaited us.

Adrar seemed as old as the Sahara. Its huts, built of mud, had stood a thousand years in this rainless, changeless land. The majority of its five hundred black-skinned Arab inhabitants had never in all their lives been a mile beyond the protection of the palm trees, nor had their fathers or grandfathers before them. This—the illimitable burning sand, the cool shadow of one grove of palms—this was the world. Rain they had hardly ever seen; snow was undreamed of; rivers, fairy tales; an ocean. . . . One of the old village chiefs took us to the tiny trickle of brackish water his women-folk lifted by buckets from a well. This trickle irrigated his palms and gave life to a cluster of wild iris—iris, even in the Sahara. The old chief's eyes sparkled with pride as he asked us in gestures, eloquently enough, if we had ever *seen* so much water. We told him solemnly that we never had. True, he had heard there was a little lake in Colomb Bechar, but that was a month's journey by caravan, and he had never been able to go so far from home. We had filled our water-bottles at that lake five hours before!

Next morning, assisted in our departure by every member of the village down to the smallest child, we struck out to find a tank of gasoline five hundred miles away.

The key to the tank-lock we had in our pocket, as it had been given to us back in Colomb Bechar. It was understood that we were to measure the number of gallons we took, refasten the lock and deliver the key at Gao, four hundred miles farther south. The price of gas at this extraordinary station was four dollars a gallon, so that this one fuelling would cost four hundred dollars. Even so, at any price, we were grateful for the Shell Oil Company's enterprise in having put it there.

On leaving Adrar, Moye and I took up another notch in our belts. This flight was to be the central span, the big effort, for our Flying Carpet. New York to Chicago, and not a hill or a house or a tree. A million square miles of blazing sun and flatness and unbroken nothing—nothing, save one half-buried tank of precious gasoline.

And we must cross this stretch. There could be no compromise. Our engine must function. There must be no sand-storms. We must not lose the piloting thread. We must not miss that tank!

Again the hours and the miles rolled by. Moye's eyes and mine were fixed grimly on the wisp of a track. We lost it—wheeled about to pick it up—lost it—found it—hide-and-seek all morning long.

The sky grew more dazzlingly, tormentingly hot as noon approached. The flat hard earth flung back its glare. Our water-bottles were lifted more and more frequently to our lips.

I had pictured in my mind, in advance, what the centre of the Sahara was going to be like. It was going to be gullied and scarred, crisscrossed by ranges of black and barren mountains where the lions had their dens and prowled at night about the encampments of the wandering Bedouin caravans.

Not one of my prearrangements came true. There were no black mountains, no gullies, no scars, no lions and no Bedouins—only an endless, endless, ash-yellow sea of sandy gravel in which no life, human, animal, bird, insect or vegetable, lived or could live. Nothing ever moves but the wind and the sand. Nothing ever changes save the alternate light and darkness. In more than a million square miles only a streak of scarlet and its two lonely passengers broke the vacuum.

Moye and I took turns at the controls. By shifting, one of us could always give undivided attention to the nice sheet of totally blank white paper that served us as a map—blank because there was nothing for the carto-grapher to record except blankness.

During my idle periods I could not keep my mind off the morbid stories I'd heard in Colomb Bechar about death on the Sahara. There was the story of the French officer who, in an attempt to get to the Mediterranean coast from the Niger River, tried to drive a small motor-car the two thousand miles to Algiers along the route we were following. He broke down in the middle of this vast waste, over four hundred miles from the nearest oasis. He had water for two weeks. The two weeks passed, and a third, spent mostly underneath his automobile to escape the murderous sun—alone, with a dead engine. On the twenty-first day his last drop of heroically conserved water had been drunk. He was loading his revolver, to spare himself the last hours of torture—when the trans-Saharan military truck, one week behind schedule, came by.

There was the story of the French army airplane transporting a general on a non-stop flight from Fez to the Niger. The pilot lost the motor track (nothing could be easier, as we knew) and made a forced landing. In doing so he ground-looped and stood his plane on end, breaking the general's shoulder. For some inexplicable reason only the mechanic had a canteen of water—one canteen for three people in the middle of this inferno. The general died on the fourth day; the mechanic on the sixth; the pilot, according to the note he left behind, on the seventh. A rescue squadron of military planes found the wreck and the corpses a week too late.

And on and on these stories spun, almost always with fatal endings.

We must not lose that track.

A new anxiety now began to assail us. We had expected to find the tank, according to information given us in Colomb Bechar, about half-past eleven. It was now after twelve. Had we gone past? With each moment our uneasiness increased . . . an iron tank on the ground—so indistinguishable in colour from the sand—so easily buried by a storm. . . .

My eyes were glued on the trail, directly beneath. Moye, looking ahead, presently noticed a half-dozen discarded gasoline tins beside the track. He decided to land . . . those tins might have some bearing on our fuel. On taxying up to them we noted a curious-looking dune of sand close by. A pump-handle was sticking out of it. There was our tank! A thousand eyes would never have seen it from above. Except for those suspicious tins, we would probably have gone on, still searching, until fuel exhaustion drove us down upon the desert for a nice long rest.

Having dug away the ton of sand, and opened the lock

with our key, we found the fuel, for all its elusiveness, intact. But transferring this precious elixir to our own tanks, one gallon at a time, proved far slower and more exhausting than we had anticipated . . . with the annihilating heat waves dancing up and down our wings, and a parching wind gleefully scattering the gasoline all over the desert. We had no time to be conscious of the fact that we were four hundred miles away from the nearest spring of water, four hundred miles from the nearest human being.

Despite our long delay, with luck we might still hope to each Gao before nightfall. But luck, this time, deserted the Flying Carpet.

The hot desert wind, which had been dead against us all day, seemed to double the force of its resistance as we left the tank behind. We were forcing our engine well above cruising speed, but the flatness below seemed to be standing still. We began to watch the desert with growing apprehension, fearful lest the sand-spouts would spring forth any moment and recommence their diabolical dance.

By five o'clock we were struggling for every mile.

By seven o'clock there was still nothing but limitless Sahara in sight. The sun had gone down in flames, and a pale moon told us night was at hand.

We must land again while there was yet enough light, and resign ourselves to spending the night wherever the Flying Carpet stopped rolling.

Again on the ground, as a precautionary measure we anchored the airplane with sacks which we filled with gravel. For supper we allowed ourselves a small ration of water, and a can of beef. Then as darkness deepened, and the desert moon rose higher in the sky, we uncovered our portable phonograph brought all the way from California, and had a musicale in the middle of this still, dead world.

The full moon gave us ample light, pouring its glow over the vast rotunda that was our concert hall. Schubert himself would have been moved and subdued by the melody of his *Serenade* speading over the moonlit Sahara. The gentle, plaintive notes of the *Song of India* ceased to be wearisomely familiar. They became soaring, pure harmony, true and beautiful. We felt we'd never heard this old, old song before. We played the *Hymn to the Sun* from *Coq d' Or*. The audacity of this clear clarion chant sent chills and fevers through our blood. Its cascade of icy notes pierced the night with sweetness and reached the stars and bade them listen to the miracle of music rising from the heart of the wilderness.

Moye insisted that *Barnacle Bill the Sailor* come next. I objected violently. This was not the time nor the place, with this peace pervading us, and the dim, far harmony still singing in the air. Moye said he couldn't hear any dim, far harmony. Let's have something snappy. But I was the more stubborn. Quarrelling we went to bed.

I say we "went to bed." We wrapped ourselves in coveralls, made pillows out of tool-kits, and lay down on the hard, hard desert.

I couldn't sleep. I was too thirsty, the gravel couch too adamantine, the monkey-wrenches under my head too unadjustable, and the wind, now that the sun had gone, too bitterly, biting cold. Moye and I shivered and shook, hardly able to believe that four hours previously our very lungs were burning from the intolerable heat. In four hours the temperature had dropped seventy-five degrees.

And yet hot and cold, weary and thirsty as I had been that day, I now found myself by no means unhappy. There was a strange perverse satisfaction in this situation. Here was a new element, a new sensation—the sensation of being, except for my companion, the only thing alive in a dead world, a world that had supported no form of life since the beginning, and would never support life till the end of time. I knew now what one would experience if one could visit a dead star wandering in space. There would be the same relentless progress of the murderous sun by day, and of the frozen firmament by night, in cloudless, seasonless silence. There would be the same appalling expanse of fixed, enchanted waste, without end, without change, without hope. In other deserts there is spring. But there is no spring here. No flower ever grew upon this boundless, barren ocean; upon this illimitable corpse no bird or beast was ever born. When God made the world, some form of life was granted to every part of it—to every part but the Sahara's heart. The miraculous Finger never moved this way. A First Day, and a Second Day, and part of a Third, out of the

Six, was all the Creation these silent moonlit sands about me ever knew.

The moment a rising sun gave us light enough to follow the motor track again, we climbed aboard the Flying Carpet and once more flew on toward Timbuctoo.

For another two hours we had to endure just such scorching heat, such dead, pitiless, ash-yellow wilderness, as the day before. For another two hours we kept our eyes glued on that will-o'-the-wisp of a trail.

At last, far off, we saw the Niger River. It seemed intrusive and out of place. Sand, sand, sand, for a thousand miles, and then, presto!—a great river with *water* in it. Water, but no trees to shade it; just a barren canal winding through the desert.

The city of our desire was still three hundred miles beyond—westward now, up-stream. Having delivered the tank key at Gao, and settled our account, we turned at right angles to our southward course, flew high above the meandering undecided river, and watched for the fabulous city which we knew from our maps lay several kilometres inland from its banks.

Timbuctoo! Leagues away, from ten thousand feet, we saw it—the goal, the promise, of our long, long journey.

CHAPTER III

THE CITY OF THE STORKS

FROM two miles above, Timbuctoo looked like a great disk lying lost in the desert, round, flat, with close-packed houses, and a square hole—probably the market place—at the hub.

We wheeled and wheeled, lower and lower, trying to realise, after having travelled across America and the Atlantic and Europe and the Sahara, that this below was the city the Flying Carpet had set out from California to find.

At five thousand feet we could distinguish mosques and minarets, forts and garden walls, and the maze of labyrinthine streets.

At one thousand feet Timbuctoo came to life. The strings of dark specks became camels that moved. The market place flowed with white-robed natives gazing skyward at the Flying Carpet. We could see that our airplane was causing immense excitement. People were leaning out windows, climbing on roofs, to watch the gold and scarlet airplane flying over Timbuctoo.

At five hundred feet one of the most extraordinary spectacles we were to meet on all our forty thousand miles of flying unrolled below us.

Right before our eyes Timbuctoo began to disappear; to be blanketed over, blotted out, by a vast dark cloud that rose up miraculously from the chimneys and the housetops. The cloud seemed alive. It was made of a million distinct and separate particles, each particle moving independently of its neighbours and yet managing to rotate in one sweeping circular motion around a central axis. I took off my flying goggles better to observe this phenomenon. No wonder Timbuctoo was considered a weird mysterious town.

22

Then a small part of the cloud floated uncomfortably close to our propeller—and the mystery was explained. . .

The cloud was not smoke.

It was not locusts.

It was not sand.

It was storks!—storks in countless multitudes, wheeling and flapping, in pairs, in squadrons, in regiments, over the housetops of Timbuctoo . . . storks, all bewildered, all agitated, by this roaring giant of a Fire Bird that came shooting out of nowhere into their midst. A million storks—or so it seemed—had risen from their nests to form this panic-stricken mass, this tossing sea, below.

Coming from the makeshift landing field Stephens and I, on horseback, rode grandly along the deep sand road into the celebrated city. Some ten thousand Moslem negroes and a sprinkling of Arabs live in Timbuctoo, and most of them were out to stare at the two men from the moon who had flown upon a miraculous gold and scarlet dragon here to earth. Crowds of laughing, shrieking little negro boys, stark naked, ran at our horses' heels as we entered the crooked lanes between walls of squat mud houses. Groups of black-skinned, white-robed citizens pressed about us whenever we stopped. Above us, on each ledge and wall and roof, stood our friends the storks, recovered from their agitation and returned to their nests. Every house in Timbuctoo seemed deluged, overwhelmed, with hordes of unemployed storks. They had so little work to do—few people were ordering babies any more.

We were looking for Père Yakouba. Father Jacob is the town's chief patriarch and foremost personality. Born in France some seventy years ago, he came to Timbuctoo in 1903, on the heels of French occupation, as a Catholic missionary. And he has never gone home. Living so cut off from the world, he chose to modify his religious vows to the extent of marrying a negress and begetting eight children. Removed from all modern distractions— there is not even a motor-car in Timbuctoo, and Paris is sixty days away by mail—he has been able to develop his scholarly interests without interruption, until he has become the great authority on native languages and native cultures in the Sudan. This rare old gentleman, with his long white robes and long white beard, stands like a beacon of light and learning in dark and savage Timbuctoo. He is the White Father, the teacher, the

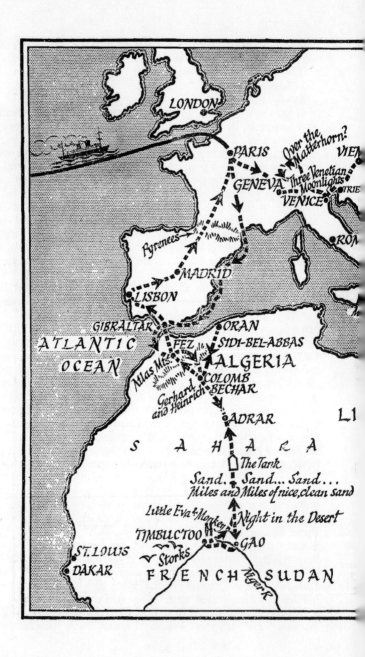

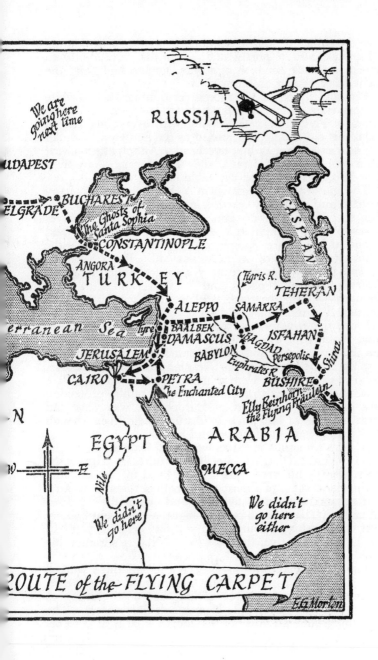

We are going here next time

UDAPEST

ELGRADE ● BUCHAREST

RUSSIA

The Ghosts of Santa Sophia

CONSTANTINOPLE

ANGORA

TURKEY

CASPIAN

Tigris R.

TEHERAN

Aleppo SAMARRA

erranean Sea Tyre

BAALBEK DAMASCUS BAGDAD ISFAHAN

JERUSALEM BABYLON Persepolis

Euphrates R. Shiraz

CAIRO ● PETRA BUSHIRE

The Enchanted City

Elly Beinhorn the Flying Fräulein

N

EGYPT ARABIA

W E

Nile ● MECCA

We didn't go here

We didn't go here either

ROUTE of the FLYING CARPET

E.G.Morton

encyclopædia, of the community; a wise and benign saint—but also a portly and a worldly saint, with an enormous black Amazon of a wife, six feet high, and the eight lusty brown children.

Père and Madame Yakouba greeted us cordially—white visitors were so few and far between, and especially the crews of Flying Carpets. Along with everybody else in town this old couple had rushed to the housetop to watch our scarlet Carpet sailing overhead. Anticipating a visit from whoever was aboard, they had brought out their best liqueur and spread the table for tea.

The moment we sat down in Yakouba's study, a baby leopard and a monkey crawled into our hostess' ample lap. But the place was no zoo. All around were shelves covered with pamphlets, books, notes, written in and about the obscure languages of western Africa—the scholarly library of a hermit-savant. Père Yakouba proved to be an extraordinary source of enlightenment. Every question Stephens and I asked—and they were countless—about the town, the people, their history and culture, Yakouba answered most patiently.

From the windows we could look out across the flat mud rooftops of the huddled town, and see nothing but ten thousand storks and a dilapidated mud minaret which rose up in the background. I exclaimed about the storks. I did not know there were so many storks on earth. Père Yakouba explained to us that the same public protection was given them here as in Europe. It was very bad form as well as bad luck to disturb them even though they drove you out of house and home.

But if I thought the storks were bad, wait till I saw the bats! Wait till night! For every stork in Timbuctoo there were a hundred bats. They lived in vast colonies in the mat ceilings of almost every room in town, squeaking and squirming all day, flying in and out of the windows all night. They were a pest, a plague, a curse, but nobody ever did anything about it. If you had ceilings, you had bats. To the native, that was one of Nature's immutable laws.

Timbuctoo makes an ideal refuge for all these winged citizens, since it is a dying community. For years, commerce—its only source of life—has been shifting to newer and more accessible French colonial centres. The dwindling population is not one-fourth what it used to be.

As the houses are deserted these bats and storks take absolute possession. Some day there will be no more people, only storks and bats, the emblems of birth and death, living in multitudes upon the mud shell of the city that once was Timbuctoo.

But even then, the ghost of the city, after the final demise, is going to be a proud ghost. No town in Africa has had such a history. A thousand years ago it was founded in the desert by a woman named Buctoo—Tin-Buctoo, the town of Buctoo—seven miles from the Niger. This woman was chieftainess of a tribe of Tuareg who dominated this part of Africa as do their descendants to-day.

The history of Timbuctoo has been a history of these Tuareg. Sprung, some say, from a lost Roman legion, they have maintained their white characteristics in the heart of a black continent. They have remained virile, proud, belligerent. Besides their light colour and fine features their most curious distinction is a heavy mask-like veil worn by the men. Boys assume this veil on reaching manhood, and never remove it. Even intimate friends do not behold the faces of one another. How many centuries back this custom began, and why, no one seems to know.

The faces of the women, on the other hand, are as exposed as those of the men are hidden. And for that one is grateful; for prettier, gentler faces will not be found the length and breadth of Africa. Their skin is pale gold-brown, their hair fine and curly, sometimes blond. There is no fear, no furtiveness, in their eyes. They stand, tall and erect, draped in long Grecian-like robes with a scarf worn across their throats and over their heads, as perfect a picture of feminine charm as I have ever seen.

Even though this romantic and beautiful race founded Timbuctoo and for a thousand years supported it, they have never really lived in it. They are nomads and shepherds, and refuse to live in any city. They have left Timbuctoo to be peopled by the blacks. But they flow in and out constantly from their desert encampments to trade.

Up until thirty years ago, when France made a conquest of this part of the Sahara, these Tuareg did an enormous business in slaves. The central plaza was one great slave-market to which buyers came all the way from Fez. Salt offered a no less profitable article of trade. Twice a year ten thousand camels made the journey across the desert to the mines, three hundred miles northward, and brought back tons of this precious mineral.

For three centuries Timbuctoo enjoyed great prosperity, reaching a climax of power during the period when America was being discovered and explored. Riches and culture from half of Africa were attracted to this thriving community. Four imposing mosques (imposing even though made of mud) raised their squat minarets above the crowded city. Arabic schools and colleges shed the light of art and science upon this outpost of Islam. The name of Timbuctoo became a great name throughout the world.

But long since, the glory has departed. Salt from Paris can be bought cheaper than the native product can be marketed. And as for slaves, while there is still surreptitious bootlegging on the side, the vast majority have become French citizens and dislike being bought and sold. The colleges have crumbled; the mosques, empty and forlorn, look down with grave reproachfulness at a city that has forgotten how to pray.

Yes, the glory had departed. The ex-slave-market has been given over to the sale of sheep. Naked black children and indolent black women and dogs and camels and crows lie about in the deep sand of the crooked lanes that wind between the lines of tumbled-down mud houses. Except on market days, nobody seems to work, there is little sign of life. The storks stand above the fading, ageing city—and wait.

Still followed by a pack of curious natives, Moye and I left Père Yakouba's house, and, guided by one of his sons, found our way to the caravansary. This turned out to be a most unprepossessing building on the town's outskirts, where visiting tradesmen could find shelter. It provided no furnishings, no attendant, no food, just a few barren mud-walled rooms. One brought one's own bed and cooked one's own meals. This place also seemed to be the head office for all the bats in Africa. They had burrowed their way underneath the ceiling mats, and there they lived by the thousand. For days on end no one entered the caravansary to disturb them. Consequently when Stephens and I presumed to intrude, their indignant remonstration was loud and long. After the first night, the evil, suffocating bat-odour drove us on to the roof, but there the storks had built a dozen nests, and resented our presence as much as the bats. Defeated, we slept on the sand in the courtyard.

Twice a year this building is packed to bursting with guests. In March and September caravans converge at Timbuctoo from all over the Sudan, to travel to the salt mines I have mentioned. This is the only salt deposit in a million square miles of Africa. Thirty years ago, the spectacle of ten thousand camels moving as one enormous unit must have been a magnificent sight. But in recent years the demand for rock salt has so fallen off that only three thousand camels are required. Even at that, three hundred tons of salt and several thousand tradesmen are still brought into the city with each returning caravan. At these times the rest-house becomes the busiest place in town, sheltering merchants who have collected here from hundreds of miles around.

Once this brief period of activity is over, Timbuctoo sinks back into its lethargy. Only on the weekly market day does the city rouse itself. Then the central plaza is a most colourful place. Dozens of Sudanese negresses, nude to the waist, sit beside piles of melons, fruits and fowls. Wild-looking negro shepherds drive in their sheep and goats from the Niger flats. Savages from the brush country and the southern jungles, wearing only a loin-cloth, wander about unnoticed. One will see tall, hawk-faced Tuareg, veiled to the eyes and carrying huge Crusadic swords, moving across the square with a humble negro close behind. They are bootleg slave-dealers with a slave to sell. Locally-made pottery of crude design is stacked in bright little hillocks. Brassware and home-made weapons sparkle in the fierce sunshine. Cotton cloth woven by hand in the native homes is being bought— but not so eagerly as the bottles of gin an enterprising half-caste is selling to young Tuareg swells. A string of heavy-laden camels just in from Marakesh, a thousand miles away, kneels before the old slave-block, waiting to be unloaded; and a dozen burros, almost hidden under sheepskins they are bearing, struggle past through the dust.

Nine-tenths of all this life and movement are given by the negro traders and their petty commerce. The Tuareg give only one-tenth; but instantly, on a visit to the market, one feels the domination of this small minority. The negroes seem subservient, oppressed, and pay obeisance in look and manner to the veiled lords of the desert. And what lords these Tuareg are!—conscious of their beauty and tall slim carriage, swaggering arrogantly from shop to shop. They look at one over their veils with fierce dark eyes that leave no doubt of the contempt in which they hold other men, or of their readiness—and ability—promptly to re-enslave Timbuctoo and all its unwarlike population the moment French machineguns are pointed some other way.

Stephens and I soon made the acquaintance of Timbuctoo's very limited white colony. It consisted of one army colonel, six young officers, and about eight French civilians including the postmaster and his extremely pretty daughter—the only French girl in town. The officers were our special friends and dined us frequently on the roof of their barracks. There champagne flowed bountifully; and the singing of these young soldiers exiled in this desert town rang out over the housetops. "We have to drink and sing," they confessed. "Otherwise, we'd perish from the heat and monotony."

Moye was content to spend every evening with our military friends, but I sometimes grew restless and chose to wander about alone in the starlight to enjoy the metamorphosis that comes over the squalid little city after dark. From dawn to dusk the sky blazes overhead with a terrible heat, exhausting and withering the spirit of the land, and revealing the fabulous, mythical Timbuctoo to be in soul and body what it now really is—just mud. But when the darkness falls, a mysterious and truly magic spirit floats down upon the town. Then Timbuctoo becomes the dream city I had come so far to see. All the drabness disappears. The houses seem no longer made of mud, but of starlight, standing haunted and half-real against the velvet sky. In the darkness, there is a strange, wry angle to every wall and roof, like the backdrop of some modernistic stage setting painted in black and silver by a madman. From the mud walls of the blunt and tumbling minarets, innumerable dead branches of trees, used for decoration, stand out at right angles, and in the night-time I half believe I see, in the ravens roosting there, the black-faced ghosts of all the slaves that had been flogged to death throughout the dark and bloody history of this savage place.

I stroll deeper into the city. Here and there a candle glows through some open door, casting across the sandy path a pale lugubrious light. A camel sleeping in the lane suddenly rises noiselessly to his feet at my approach— a shapeless swelling apparition in the dark.

These lanes are not deserted after nightfall. The traffic of the day has passed, but the traffic of the evening has just begun. Dark figures of women drift up to me through the sand, and stand, and do not speak. They are not prostitutes, but rather primitive daughters of a primitive black Eve, hunting love and inviting into their arms the first person they can find.

Nevertheless I reach the courtyard before the Central Mosque. It is utterly deserted. But here the night wind stirs, and brings from the far-off edges of the city the faint, melancholy wailing of Arab pipes. I stop to listen. From out of the air there also comes the distant throbbing of a drum; but the wailing and the throbbing are so faint, so far away, they only lend to the illusion that one is but half-awake, wandering in a labyrinth of dream houses, among dream people, all buried in a starlit shroud of sand.

CHAPTER IV

THE TWO SLAVES

LIFE in our caravansary was not especially comfortable—in fact it was not comfortable at all, for with each hour our mortal enemies, the bats, became more bold and more disagreeable. One morning, after they had given us a particularly unpleasant night, I remarked to Moye that we should have servants to help us in our battle against the varmints.

"It would take an army of slaves," he said gloomily.

While I felt that an army of slaves might be too many I did believe that a few would solve our problems. So I suggested that we go out and buy some. It would be rather opulent and luxurious to sit back and order slaves to do our bat-fighting for us. They might also be trained to wash dishes, at which neither Moye nor I was much good. To me this idea seemed in no way shocking, for both my grandfathers had been slave-owners in Tennessee, and I had been brought up believing in the sanctity of the institution.

The problem of finding just what we wanted was not at all difficult. True, any French official would have looked at us with shocked surprise if we had asked for his assistance in securing slaves, and yet they *were* being bought and sold surreptitiously. The bargaining, of course, would have to be done privately and not on the auction block.

The most reliable dealers, so we learned, were the Tuareg chiefs, and the best place to confer with these chiefs would be in their own encampments, some of which were situated no more than ten miles from Timbuctoo.

So Moye and I engaged an interpreter and three camels and visited the nearest camp.

On the way out the interpreter explained that we could no doubt buy as many slaves as we wanted from the

Tuareg, but that we had no legal hold on them whatsoever, since slavery is not recognised by the government. If a slave purchased by a white man in Timbuctoo wishes to walk out on his master and declare himself free, no power can stop him. Consequently, we must understand that any slaves we bought as investments would be exceedingly bad risks. The Tuareg, who are more or less independent of the French social laws, can use as drastic means as necessary to keep their own slaves in bondage.

On arriving at the camp we found about one hundred people living in crude tents made of hides. The furnishings were of the simplest order—a few straw mats and a wooden bowl or two. Even in camp every man was wearing his veil and his long two-edged sword with the cross on the handle—all that survives from the time when, before the tidal wave of Islam, the Tuareg were Christian.

Most of the tribe was out of sight, shepherding the flocks of goats which alone can subsist upon the scattered desert thorn bushes. But the chief was there, veiled to the eyes, and received us cordially.

Stephens and I soon noticed the dozen or so negroes in various labours about the tents. I asked the chief if they were slaves, and he admitted, quite frankly, that they were.

"We're in need of two ourselves," I said, "—to help us wash dishes and fight bats. We were directed to you, and told your prices are very reasonable. We're not French, and guarantee not to embroil you with the authorities."

"I really haven't any one for the market, just now," he replied,"—unless you might like those two little ones over there. I'm willing to sell them to you."

We followed his gaze and saw a boy and a girl each about ten years old, dragging a bleating, struggling goat by its hind legs into the bramble corral.

Moye and I had thought of buying only fully mature slaves, but on considering the children saw no reason why they couldn't fight bats just as well. In fact they might adapt themselves to our household requirements even more quickly than their parents.

The chief called the boy and girl over to our tent. They obeyed, grinning broadly. I never saw blacker skin—and *all* of it was showing. They were rather pretty children, judging from negro standards, and apparently about as healthy as the goats they herded.

"How much?" I asked the chief.

He thought a bit. "Two hundred and fifty francs each," he said. That was ten dollars apiece.

We were very much surprised at such an absurdly low price. I knew for a factt hat full-grown slaves sold for one hundred dollars, or even five hundred if the slave possessed especially good qualities. Ten dollars! There was a catch somewhere. They must be deaf and dumb or feeble-minded. So I offered five dollars for the pair.

The chief groaned with agony. Five dollars for these two handsome children! He pinched their flesh so we could see how firm it was, made them show their teeth, and extolled their strength and beauty to the skies.

We finally compromised at five dollars each.

Then without stopping to think what on earth we'd do with two negro children, where they'd sleep, what they'd eat, and where they'd go when we flew back north again, we paid down the money and found ourselves the owners of two real slaves.

The children seemed delighted. They were going to Timbuctoo—with the two white men. They couldn't imagine a more beautiful adventure.

We got back upon our camels and each of us lifted a slave aboard to ride astern. The camels were of the one hump variety, with a sack saddle behind the hump. Consequently the children had to put their arms around our waists and hold on tight to keep from sliding down the camel's tails.

But they loved it. Whenever the camels decided to trot a bit, our slaves shrieked with laughter. And no wonder. Many an American child would have paid his last penny for the privilege of riding the rear end of a real camel ten miles across a real desert.

The boy was riding behind Moye, the girl behind me. "What shall we call them?" Moye asked as we bounced along.

"Alice—Annie—Lilly—Lulu—Mabel—Violet," I suggested for the girl.

"Adam—Eddie—Felix—Gus—Jimmie—Moses—Oscar —Pat, for the boy," said Moye, going down the alphabet.

But before we got home Moye asked how "Little Eva" (not "Topsy") was faring on her pillion, and I inquired about the comfort of his own little monkey. And these two names just stuck—Little Eva and Monkey.

On reaching the caravansary we looked about to find beds and mattresses for our slaves, forgetting that they'd slept on mats spread on the ground every night of their ten years. Then we went out to buy fruit and canned milk and spinach. We'd always heard that growing children should be made to eat lots of spinach.

Had they come down from the moon Little Eva and Monkey could have been no less accustomed to our civilised manners. They'd never slept inside a house, in fact had seen very few, for the children of the nomads visit the towns but rarely. They had never seen a tin water bucket, or a European broom, or a blanket, or soap, or furniture, or any of the kinds of food we ate or clothes we wore. Teaching them anything was exceedingly difficult, for we had absolutely no medium of instruction. What they did learn was learned parrot-like. For instance, Monkey, following my example, would seize the broom and lambast bats for dear life—until he crippled one. Then he'd pick up the revolting little animal, and, the moment my back was turned, run away to play with it, entirely forgetting that bats were the enemy.

Or Moye would take little Eva and a tin bucket to the reservoir and fill it for her at a place where the water was clean, and then carry it for her back to the caravansary, and put the water to its various uses, hoping she'd observe and imitate. But when sent off alone to repeat the chore, she'd fill the bucket where she found the nicest bugs and water weeds, get tired on the way home, leave her bucket behind and wander off. Then Moye would have to go looking for her all over Timbuctoo. She was always delighted to see him. He simply could not make her understand that she was a *slave*.

For very good reason we decided that it would be fitting and proper to have our slaves bathe now and then. They never had before—which was the best argument in favour of beginning. So I took them over to the canal that connects Timbuctoo with the Niger and instructed them in the use of soap and water. Quite unlike most children they fell in love with the idea—getting their bodies all slick with cheaply perfumed lather. In fact they liked it so well that they were for ever running off to the canal to apply the soap. This might have been a habit to encourage if they had not spent all day doing it, and come home with layers of sand sticking to the lather which they had only half washed off. Then Moye and I would have to get out the wash-cloth and water bucket and scrub the sand away from their hair and ears.

There was something of this sort to do every minute. Looking after Monkey and Little Eva became a twenty-four-hour-a-day job. Moye was finally driven into remarking that he didn't know who were the slaves—they or we. They were as free and as happy as the wind, enjoying life and liberty as they never had before, while Moye and I, the distracted slave-owners, found ourselves more and more shackled with the responsibility of our two little savages.

But with it all, it was rather amusing to have them trotting and grinning along behind us when we went walking. At these times we would absolutely *insist* on Monkey wearing the red pants we'd bought for him and Little Eva her red sarong. We had red turbans for them too, and red leather sandals, and a string of red beads which hung around their necks and down the front of their black and shining chests. In all this elegance they were supposed to wait outside when their royal masters entered a shop or house, but if the wait was too long they'd be sure to shed their finery, pants and everything, and go wandering blithely off to get lost in the maze of streets.

After a week of this slavery business it began to be apparent, even to me, that we could never expect any actual service from our slaves. Indeed I can't remember that they did one useful thing. Moreover the date of our departure was approaching. We decided to assert our independence and make some immediate disposition of the children. There was only one thing to do—take them back to the Tuareg camp.

Once more with our camels and interpreter we found the chief, and explained to him that he could have the children back again for the same price we had paid for them—five dollars each. He understood, but to our consternation said he didn't want them, that he was feeling the local depression, and that food was so scarce he was having to reduce rather than increase his retainers. This was why he had sold them at such a low figure. We then agreed to *give* him Little Eva and Monkey, free, if he would only take them off our hands. He shook his head. His family was much too large. The thing he least wanted was to have those two young appetites to feed again. As a last despairing resort we offered him money if he'd oblige us and take back the slaves. How much would he ask?—only name his price!

"Ten dollars each," he demanded—as before.

"Two-fifty each," we suggested—as before.

As before, we compromised at five.

At last—we were emancipated!

It was not without some sentiment that we parted from Monkey and Little Eva. They, likewise, seemed genuinely sorry to see us go, for never in all their ten years had they been so amused as by these two crazy Americans. Moye and I bade them a last farewell, and then turned back to Timbuctoo, knowing exactly how the children of Israel felt when, delivered at long length out of bondage, they made the exodus from Egypt.

We had waited until the last day to return our slaves, and now had only one more night to be in town. At dawn we were returning to our Flying Carpet, and once again crossing the Sahara the way we had come. Moye was dining with the army officers—just as we had done so often in the days before Little Eva and Monkey came to bless our happy home—but since this was the date of the annual *fête du mouton*, an Islamic holiday, and my last chance to explore the starlit mysteries of Timbuctoo, I chose to prowl the town alone.

Toward midnight I came to the central market place, and found several groups of natives seated in circles on the sand, singing and swaying to the rhythm of the drums and the clap-clap-clap of hands. There was no light but the deep blue desert stars, but they were bright that night and sufficient for the feasting and the revelry. The idea occurred to me that on this festive evening the citizens might enjoy the music of my phonograph. So I fetched it, along with the familiar records, and placing it on the ground before the old slave-block, prepared to give Timbuctoo a concert.

A circle soon gathered. I wound up the music box, and *Happy Days Were Here Again*. My audience rapidly grew to fifty natives—to a hundred—all laughing, all curious, all tipsy, all delighted. The old mud minaret, looking down, swayed just a trifle I'm sure to the cadence of the Happy, Happy Days. These dark-skin Sudanese seemed to comprehend the jazzing, joyous music, and tried to accompany the tempo with their pulsating drums.

37

I tried Ravel's *Bolero* next. It worked. The hypnotic, haunting beat of its lilting strains, increasing in volume and passion, echoed against the ancient mud walls of the square, and brought forth more and more natives, singing and swaying, drunk on music—and gin.

But I saved the best till last—the *St. Louis Blues*. If there ever was a proper place, a proper time, to unleash this immortal negro masterpiece, it was here—music by the negro and for the negro. Moaning and sensual, it seemed to harmonise with the sensual rhythm of the barbaric drums, to be in accord with the beat of clapping hands, to belong here as much as the black houses and their black inhabitants. This was the savage soul of Africa come home from exile and proclaimed by the night wind to all the savage city.

I leaned back against the slave-block, watching, enjoying this scene the music had evoked—a hundred white-robed negroes chanting and swaying and hand-clapping in the starlight . . . Timbuctoo! . . . so it was like this . . . not really very extraordinary after all, when one had actually covered the miles that magnified its mystery, and had sat in its market square, and played familiar American phonograph records with great success to a group of swaying natives. I could have closed my eyes and almost believed myself back in the Cotton Club in Los Angeles.

No—this place, for me, was no longer the most mysterious of towns, no longer the symbol of remoteness, of strange glories and weird secrets. Yet it had not disappointed me. For to-morrow, when I climbed back into the clouds and looked down to say farewell, I would see, not just a little desert mud-pile with an immortal name, but a city that had become a symbol of attainment. Moye and I had dreamed of travelling in the Flying Carpet to the most remote and outlandish corner of the earth. And we had arrived there. We could feel confident, now, of flying on to any other dream city to which we might aspire.

The Flying Carpet had kept the faith. We had been to Timbuctoo.

CHAPTER V

THE FOREIGN LEGION—YEA AND NAY

A MILE below our Flying Carpet, Algeria drifted by. Green wooded hills, green fields of wheat, a green, green world but for the blood-red meadows where the poppies grew. A streak of gold and scarlet against the Algerian sky, the Flying Carpet, scorched by the Sahara's sun, heavy with the desert's dust, was returning to a verdant land. Two thousand miles behind us, across the terrible Sahara, lay the city of Timbuctoo from which we had come. Two miles ahead of us, beyond the vineyards and the gardens, lay the city of Sidi-bel-Abbes to which we were bound.

Moye Stephens and I looked down with searching eyes at the approaching town. How peaceful and poetic it seemed in its gown of green. How gently the poplars waved above the flower-hidden walls.

And how this sweet expression lied! For Sidi-bel-Abbes is one of the grimmest cities in the world. It is the school to which two hundred thousand men throughout three generations have come from every country on the globe to learn to shoot and bayonet their fellow-men. It is a martial city, a city of soldiers, the toughest, wildest, ablest soldiers in the world. It is the home of the Foreign Legion of France. Those imposing buildings, rising through the trees to dominate the town, are barracks that house a regiment. And down the boulevard lined with cheering multitudes this regiment marches, with banners flying, drums rolling, fifes and trumpets piercing the sky—a grand and glittering parade—the Legion celebrating the anniversary of its first hundred years.

To witness this *Centenaire de la Légion*, visitors had come from all over Europe, and we had hurried back north ourselves from the Niger to be on hand. We were exceedingly curious about this unique army, so highly acclaimed, so bitterly damned. We wished to find out for ourselves if it were as colourful and as controversial as the story-books had painted it. The Legion's capital, *en fête*, seemed to us the proper place to begin.

Three days of pageants, concerts and speeches offered us one very pleasant picture of Legion life. But this was by no means the customary, typical picture. So I was glad when the celebrations had come to a close, and raw recruits, rather than brass bands and orators, were entering the city again.

Sidi-bel-Abbès had never known such a heavy inflow of new recruits. Times were hard in Europe. Millions were out of work, hungry, lost in almost every country, and the Legion offered a refuge. They were coming in such numbers that the bureaux in Marseilles and Oran, where new men were generally issued their uniforms, were swamped and sending the overflow straight to Sidi-bel-Abbès.

A few days after our arrival, I went to the railroad station in the early morning to watch a train-load of these unequipped *bleus* come in. They were of every race under the sun: Poles, Turks, Negroes, Spaniards, Italians, Russians, Roumanians, Belgians, and, above all, Germans. More than half were Germans. What a babble of tongues one heard as this band descended on the city! Every tongue but English—for one sees very few Anglo-Saxon Legionnaires.

Yet however much their languages differed, they all looked alike. They had been travelling a week in their civilian clothes, and were now a grimy army of tatter-demalions, unwashed, unshaved, ragged, exhausted. Some had newspaper bundles, a few carried old straw suitcases. Some had no hats, some no shirts, some no shoes. Not one in fifty seemed capable of presenting a spruce appearance had he the opportunity.

As the hopeless and disreputable column slouched down a road leading to their barracks, I joined them. Was this the famous Legion—*la brave Légion*—that had conquered Africa for France, that had brought glory upon glory to their flag, that could outmarch and outfight any army in the world since Stonewall Jackson's?

Yes, the very same. This grime and beard and tangled hair will be washed off and clipped away. These rags will be burned and a smart new uniform issued to replace them. These miserable bodies will be straightened by exercise, these unhealthy faces tanned and toughened. In six months this pack of starving vagabonds will go marching back up the boulevard behind the stirring trumpets, clean, erect, shining, dangerous.

Their physical metamorphosis is wonderful. But their spiritual change, the change that will take place in their souls, is a miracle. To-day they are a rabble, a miscellany of all the tongues, traditions and trades on earth. They can neither speak to one another nor understand one another's ways; they are strangers met in a strange land, and the utmost they have in common is a vague mutual desire to forsake whatever life they have known before. But by to-morrow, no more united body of men will be found on earth. Subtly levelling all barriers between them, a new spirit will bind each man to his fellow and all men to each; they still may not speak alike, but they will think alike, feel alike, live for the same purpose and die with the same resolution. They will be more than a mere uniformed army—they will be a single embodied Idea, the Foreign Legion of France.

How does one join this army? Engagement is very simple. Recruiting stations are found in every large French city, though Paris, Metz and Strasbourg do the biggest business. The last two get the Germans. Of course an age limit exists, good character is demanded and a medical examination must be passed. These interrogations, however, are merely a matter of form, since very few of the recruits understand French. They give any name and any age they choose, laugh openly about their good character, and get by the medical officer if they can stand on two legs. Consequently one finds all ages from sixteen to sixty, and all types.

But more specifically, exactly *who* joins this Foreign Legion? First of all, young Germans. Every other recruit is a peasant boy from Germany, who has run away from home because he was ill-treated, or hungry, or adventure-bent—just simple-hearted children. And almost half the remaining half are German too, ex-soldiers and labourers out of jobs. A good ten per cent will always be French, who technically are not allowed to join, for it is simple to claim one's self to be Belgian or Swiss, as no birth certificate or passport is required.

This French ten per cent are usually the villains, for they are likely to be fugitives from justice, thieves, embezzlers, crooks of all sorts who must join the Legion or face the courts.

The remaining fifteen or twenty per cent are truly international. These come from every walk of life, though the great majority are from the lower orders. Exceptions to any generalisation, however, meet one at every turn. In Bel-Abbes (as the Legion calls its home) there is a military band of one hundred and fifty pieces that claims to be the finest of its kind in the world. Every member of that band is—must be—a good musician. And every member is a Légionnaire. At the other extreme, in Colomb Bechar, one finds the infamous *Compagnie de Discipline*, the penal prison for the Legion, where three hundred murderers, bandits, criminals incorrigible, have been collected. They too are Légionnaires.

But the average Légionnaire is neither musician nor murderer—just an unhappy fugitive, an unfortunate outcast, a *pauvre malheureux*, seeking forgetfulness from the past and shelter for the present. He loses his name when he joins up, and finds a new one. He changes his physical appearance, his language, his entire world. He denies and dismisses all he was. He is reborn again of a mother who understands and forgives. But in payment for this rebirth, he must sacrifice all else for her and fight for her and suffer and hunger and thirst for her—and die for her, unhonoured and alone. The new mother is not unappreciative of this fidelity. She grants him, along with her stern protecting love, two dollars a month.

When my band of recruits and I, marching on into Bel-Abbes, reached the main street, Légionnaires by scores came to the curb and shouted insults and mockeries at their newly arrived brothers. "Look at that trash!" "*Imbéciles!* You'll be sorry!" "Won't they terrify the Arabs!" "*Bêtes!* You're as good as dead!"

I was walking behind, talking to the sergeant, but apparently looked the part of à recruit, for one of the sidewalk mockers shouted out to me in my own language: "Hey—aren't you American?"

"Right!" I replied.

"Me too!"

As the *bleus* had almost reached the barracks anyway,

to my countryman's great surprise I stepped out of the column and made his acquaintance.

Paul, from Boston, turned out to be the only Légionnaire from America in Bel-Abbes—a rolling stone who had given up the sea for soldiering.

"I was in hopes you were going to be a real *bleu*," he said. "I'm tired being the only American."

I expressed regret that I could not swell my country's quota.

"There's only one Englishman, too—named Charles. Let's find him." We did find him—a young man of good breeding, unusually well-informed and very much a gentleman, who had quarrelled with the traditionally stern father and joined up in a melodramatic moment. His like was rare and wonderful in *la Légion Étrangère*.

Next we found Moye, and all the Anglo-Saxon representatives in Bel-Abbes were assembled. Paul and Charles were off duty, so the four of us had lunch together.

"Now let's hear all about the horrors of the Foreign Legion," I said as we drank our Arab coffee, "—from two veterans who know: buryings in sand, prison tortures, buckets of blood and sudden death. . . ."

"Bosh!" exclaimed Charles. "Who told you that?"

"Books—and the movies."

"Well, it's not true—or rather, it's only partly true. Do you think if we were treated as brutally as that, there'd be six hundred new recruits pouring in here every week to enjoy the fun? Six hundred a week since Christmas! And that inflowing stream never seems to slacken, either. We've increased from twenty thousand to thirty thousand in the last five years. We'll be fifty thousand before long. This in the face of the fact that Germany, where most of us come from, commissions the most fearful and hostile books to be circulated to discourage volunteers from serving France. I've been in the Legion more than three years, and I've seen it inside out, and I'm still glad I joined. By now I've an outlook about as tough as any one's—and yet, despite all the terrible hardships and dreariness, I do find a romantic, adventurous quality about our outfit that can not be denied.

"Naturally the adventure is not served out equally. One man gets stuck in some dull, dirty post for his whole enlistment and doesn't see a thing, while the next man fights Arabs all over North Africa and may go to Syria or Indo-China as well. Personally, I've marched over Morocco from end to end, and to me it's still the most fascinating country in the world. I'll hate to leave; in fact, I'll probably re-enlist!"

"Do Légionnaires ever re-enlist?" I asked, surprised.

"Do they! *More than half!* And after they've had five years of it, too. Every other Légionnaire you meet is serving a second term, or third, or fourth. So the 'horrors' can't be so bad as they look in the movies. Besides, things are getting better all the time—food, clothing, discipline. The pre-war Legion wouldn't recognise us—or speak to us—we are so *de luxe* in comparison to what they knew."

"I'm afraid they made the better Légionnaires," interrupted Paul. "At least for books!"

Charles ignored Paul's cynicism.

"Take for example the prison system," he continued. "Up to 1928 I admit *it was awful!* I'd just entered then and I was often in the *boîte*, so I know. We had to exercise six hours a day with sixty pounds of sand on our backs, in this relentless sun, and living on starvation rations. Most of us collapsed, a few of us died, under such barbarous treatment. But it's been abolished now."

"And there's a lot *more* to be abolished before this prison here pleases me," exclaimed Paul. "I was in it last winter, and I almost froze to death. The same old stone cells have been there a hundred years. No windows—just a slit in the wall. No plumbing except a hole in the floor. I had a slab of cold stone for my feather bed, and one blanket about as big as this table. The temperature fell below freezing every night—and me too."

"I'd like to see the *boîte*," suggested Moye. "Can we get in—and get out again?"

"Sure—we'll take you."

So off we went to visit the imprisoned Légionnaires. About half the cells were occupied—more than usual. It was just lunch time, otherwise all the prisoners would have been out on some construction *corvée* in town.

"What are you doing in the *boîte*?" I asked in French of an innocent-looking youngster who peered at us through the bars. He was German, and didn't understand a word of any other language.

"He's a *bleu*—tried to run away," explained the guard, "and so is this one, and this one, and this."

A bunch of little boys being kept after school! I was chagrined, having come to see desperate criminals paying for their crimes.

"Haven't you anything except *bleus* who tried to run away?" I asked.

The guard explained: About three-fourths of his prisoners were recruits caught escaping—usually before they had been in the Legion two weeks. They expect glamour; when the newness wears off and they learn there are to be no palm trees and dancing girls, no desert and oriental romance for a long time yet, but only drill, drill, drill, they decide to quit. That's not so easy. They don't know the language or the country. They have no money. The neighbourhood teems with agents and police. The *bleu* has about as much chance of disappearing as a runaway elephant. The story is so common-place it's not even called desertion, just "absence without permission." The poor recruit is caught, marched back and given eight days in the box.

The place was no chamber of horrors, obviously; but it was dark, dank, unpleasant, so we turned to go.

"What do the others get shut up for?" I asked my companions, as we walked back across the courtyard.

"*Pinard!*" Charles replied, shrugging his shoulders.

"What's that?"

"That's our red, red wine."

Pinard, as I soon learned, is the *raison d'être* for the average Légionnaire. *Pinard* has always been his god. It is now. It will be till the Legion perishes. *Pinard* has welded the Legion together, preserved its morale, won battles, conquered Africa. Bottle-brothers—Légionnaires.

Drink, drink, drink! Half the *bleus* are already drunkards when they come here; and they have ample opportunity to indulge, in Bel-Abbes. At times there's little to do except dissipate, so the other half soon learn, soon fall. The monotony, the weariness, the homesickness, the hardships—all these things the *pinard* washes away. It's issued regularly—whether as food or drug, I don't know. If it's medicine, it's a convulsive cure—but for the moment, it works.

We wandered into the barracks canteen, the Legion's high altar to this great god booze. The place was crowded, but we cleared a table and sat down. Above the roar of languages, coins clinked unceasingly on the bar.

"Where do they get the money?" I asked, turning to Paul, who seemed more at home here than Charles. "You say your pay is two dollars a month—you can't stay drunk thirty days on that."

"Hardly!" Paul replied. "But you see, there's a bounty of sixty dollars paid to each *bleu* during his first year, and he gets twenty of it the first week. They all make good resolutions to save it, but the old Légionnaires won't let them. *They* see to it that the money goes for *pinard*, and quick. Recruits are coming in almost every day, so there are always fresh bounties and more wine. If you want to see real drinking, though, come back here to-morrow night. It's pay-day."

We did come back, and Moye and I sat marvelling. *Pinard* was chosen for the Legion's drink because a little goes a long way; any quantity of it makes a man crazy— and these men were pouring it down. The canteen was an inferno, with scores of soldiers brawling, laughing, singing and shouting in ten languages. Tobacco smoke thickened the air, oaths turned it blue. Bottles and bodies were strewn across wine-splashed tables—or under them. Benches were overturned. Drink, drink, drink—a madness, a frenzy, a demoniac worship of the idol alcohol. As the night advanced, those who were too paralysed to lift another glass were stacked in corners while stouter drinkers held on and poured it down till dawn.

Next day found a good percentage of the most savage drunks in prison, more than one ill and battered, and scarcely any one in the whole barracks really sober. As a rule, however, the officers are wonderfully patient and overlook most of these little binges. I saw one Légionnaire who lay prostrate in the gutter rise tottering to his feet at the approach of an officer, draw himself to rigid attention, salute with a smartness that was inspired, and then—plop!—back into the gutter he collapsed. The officer just laughed and passed on.

But drink is by no means the Legion's only diversion, though it traditionally takes precedence. In Bel-Abbes there is the *Village Nègre* too—the Street of the Women. Our friends led us there one night, to show us a spectacle I shall never forget.

The street itself was so narrow we could reach out and touch both walls, and was unlighted except by candles glowing through open doors. But the stars were bright and the moon generous. Not only Légionnaires in swarms, but Tirailleurs, Spahi, Zouaves, Senegalese, the Goumier native police, and the Arabs themselves, streamed with their bright uniforms and white burnooses up and down the lane. It was a holiday. The women had put on their most bizarre gowns and heaviest jewellery. Gross negresses cried shrilly at passers-by. Painted Jewesses reached out to seize us from the crowd. Arab girls with raucous voices shrieked insults at each other across the alley. A few French *filles*, too old for Paris, competed savagely with their native sisters, striving in this last outpost of degradation to postpone the end another year, another month.

Out of doorways dogs snarled and yapped at our legs; nightmare-size rats scurried beneath our feet. Small children, amused by what they saw, laughed in the midst of the crowd. Through the whole street came the sound of the yelping tin phonographs. And down through the narrow crack between the roofs, the kindly moon poured her magic light to add an unreal touch of romance to the only love the Legion knows, to make bearable the only women it is allowed to touch.

With so many desperately gay soldiers, of so many breeds and colours, wandering about the streets at night, fights are frequent. At this the Legion excels, and woe to their opponents, for however much they may hate and betray one another individually, steal from one another and brawl among themselves, let any outsider attack one of them and every Légionnaire in sight comes swooping down to fight like a wildcat for the uniform. Against their meanest street enemy, as against the most formidable army, the Legion presents a phalanx-front. Not a night passes but from some obscure corner of Bel-Abbes one hears the cry of "*La Légion! La Légion! A moi! A moi!*" The cry is never raised in vain, and the enemy, however just his quarrel, is lucky to get away alive.

This *esprit de corps* is the Legion's flaming flag. The *tricolor* for them has little meaning, since they most emphatically are *not* French. Neither are they Germans any more, nor Russians, nor Spaniards. They are *Légionnaires*.

They groan and grumble at their lot; they curse the food, the drill, the sergeants, one another, themselves. They preach revolt and mutiny as a creed. They desert whenever they see a chance. They are a dissolute,

47

savage, drunken crew and an abomination to all honest citizens. They join because it is their last resource, endure because they must, drink vile *pinard* until they get the *cafard*—the desert frenzy—run amok, and shoot their officers or hang themselves.

But—when it comes to their main job, the job for which all else is only the hard, the bitter school—fighting Arabs —they are incomparable. In the history of high deeds, the Legion must be listed beside the Theban Band and the heroes of the Alamo. At the first whiz of a hostile bullet, they crystallise into such activity, such passionately devoted unity, such courage, such sacrifice, such utter contempt of danger and death, as few other armies have ever known. They'll risk their lives a dozen times for a fellow Légionnaire they've all but murdered out of hate in times of peace. A sergeant will give his last drop of water to a soldier he has detested from the first. What matter their numerous personal sins when, at the test, they never, never fail? They know all the vices, but not cowardice.

This extraordinary fighting efficiency, this indomitable spirit, is the first and greatest tradition of the Legion. It has been born of countless heroic battles throughout the century since Louis Philippe first organised the service.

Nor have those battles all been fought in North Africa. Hundreds of Légionnaires perished for Maximilian in Mexico. Their graves are strewn across Indo-China, French Sudan and Madagascar. During the World War, the major part of the Legion, combed clean of Germans and containing at that time many Americans, was transferred to France. There, the First Regiment suffered more casualties and won more honours than any other Allied regiment. Four times it was annihilated. Four times it was re-recruited. Into every desperate battle it was flung. Its flags won the *Croix de Guerre*, the *Médaille Militaire*, the *Légion d'Honneur*, and so many citations that one general exclaimed, "The folds of this flag are not broad enough to hold all its claims to glory!"

It was Charles who told me all this, and more. And his voice filled with pride in the recital of the tales—the tales of the unconquered banners these drunken brawlers have held high. As I listened to him, I began to understand how the Legion can gather up the dregs of men and forge their souls, like steel, in to a single sword flashing over the frontiers of France.

CHAPTER VI

THE LEGION MARCHES

When the Flying Carpet and its crew had been in Bel-Abbes about two weeks, our Legion friends—now numerous—were ordered into the wilderness for their annual two weeks' manœuvres. Rather than be left behind in an empty town, I decided to go with the army, especially since it might be interesting to see them wage their mock war against mock *dissidents*—"dissenters"—the term used for hostile Arabs.

From several directions columns were marching to a concentration point called Bedeau, sixty miles south of Bel-Abbes. The garrison at Geryville, a hundred and fifty miles beyond Bedeau, had the most rigorous schedule, having been ordered to arrive on foot within five days—so I chose to join them. Mock war or not, their orders promised real marching, and I was interested in seeing the Legion machine in motion.

Moye Stephens had accepted an invitation to an aviation meet at Oran, fifty miles away, so I made the trip to Geryville by motor-car without him, arriving just as the detachment of two hundred men was departing. It was three o'clock in the morning—the usual time for marches to begin, since an early start permits the column to reach its day's destination by noon and thus avoid much of the scorching heat. But now the night was freezing, and as the men lined up they kept their heavy service overcoats closely buttoned. Under this overcoat each man wore his full uniform, with eighteen feet of broad *ceinture bleue* (the dark blue foot-wide sash that distinguishes Légionnaires) wrapped around his waist; and in addition, each carried two half-gallon *bidons* of water slung from his shoulders, cartridges, firewood, sometimes a pick and shovel, a haversack, a mess-kit, food, one section of a field

tent, and a five-foot rifle! I surveyed my own equipment
—a sweater, thin shoes, one *bidon* and a camera—and
decided that if Légionnaires could march *with* a whole
commissary on their backs, I would be able to keep up
without.

We had thirty miles to do that day, and I'd not walked
a mile in months—flying carpets had been my only mode of
travel. Scarcely had we left Geryville when I began to
regret it. The *pas de route* order was given, and the Légionnaires broke step, adjusted their burdens any way they
liked, took up a reef in their *ceintures* and moved. My God,
how they could march! The kilometres rolled behind like
knots behind a battleship, smoothly, steadily, mercilessly.
The pace was never less than four miles an hour. We
marched fifty minutes and rested ten, marched fifty and
rested ten. The moment a rest order was given, the entire
company fell to the ground where it stood, and lay like
dead men—and I'm sure I was the deadest of all.

As soon as the sun rose heat began to torment us. I
drew off my sweater and unbuttoned my shirt—still the
sweat rolled down my face. But what of the Légionnaires,
in overcoats that were bound to them by a dozen other
burdens? They dripped far worse than I did, but while I
struggled to keep up, they *sang*—lusty German marching
songs, always, always, German.

And these had once been unhealthy wrecks such as I
saw slouch out of the train that morning at Bel-Abbes!

About eight o'clock we had a half-hour halt for breakfast. Each soldier carried his own food, but I had joined
them too abruptly to have thought about such things, and
consequently I had none. However, for five francs a
Légionnaire eagerly sold me his entire ration. Thirty
miles on an empty stomach was nothing to him; besides,
he'd forage among his comrades, and that night get
gloriously drunk with the money. For another five
francs he'd have sold me the captain's meal as well!

We were now in a wilderness of brush and gravel, and
my light shoes were giving out rapidly. I'd always considered myself a fair walker, and had done thirty miles a
day frequently—but not so unprepared as I was then. By
ten o'clock I trailed behind. So, however, did several
others; I was not quite the last straggler. Nor the most
unfortunate—for some of the soldiers' heavy boots were so
old or ill-fitting that, having removed them, their owners

50

were walking barefooted on ground that seemed to sprout with thorns.

When I finally did get into camp that afternoon, an hour behind the head of the lengthening column, I found the place dotted with pup-tents sheltering six men apiece, each man having carried his sixth section. Under every tent were the six Légionnaires, lost in sleep and exhaustion, their swollen feet extended from under the flaps, their bodies huddled against the welcome earth.

At least there was hot food, for the two-wheeled kitchen wagons had gone on ahead and were waiting for us. I ate—I can't remember what; then I found the well—it was decidedly saline, but who cared—and drank and drank and drank. An officer offered me a blanket, and I fell upon it, almost dead.

At twilight the camp began to come to life. *Pinard, pinard!* It flowed like water, for every soldier had a full pint issued to him and more could be bought. Aching bones were eased, blistered feet healed, the sun and the sand and the insects forgotten, in the benison of the red, red wine. The soldiers drank, laughed, jested, sang; they gulped their evil-smelling soup from tin plates as though it were ambrosia, and forgetful of all the day's hardships, rolled over to sleep again as happy as children on a holiday.

But the next stretch was unmitigated hell for even the toughest Légionnaire, while for me—well, we had to cross thirty miles of sand desert without a tree or a stream, a firm foothold or a patch of shade. And stragglers there were aplenty that day, for the sand was deep and the sun annihilating. The officers drove their men with more and more brutality. They *must* march—*marche ou crève*—march or die. But some absolutely, physically, could not keep up. They preferred to *crève*—and so did I! I was unable to walk another yard. For even had it been possible to force my swollen feet to move, my shoes were in pieces and useless.

So falling back in ignoble defeat, I persuaded a kitchen-wagon driver to let me board his steaming stove. It was hot, but at least it had special wheels to conquer that clutching sand. He had been ordered to follow the column to pick up stragglers, so our strange ambulance was soon loaded to capacity, but still the limping stragglers multiplied. As a last resort, ropes from the wagon were tied to the exhausted soldiers' belts—not so much to compel them as to assist them, but it worked both ways.

That afternoon I reached the second encampment just in time to witness a painful scene. The captain was standing before the well, with his riding whip uplifted, lashing across the face every Legionnaire who tried to rush the reservoir. Half-way across the burning desert that day the men had drained the last drop from their *bidons*; they came staggering into camp perishing from thirst—and the captain stood between them and the water, beating them off.

But this was not just the legendary Legion cruelty. The water was impure, and when gulped down in quantities by thirst-crazed men it brought on violent dysentery. An hour later when they had somewhat cooled and relaxed, it would be less dangerous. The officer knew the necessity of protecting his men—but it was a most thankless and futile task. Their clamours increased in violence. They came at him by tens rather than by twos. His own wrath rose, but by sheer weight of numbers he was forced from his post, cursing and lashing, and the scores of Légionnaires fell like thirst-crazed beasts upon the unhealthy well.

Other than this one justifiable incident I never, in all the weeks of my close association with the Legion, saw any officer strike a Légionnaire. That form of treatment has gone forever, along with the sacks of sand. The fire-breathing sergeants of cinema and story-book fame are fiction. Discipline is at times stern, necessarily, to fashion hard-boiled, Arab-eating soldiers out of German farmer boys; the routine is harsh, to build up the extraordinary endurance demanded of them. But they're all in it together, and each captain tries to keep his men as happy and devoted as the hard life allows. The officers I met were invariably hard-bitten fellows, but likeable, with a knowledge of men and a sense of humour. During our march the lieutenants walked every step of the way when they could have ridden had they so chosen. It is this spirit of all-share-all which, along with the *pinard*, holds the Legion together in such close unity.

Many times I saw officers tolerate breaches of discipline that would be court-martial crimes in other armies. The very night after our thirty-mile desert crossing, in the little *bistro* at camp, a Polish soldier of the lowest sort got violently drunk, and when the captain entered, poured upon him a torrent of abuse for making his men march, march, march, "just for a game." The captain sat very quietly, taking little notice of the frenzied soldier. Only when the Pole advanced threateningly with a bottle uplifted did he order him seized.

"What will you do with him?" I asked as he was led away, expecting to hear at least a sentence to the guillotine, since this was the "brutal Foreign Legion."

"Nothing," the officer said calmly. "He's drunk—a touch of the *cafard*. He's marched a hundred kilometres in two days, and I know how weary he must be. I've never found that punishment improves them so much as persuasion. They're only kids still, you see—just *gosses*!"

And I was to become so accustomed to this humane paternalism that several weeks later, when I saw a sergeant-major pedal his bicycle into a group of Légionnaires and in a blazing, tyrannical fury call them every *espèce* of animal for not getting out of his way, I stared at him with speechless amazement—and so, to a less speechless extent, did the Légionnaires.

The real hardships of the Legion spring from the nature of the Legion's task rather than from the ill-nature of its officers. On the third day of our march, I remarked to a veteran who tramped beside me that I couldn't imagine anything worse than the previous day's march.

He burst out laughing.

"That!" he exclaimed. "Oh, that was a tea-party. That was just play. I've been on forced marches in the enemy's country that *were* hard. At those times we have to carry twice this much equipment, and there can be no straggling either. A straggler's as good as dead—worse, because he'll be captured and tortured to death, and he knows it.

"Then when you've driven yourself sixty kilometres in one day and finally reached a water-hole to camp, there's no falling down unconscious to rest. Not much! You take the pick-axe from your raw shoulder and dig rocks and earth for a temporary barricade. The walls must be four feet high and three feet thick and extended enough to shelter everybody. Sometimes this work takes as much sweat and struggle as the march.

"When the wall is finished you have to creep out for wood and water. And water often costs lives. The *dissidents* hide near the spring or the river, and wait for Légionnaires there. Many a man has been found, sprawled over the water-hole, with his throat cut, and maybe still grasping his *bidon* in his hand.

"After the water has been fetched, tents have to be raised and rifles and machine-guns cleaned. Then each man must take turn at guard duty. For food you get perhaps a tin of sardines and a cup of flour and some raw rice—and then if you get two hours' sleep you'll be lucky. Oh, the Legion," he exclaimed, shrugging, *"elle 'trappe toujours*—she always catches it!"

The veteran Legionnaire who told me all this as we marched along was a Belgian corporal serving, though he was not yet thirty, his tenth year. Here was someone who knew, and, to my delight, someone who was willing to talk.

I had first noticed him on the second day's march when, seeing a young soldier suffering under the weight of sun and sand and overcoat and pack, he had lifted half the younger man's kit and piled it on his own tremendous but already overburdened shoulders.

"Are many of you as decent as that?" I asked him now, referring to the incident.

"Oh, that—that wasn't anything. He's my *copain*, you see, my comrade. He's been sick in Geryville with fever and right now ought to be in the hospital instead of this cursed desert. And he'd do as much for me—we've been pals for a long time."

In the midst of their cruel world, barren of almost everything but hardship and danger and death, these toughened men hold to their friends with a patient devotion that is, at times, rather touching. Most of them are simple young animals, too healthy in body and too high-spirited to go through life empty-hearted. But they have no homes, no wives, no books, none of the usual attachments—and so they offer their whole souls, with a sincerity that compels admiration, to their regimental flag and to their friends. They have little in goods to give one another, but they are generous in spirit, and many an Achilles has lifted equipment from the exhausted shoulders of Patroclus, and many a Légionnaire David has shared his last ration or his last *sou* with Jonathan his friend.

But do not get the idea that a Legion camp is a congregation of brotherly love. Most emphatically, it is not. Sober, the men will scheme against each other, rob each other, hate each other; drunk, they will fly at each other's throats with murderous purpose. A few of the surliest characters remain solitary year after year. But throughout the ranks, almost every man has found some special friend whose fidelity makes the enlistment easier to bear. Extraordinary tales are told of Légionnaires who have re-enlisted rather than leave behind a *copain* whose term was not yet up, of great sacrifices and great risks endured, of lives laid down, for a comrade.

One of the most moving—and most tragic—stories of Legion friendship was told to me by this same Belgian corporal, as we tramped on towards Bedeau.

"I'll tell you about Hans," he said, "—a *bleu*. He claimed to be twenty, but he could not really have been more than seventeen. His family were provincial German farmers, and he grew up in some remote village in complete innocence of human evil. When he heard about the Legion, with its romance and adventure, his little village suddenly seemed too small, and he ran away."

At length, the corporal continued, Hans found himself in Bel-Abbes. There the toughness and brutality he encountered terrified him; in his worst dreams he had not imagined a life like this. The older Légionnaires bullied him, cheated him, made life hell for the baby-faced recruit. And then, when Hans was most in need of a friend, a Russian named Nicholas, two years in the outfit and several years older than the boy, took him under his wing, and felled every other Légionnaire who dared mistreat the little *bleu*.

Hans' juvenile inclination to hero-worship went out in full force to his champion. They became fast friends, sharing alike their wine and their wealth. Thus they came in time, still together, to the Legion barracks at Fez.

Straightway, to celebrate their arrival, Nicholas became magnificently drunk, committed some harmless *bêtise*, such as insulting a sergeant, and into the *boîte* he was bounced. But being a very lively lad, he soon tired of prison and decided to play sick in order to enjoy a visit to the infirmary—just to break the monotony. So, along with another "invalid" from gaol, he was marched to see the doctor, escorted by a corporal and an armed guard. And who should the armed guard be but Hans!

It was a spring day; Nicholas was out of that cold dark prison, back into the warm sunshine and the wind—and there was Hans, his pal, happy to encounter him even in this somewhat constrained manner. Nicholas felt a sudden overflowing of *joie de vivre;* he had to express it somehow or burst. "Let's run off," he whispered to his fellow prisoner, not meaning to run very far. "Let's desert—for the afternoon."

Like two wild goats let out of a stockade, they darted away from the astonished corporal, laughing at their own impudence. The corporal was new, inexperienced; he had never before had to meet such a situation. He shouted at the escaping culprits to come back, but that only made them run the harder. He threatened to shoot—they knew it was only a bluff, and anyway, they were two hundred yards away by now. They did not stop.

But the corporal *was* in earnest. It was he who would catch hell for this escapade. He commanded Hans, who stood by grinning with delight, to fire over the prisoners' heads—just to frighten them. Hans had never fired upon a human being in his life. He'd never even seen the *bled* (the waste land where the forts are), much less a hostile Arab. He had drilled with his rifle, but even in practice had shot it only enough to prove himself a hopelessly bad marksman. He fumbled at the trigger.

"Fire, fool, I tell you!" shouted the corporal. The prisoners were over a thousand feet away, and running hard. Hans, now shaking with excitement and confusion, fell on one knee, pointed his rifle vaguely in the direction of his fleeing pal, and fired.

The Russian Legionnaire, a third of a kilometre distant, plunged forward on his face.

Uncomprehending, dazed, faint, Hans knelt there like stone. A dozen guards, attracted by the rifle report, picked Nicholas up and, carrying him back to where the corporal waited with Hans, laid him on the ground.

Nicholas was dead—a clean shot through the head.

With one bitter cry Hans crumpled to the ground, and for weeks after he remained in the mental ward of the infirmary, tortured day and night by horror and remorse.

As the story ended, I plodded silently onward through the dust, behind the column of Legionnaires. The soldier, marching beside me, kept silent also; he seemed to be as much moved as I by the poignancy of the tale he had just related.

"And the poor corporal," I said at length, "—how miserable he too must have felt."

"How miserable he too must have felt . . ." the soldier repeated after me, very slowly. "How miserable I know he will always feel. You see, the corporal was . . . myself."

CHAPTER VII

HEINRICH AND GERHARD

THE Foreign Legion quarters at Colomb Bechar are surrounded by a wall, the front entrance of which is guarded
to the teeth by barbed wire, a half-dozen sentries, two
pill-boxes, a guard-house, and Lord knows what else.
But at the time of our visit, in the back wall there was a
break in the masonry, where the bricks had been removed
for the extension of a pipe line, and, for the time being,
not replaced. And this very convenient exit was wide
open day and night, so that any Légionnaire who chose
could walk out of camp unchallenged whenever it jolly
well suited him, and home again. There was just one
little catch. He had no place to walk to, except out across
the miles and miles of nice clean sand.

Colomb Bechar—this was our third visit here. It was
the place where, *en route* south to Timbuctoo, we had
waited six days for the sand-storms to subside—six days
spent picking grit from the airplane engine. And on our
way north, we had again paused here, but only long
enough to fuel.

So, when Moye had finished flabbergasting Oran with
his air-acrobatics and I had returned to Bel-Abbes from
the manœuvres, we flew back this time to Colomb Bechar,
having had no opportunity before to absorb its character
as one of the most active desert Legion posts. After all,
when you've a Flying Carpet, four hundred miles isn't
much, and it was an easy flight this time, as there were
no sand-storms to struggle through.

Colomb Bechar itself had not been under attack in
recent months; but the garrison was ever on the alert, for
they never knew when the *dissidents* might swoop down to
make raids on the wild regions in the neighbourhood. It
was because of this constant warlike air that everybody in

Bel-Abbes had insisted we must, if we really wished to know the Legion, fly back and meet the five hundred veteran Légionnaires posted here.

The first thing we did on landing on the familiar field was to persuade a Legionnaire to buy us complete Legion uniforms, *ceinture bleue* and all. Wearing these, we made ourselves at home in the community. Moye took to his uniform as if he'd been in the Legion all his life. No soldier in town better looked the part of the sun-tanned tough campaigner. My own uniform was twice too big, and my *képi*, my cap, too small, so that Stephens suggested I play the part of his orderly since I looked just like it. Certainly I was neither smart nor terrifying in my khaki clothes—just gauche.

Thus inconspicuous, Moye and I did as the real Légionnaires did and went where they went. We laundered our clothes in the same stream at the same time, went swimming in the same pond, learned to know the Legion *argot*, a hodgepodge of French, German and international slang, drank our share of *pinard* with the rest, and made friends.

Our two best friends were Heinrich, the company's thirty-year-old giant, and his *copain*, Gerhard, just as German, but some seven or eight years younger, whose intelligence and attainments were decidedly superior to most Légionnaires'. Heinrich, serving his second term of enlistment, was when sober as fine and effective a soldier as one could hope to meet. Why he had joined, even Gerhard did not seem to know. He had some tale of deep dark crime, but so had they all, especially the youngsters who had joined just from a desire to find adventure and were unwilling to admit any motive so innocent. Heinrich knew every post in Morocco. He had fought through a dozen battles, yet always came away intact— how, one wondered, for with his colossal physique—he was six feet six and weighed two hundred and twenty pounds—he made an excellent target. His capacity for *pinard* was legendary, as were his bull-like rampages whenever he became, at long length, drunk.

The only person who could handle him was Gerhard, whose manners were as quiet and as charming as Heinrich's were brutal. When the giant went on a binge and threatened to exterminate Colomb Bechar, the police quickly summoned Gerhard, and while everybody else was running for dear life, Gerhard, who measured a foot

59

shorter than the gorilla and was a hundred pounds lighter, would order him home with the tone of an indignant and exasperated parent, and Heinrich, meek as a lamb, would promptly go.

They occupied a *marabout*, or permanent barrack tent, along with six others—or rather eight, because Moyse and I were always there. Ten mattresses, like spokes of a wheel, radiated from the tent pole, and on them slept a most curious collection of Légionnaires. Beside Heinrich and Gerhard, there was a nephew of the recent Shah of Persia. He had been sent to St. Cyr, the West Point of France, with an unlimited bank account, but his wild dissipations had caused him to be expelled from the military school. So he joined the Legion. He was the most agreeable and generous person in the camp, and unquestionably the *worst* soldier.

Next to him was the vivacious little Belgian, Max, who had secured our two uniforms for us. He insisted he had bought them honestly from the commissary with money we gave him for the purpose, but he stayed drunk so long afterward we began to suspect he had "decorated" himself with his neighbours' gear and spent the money on *pinard*—which, we later found out, was true. The two unfortunate soldiers who had lost their entire wardrobe had to replace it piecemeal from somebody else, and those in turn invaded the next tent, until some poor innocent recruit, ten "decorators" away, got caught without his pants or his *ceinture* and sent to prison for two weeks.

Next to Max slept a Russian boy who proved so non-committal and so remarkably sober I was never able to find out his history. He was a complete enigma even to his own tent-mates.

Next to the Russian came old Petruska, the Yugo-Slav corporal. Petruska had fought through the Great War in the Austrian army, had huge walrus moustaches, and more tattooed flesh than any man in history. He was a born soldier, but completely helpless in any other sphere. Realising this, he had dedicated his life to the Legion and would follow it to the end.

The other two men were just simple stupid Germans undistinguished in any way, except Johann who was *so* stupid that even after a year in the Legion he had learned, beyond necessary drill commands, only one word of French —*pinard*.

We had lively times in that *marabout*. Fortunately, access to it at all hours was a fairly simple matter—through the temporary break in the back wall. Taps came at nine o'clock. Then the inspecting sergeant made the rounds. Moye and I had to keep out of sight until this was over. During the day we enjoyed complete freedom to come and go, but at night the post was closed as tight as a drum (except for the gap) and bristled with sentries who had strict military orders to arrest all intruders. Moye and I had to be *very* cautious when we crept through the gap and into the *marabout* carrying a bottle of *pinard* under our arm, and fruit and cigarettes. We couldn't have any light, and weren't supposed to talk, but Heinrich did as he pleased, so we held forth half the night.

The Legion tales I heard in that tent would fill this book. Two stand out in my memory:

Some three years before my visit to Colomb Bechar considerable excitement had developed there over the remarkable case of a certain Austrian whose name, shall we say, was Schantz. Herr Schantz had fallen heir to a huge fortune in Vienna left him by his father's will, and the executors were trying to find the beneficiary, whom they knew to be for some unknown reason hiding in the Legion. They had succeeded in tracking down his regiment, even his company. His assumed name, however, baffled any further identification.

As a last attempt to find the missing man the executors of the will received permission to have the sergeant-major, to whose company they were sure their man belonged, announce the bequest publicly at assembly. This was done, all the details being described so that there would be no mistake. The sergeant-major ordered "Schantz" to step forth and receive his legacy. There would be no penalties, no questions—just a paper to sign and a million dollars to spend.

Nobody moved.

"What! A million dollars, fool!" The examiner's eye swept the ranks, blazing with impatience at the stupidity of the secretive Austrian who preferred to remain unknown at the price of a million dollars.

But all his pleadings and threatenings were of no avail.

He then tried individual cross-examination of every man in the company. Half the men were quickly eliminated—they were obviously not Austrians. Most of the other half were likewise ruled out, it being evident at one glance that they were of peasant birth and breeding, whereas it was known that Schantz came of a cultured and distinguished family.

Only four remained, all four Teutonic, with speech and manners that would qualify. But not one of these four would confess to be Schantz. The more the sergeant-major bullied and argued, trying to solve this mystery, the more stubbornly non-communicative they became. He finally had to admit he was defeated, for every attempt to locate the missing man had proved a complete failure.

—A failure until two years later when Schantz himself, discharged honourably from the Legion, appeared in Vienna to claim his fortune.

Schantz was the sergeant-major!

The other story came from Gerhard with supplementary remarks from Heinrich who vowed that he, together with his friend, had gone through the experience I am about to retell. I've put it in quotations, but make no attempt to record the exact phrases, for they were spoken by a German talking Legion French. The thread of the story is as he told it.

"From the books you read about the Legion and the moving pictures you see," began Gerhard, "you would think the fighting we do is all done in the desert. Well, it isn't, though you'll never make the public believe it. For a Foreign Legion story the public must have its forts half-buried in sand, decorated with a few palm trees and domineered over by a sadistic beast of a sergeant. We do have posts in the Sahara with palm trees—Colomb Bechar right here is one of them—but I should say well over half our fighting, and two-thirds of our casualties, have so far happened in the Atlas Mountains."

"Right!" exclaimed everybody.

"But the public won't have it that way. It's like a story I heard once in Turkey from a German newspaper correspondent. He had just been investigating a terrible Armenian massacre, and found out that it was the Turks, some five thousand of them, who had been massacred by the Armenians. 'But I can't tell the truth about it,' he said. 'The public wouldn't believe me. You *must* have the Turks massacre the Armenians. My readers insist upon it. And so that's the way I had to write my story,'

"Well, that's how it is in the Legion. You *must* have sand. To be sure, I've had my fill of sand, but all the really murderous fighting *I've* seen has been nearer the snow than the palm trees."

"Same here," agreed Heinrich.

"The tribes of Chlurs we have to face in the Moroccan mountains are the most desperate and cunning fighters. Fighting is their passion, their religion. If they weren't shooting at the French they'd be shooting at each other; but their pet abomination is the Legion. They are fired by a fanaticism that makes them terribly dangerous; we expect no quarter, and consequently give none. The Legion's wounded often have no chance of being rescued by their comrades, so it's the customary thing—the sensible thing—for a prisoner or wounded man to shoot himself rather than be tortured slowly to death, as he is absolutely sure to be, by the Chlur women. For these women, the torture of captives is a time-honoured ritual—their specialty, since they have proved themselves more artistic, more pitiless, than the men, in inventing horrors for their victims. They always mutilate him first, and then, when he shows signs of expiring at last, they cut open his abdomen and fill it with stones. The torture sometimes lasts for days, though, before the soldier is allowed to die."

"So you can understand *why* the Chlurs get no quarter in return," exclaimed Heinrich.

"They always half strip themselves in preparation for a fight," Gerhard continued, "wearing just a rag of a brown shirt and a loin-cloth. Their entire kit consists of a leather bag slung from the shoulder. In it they carry gunpowder, round lead bullets they've made themselves, and sometimes a page of the Koran, not a word of which, most likely, they can read. Their weapons usually consist of a long ugly home-made knife and a flintlock gun bound together with bits of brass and copper wire. Lately you find Chlurs with modern rifles they've captured or stolen. With any sort of rifle, new or old, they are wonderful marksmen.

"The fighting is mostly guerrilla warfare, at which the mountaineers have the advantage, as their brown half-naked bodies mingle with the brown rocks and make them hard to see. Only occasionally have they been known to meet the Legion in force in open combat, usually contenting themselves by ambushing small parties or sometimes a company.

"Just about a year ago, before we were transferred to the desert, Heinrich and I were fighting with our company in the mountains out from Rich. Our column, about five hundred strong, had been following a valley deeper and deeper into enemy territory, and every foot of the way was being contested by snipers on the rocks above. We were trying to establish a telephone line at the same time so we could keep in touch with our main post. We reached the 'kasbah'—that's what we call the mud-walled native towns—and fortified ourselves there as best we could.

"But straightway the Chlurs cut the new telephone line, and our commander ordered out a small party of linemen to repair it—with nearly a hundred soldiers to protect them, as they were almost sure to be attacked.

"The Chlurs were just waiting for this chance. They swooped down from the top of the ravine with an over-whelming force no one had suspected they possessed, and placed themselves between the detachment and the kasbah.

"The Légionnaires knew there was no hope for them to get back to the town against such odds—no chance to reach their comrades; but they meant to sell their lives as dearly as they could.

"The fighting was hand to hand and as ferocious as fights only can be between Légionnaires and Chlurs, who hate each other with a desperate, venomous hate. When that terrible battle was over, even though the Chlur casualties, in proportion, were enormous, the out-numbered Légion-naires had been butchered to the last man.

"Fired by this triumph, the natives turned toward the kasbah, and drove back into its walls those of us who had gone out to rescue the ambushed detachment. For eight days the most determined assaults were made upon our barricade. The Chlurs seemed inexhaustible. Our entire force might have been slowly depleted by the assaults, starved out and completely annihilated, had not four more companies come from another direction to save us.

"As soon as things were quiet again, we had the sad duty of collecting and burying our hundred dead comrades, up the river bed, who had perished there on the first day of fighting. We had been much too dangerously engaged to do it before, and by now you may be sure it was a painful, sickening job. Their bodies had been lying in the open all that time.

"We had about forty mules and a hundred canvas sacks.

This lugubrious procession moved slowly along each bank of the river until we came to the place where the slaughter had taken place.

"It was a heart-breaking sight. Each body was completely naked—clothing is valuable loot to the Chlurs—and in a fearful state of decomposition. Every Légionnaire had been mutilated, and many decapitated. It was difficult work—a lot of the bodies falling to pieces as we tried to slide them into their rough shrouds. Occasionally one of us had to pick up a head or an arm separately and drop it into the sack. Of course there were as many Chlur bodies as Légionnaires. Those corpses we collected into a great pyre to burn.

"As we moved on up the ravine, we came to a sharp turn, and suddenly ran into five bodies close together—all Chlurs. Most unusual. Then Heinrich and I, who were working together, noticed an overhanging cliff just above, half hidden by green vines. Behind the creepers we found a level recess in the rock. There lay a naked body, face down with legs and arms spread out as though crucified. The blond hair showed immediately that it was a Légionnaire. Evidently he had crawled into the cave after being wounded, and before dying had done a little sniping of his own, right into the midst of the Chlurs, for a few empty cartridge cases were scattered near by—and there were five bodies piled below.

"Right in front of the Légionnaire's head we found a flat piece of slaty rock, and upon it a long splinter of slate. We suspected that meant a message, and bent down to find a faint scrawl, scarcely legible, in German. It said: 'Tell my father——' And then there was an address in Duisburg.

"As we were putting the body in a sack, Heinrich noticed a long scar across the left side of the face. There was only one scar like that. I knew this was Karl Müller. His identification tag proved I was right. We had been *bleus* together in Bel-Abbes, and shared the same barrack room; ten days before he had marched beside me.

"I wrote a etter to the address in Duisburg telling how Karl had died, and explained that his last hought had been for his home and his family. Nearly three months later I received reply, very politely worded and written in a fine hand. The writer thanked me for my good intentions, but said this man Karl was no son of his.

65

"To this day I don't know any more than that. I'll always be puzzled."

This was Gerhard's story. And I must say that it all sounded authentic enough to me, knowing as I did that nothing can be stranger than the truth about the Legion. But he may have read it in a story-book the day before.

One never can tell.

Moye and I were finding our life as Légionnaires so amusing we might have forgotten all about our Flying Carpet and the dust it was collecting in the military hangar, had not Max, our Belgian tent-mate, ruined everything.

It was like this:

A fête day celebrating some historic Legion victory had come to the post at Colomb Bechar. Every soldier was given double pay for three days, double wine ration, and relieved from all duties. On top of that, another contingent of four hundred Légionnaires had just marched in from six months' service on the desert, and were turned loose on the town. Everybody got as drunk as possible, made wrecks of the *bistros*, drove the few civilians, fearing for their lives, indoors, and roved in boisterous gangs up and down the village's single street. There were a hundred fights, dozens of broken heads, but no murders—just the Legion expressing itself.

That night poor Gerhard was busy indeed, for he had not only the ebullient Heinrich to manage but all of his other tent-mates as well. So he called on me to help, which, though I was in my civilian clothes, I gladly did. We needed Moye too, but couldn't find him. Between us we finally pushed, pulled and carried Heinrich, Max, Petruska, the Persian Prince and the two Germans home to the *marabout*, via the gap in the back wall.

In various stages of undress every one except Max immediately went off to sleep. But Max was incorrigible. He shouted and sang. The sergeant on duty walked past the tent's entrance to shut him up. Ten minutes later Max grew more violent than ever. He had torn off most of his clothes and at three in the morning went galloping around the camp yelling at the top of his lungs that he was a cannibal, and was going to kill and eat the first sergeant he met. Sergeants on guard duty fête nights are supposed to be lenient, but this was too much—too much at least for this sergeant. He made one leap at the cannibal and

66

dragged him kicking and laughing into our *marabout*.

"Where did you get all this drink?" he demanded sternly of Max, turning on his flashlight and seeing the Belgian's bed littered with bottles.

"I bought it, ha-ha—I'm rich."

I listened under my blanket, scarcely breathing.

"Who gave you the money?"

"He did,"—pointing to where I was hiding—"to buy his uniform with. But I just decorated myself with Jacques', ha-ha—and kept the money, ho-ho."

In vino veritas!

The sergeant, with one sweep, ripped the blanket from my face. There I lay completely dressed in civilian clothes.

"Who in hell are you?" he asked.

I couldn't think for the moment just *who* I was.

"Where are your papers?"

I didn't have any.

Now I had got myself in a mess—caught without permit apparently hiding in a military post at night. . . .

Gerhard kept his head. "Come outside, Sergeant. I'll tell you the whole story."

Suspiciously the sergeant complied, but he wouldn't go two feet beyond the *marabout's* entrance.

That was far enough. I had long before noticed a rip in the rear flap of the tent and I made one headlong dive through it. The wall-gap was only fifty feet away. I heard sergeant-shouts behind me, but reached the gap and disappeared into the night. Gerhard, I knew, could take care of himself.

My escape was not altogether successful. Next morning the colonel called me into his office and suggested that I keep away from the fort at night—"for what would happen to your *Tapis Volant*," he asked with a smile, "if a sentry mistook you for a Chlur, and *shot*?"

CHAPTER VIII

LA BRAVE LÉGION

A FEW days after the *marabout* episode, Moye and I said good-bye to all our good friends in Colomb Bechar and turned to the air again. This time we were on our way to Rich. Gerhard's story about the murderous battle near this post had made us resolve to visit it.

Rich, one hundred and fifty miles straight west from Colomb Bechar, was a key-station right in the heart of the snowy Atlas. However, it was almost as big as the Legion camp we had just left, and not very different. We wanted a brave little fort, lonely and lost, deep in the enemy's country.

A small convoy happened to be going up to just such a fort as we sought, some twenty-five miles away, and so, having left our Flying Carpet behind on the military field at Rich, we engaged two burros and went along. Our column consisted of three Goumiers (native mounted police), the two itinerant *houris* they were escorting to the mountain post—and us. Having no firearms, Moye and I busied ourselves, as we trotted up the Legion-built mountain trail, with prayers to both Allah and Jahveh for safe deliverance from the savage Chlurs who infest this region.

To our relief, we arrived unmolested, and the lieutenant in charge (I think it best not to name him or his post) gave us the warmest welcome. Moye and I were the first non-military white guests he'd had the entire half-year of his command. As for the circuit-riding ladies, they were received literally with open arms.

Two sergeants, four corporals, and about thirty-five men garrisoned the fort, and they, along with their officer, had not been one kilometre beyond the walls for six months past.

The fort itself, about one hundred feet long on each side,

was built like all forts in Morocco, with an outside high blank wall and protruding bastions at the four corners. The entire place was surrounded by barbed wire, even the single front gate having the protection of a great movable barricade of tangled barbs. All the buildings were huddled against the wall inside, leaving only a small court in the middle. Here in this stark stone blockhouse, Légionnaires practically go to prison for twelve months, even eighteen months, at a time.

Fortunately, there is always enough *pinard*. Food may give out; *pinard* never. If the Légionnaires cooped up in this bleak cement hot-box were twice as drunken as those elsewhere, surely they had twice the provocation. The same routine tasks over and over, the same scene, the same faces. Even the excitement caused by the arrival of fresh supplies is afforded them only once every two months.

The favourite interest in these posts—indeed, almost the only interest—is the regiment of *dogs* with which every fort abounds. Each soldier has his dog, for protection as well as companionship. These faithful animals hate Chlurs no less than their masters, with whom they stand guard in the bastions, to sense and to see midnight prowlers long before the Légionnaires. Indeed, no sentinel at these outposts would ever think of standing watch without his dog. When the master is transferred the dog is transferred too. During my visit to Colomb Bechar, at the time the four companies came back by truck train from the desert, the last truck was filled completely with dogs, at least fifty, big ones and little ones, of all colours and mixtures. Whenever the truck stopped or slowed down, half the dogs would jump overboard and go running and barking in all directions. The poor distracted guards, had they not been so good-natured, would have gone raving crazy trying to keep their canine Légionnaires in hand.

Our particular fort was located nearly a mile high in the mountains. Consequently snow blankets it all winter long. But in summer a furnace of heat half cremates the garrison. To enter then is like entering a house of the dead. The sentinel stands immobile upon the bastion under the paralysing sun; the flag hangs limp as a gallows-corpse; every one seems burnt out completely. It was May when we arrived, and May is high summer in the mountains of southern Morocco, so I know about the heat.

But summer and winter, the sentinels must watch . . .

eternally. For even the most torpid and hateful security, the Legion has learned, can be gained only through unending vigilance. One careless moment—and a Chlur comes wriggling through the darkness into the post. There is a strangled gasp from the sentry. He is found with his throat cut and his rifle and ammunition gone. If there is an attack in force, it likewise comes without warning, and always at night when there is nothing to shoot back at except the flash of a rifle. The men in my post never knew when they might again be assailed— to-night, perhaps, or not for a month. They could only wait, always apprehensive. At any moment the Chlurs might descend from some mountain-top like terrible jinns, appear as if by magic before the fort, and make a rush at the gate. Fortunately they have no campaign tactics. If they did, along with some unity and discipline, the little fort could only delay their triumph, not prevent it.

Sometimes a Légionnaire is shot or captured outside the fort. And he usually comes back, thrown over the wall, in pieces; or if not his entire body, certainly his bloody butchered head with eye-sockets empty and lips and ears sliced off. And one may be sure this butchery was done before, not after, death.

Whatever dreams of desertion Légionnaires imprisoned in their blockhouse may entertain—and they nearly all do entertain such dreams from time to time—these occasional ghastly reminders of Chlur manners certainly deter them; for a Légionnaire, deserter or otherwise, is a Légionnaire, and the Chlurs do not stop to argue the fine points of his military standing.

Our column had reached the fort about dark, just in time for supper. It was pay-day—the Arab maidens whom we had accompanied knew their calendar—and along with the evening meal, *pinard* was flowing fast.

A full and phantom moon had risen over the peaks of the Atlas, making the white walls of the fort radiant with soft warm light. A ladder led up to the flat roof of the barrack room, from which one could overlook the wall and view the imprisoning mountains aspiring with vast sweeps of snow and shadow toward the moon.

As the heat of the day still clung to the barren courtyard, the Légionnaires had shed most of their clothes for coolness' sake.   One of them possessed a phonograph, war-torn and weary, and this, with a few mistreated records (the needle had not been changed in years), was carried by its intoxicated owner to the roof, to entertain his comrades who were by now *decidedly* hilarious themselves.

The shell-shocked machine squawked out some ancient waltzing tune, and everybody danced—hulking soldiers in grotesque couples, unshaven and half-clad, stumbling around together in the moonlight, laughing and shouting the entire catalogue of obscenities, some wearing hobnailed boots, some barefoot, some with great moustaches drip-ping *pinard*, some with their muscled backs flaunting tattooed dragons and flags and bathing girls.   Some danced alone, a clumsy *danse du ventre* to the beating of fists against tin soup plates.   Every one staggered and laughed and sang.   More wine was brought up, more wine, more wine.

Even without the two Arab girls the party would have been a great success.

When morning came the entire garrison was in a depressed and savage mood.   One first-class fight had occurred between two Alsatians, and the lieutenant, just to appease his own throbbing head, had thrown them both, with a ten-day sentence, into the prison cell.

This cell was used irregularly.   For days it would remain empty, and then the lieutenant, struck with a touch of the *cafard*, would suddenly fling into it the first soldier he sus-pected of some mild *bêtise* that would have passed unnoticed the day before.   Nobody minded.   The prisoners sang or slept.   It really didn't matter much, living in a blockhouse, whether you were in a cell or out.   You got the same food —only no *pinard*—and you didn't have to stand guard.

Before the day was over, a corporal unlocked the prison door, so that the two culprits, along with half the garrison of Légionnaires and their dogs and Moye and me, could go swimming in the dammed-up irrigation ditch below the fort.   They all splashed in the muddy water as noisily as a troop of innocent schoolboys—but their rifles were stacked on the bank within easy reach.

As we footraced back to the fort, I saw the lieutenant standing on top the walls watching this string of grown-up children flying along the path pursued by their barking and excited dogs.   And right in front were the two Alsatians, who, however, on reaching the courtyard, decided not to go back to prison. They were tired of it, and anyway, the lieutenant had evidently quite forgotten he had sent them there.

Everybody seemed happy and serene that night. The evening before had relaxed their taut, monotony-strained nerves, and they were now ready to endure another month.

The lieutenant, once the atmosphere had cleared, found time to be a most hospitable and pleasant person. He had served five years as an officer in the Legion, and though he was sometimes a severe and erratic disciplinarian, in his heart he loved his Légionnaires as his own sons. He knew their vagaries; but he also knew they *could* fight and *would* fight, fight to the last breath for the Legion, and die without a whimper, should he so command. He had seen them do just this, time and time again, and was eager to talk to us about their exploits as long as we would listen.

All the forts in this section of the Atlas, so our lieutenant explained to us, had been built with blood and bayonets, as well as bricks. The construction of each one had meant a battle, for this rugged valley had been the chief retreat of the *dissidents* who resisted the Legion's encroachments with every villainy they could command.

One such post up the line, Aït Yacoub, established only two years before, had cost the life of a Légionnaire for each foot's length of its four walls.

From our own fort, two full companies, equipped with building tools, cement and supplies, had moved upon this very dangerous enemy headquarters, with orders to erect a blockhouse there. But the walls were no more than three feet high before the soldier-masons were viciously attacked by the outraged Chlurs. Instantly, trowels were dropped and rifles seized—and the assault of Allah-yelling demons was beaten off with terrible losses.

Seeing the new fort could not be taken that way, the Chlurs lay siege to reduce it slowly. Day after day passed with them pushing this long-range battle ever closer. Behind the barricade water and food were giving out; ammunition had to be conserved with the utmost care.

Meanwhile an airplane scout had flown over the fort and grasped the alarming situation. There were no available bombs, but the pilot was able to return to Rich and bring back an equally precious burden—bullets, which he managed to drop within the walls. Each time the plane swooped low, every Arab rifle was turned upon it; each time the pilot managed to get away, to bring back more bullets and more food. The besieged Légionnaires signalled to him that they now desperately needed medical supplies for their wounded, many of whom had been lying half dead for days without even a bandage. The next trip the pilot came loaded down with these supplies, but dropping them smashed to bits every box and bottle. Each succeeding attempt resulted in the same tragic waste.

And all the while the Chlurs were swarming down in ever-increasing numbers like vultures circling a stricken animal. They had even fought to a standstill the *groupe mobile* that was trying to push its way up the valley from Rich to relieve the surrounded fort. Driven to reckless measures, the fort's commander sent out forty men, a third of his effective force, to try to form a junction with this main body halted by the Chlurs not far away.

But forty were not one-tenth enough. Half the forty were annihilated before they'd gone a mile. The others, seeing their mission was impossible, faced about and tried to reach the fort—twenty against two thousand. As they fell, each man who could, quickly shot himself, for the Chlurs were close behind, brandishing their knives. One young German stooped to pick up his wounded *copain*, but as he did so a burnoosed figure leaped upon him, caught him by his mop of yellow hair, cursed him in German for being a traitor to his own country by fighting for France, and with one terrific blow of his sword severed the boy's head from his body.

Only two of the forty Légionnaires got back. It was they who told the terrible story of the young German's death. They had both been wounded, but had fallen into a grass-hidden ditch, and the Chlurs had swept on past.

This appalling experiment left the captain at Aït Yacoub with only seventy men, and these seventy were dropping fast, for the Chlurs were now sniping at them from above as well as from all sides.

Only the airplane kept the Légionnaires' courage and hope alive. Back and forth it flew, miraculously invulnerable. By the sixth day, the sight of the lines of wounded men, stretched out unsheltered from the sun and dying by inches for lack of medicines, drove the pilot to a desperate resolution. He went home to his post, took one long draft of the red *pinard*, filled up a case with morphine and disinfectants, swooped back down over the heads of the besiegers, and right in the middle of the murderous circle *landed*, on a patch of rocky ground no other pilot on earth would have dared risk. With bullets whizzing past him from every angle he calmly unloaded his precious morphine, signalled to the near-by fort, climbed back in the cockpit and charged full speed at the wave of Chlurs rushing forward to destroy his death-defying airplane with its thrice-cursed pilot.

There was a race for the precious box. The Legion got there first.

And the astonishing aviator almost escaped—not quite, for one last long shot from the hilltop caught him in the chest. Half conscious, he managed to land his bullet-ridden plane at Rich, though neither he nor his faithful machine could fly again.

Only twenty-four men were now left alive at Aït Yacoub, but their flag still flew—and at last, six thousand of their comrades were coming to the rescue. The field-pieces began to drop a curtain of shells about the unconquerable post. A distant bugle note floated above the noise of battle. The defenders knew what that note meant—the Chlurs knew too. The Legion had come in time. The bugle and six thousand cheering Légionnaires rushed down upon the blood-stained field and swept the little fort into their arms.

As Moye and I, seated in our lonely post, almost in sight of Aït Yacoub, listened to many such stirring stories of fidelity and heroism, our admiration for the Foreign Legion soared anew. We understood at last, fully and profoundly, what it means to be a Légionnaire.

Humbly, before such brave and hardy men, I'll tell you what it means:

It means, first of all, one must be an able and courageous soldier, and an engineer, a builder, a coloniser, as well. A Légionnaire must wield his spade as skilfully as his rifle. He must build roads, cleanse the villages, and irrigate the desert that trees and grain may grow in the wilderness.

It means one must march, march, march or die, be ready for every bitter hardship, disdainful of every danger. It means one must fight under a copper sun in the inferno of sand, and among the mountains where the slopes are white with snow.

It means one must serve under a foreign flag—a flag that has seen die in the shadow of its folds a great number of these stepsons of France.

To be a Légionnaire is to forget one's home, to forget one's name, to deny one's self every thought of sons, every contact with women whose love is not for sale. It is to make an endless emptiness of one's heart.

To be a Légionnaire is to go hungry, to drink water that is salt and crawling; to fight to the last cartridge, and when that is gone, with the bayonet, and when that is broken, with a club; and to kill one's self unhesitatingly rather than fall into the hands of the torture-loving Chlurs.

It is to guard the traditions of the thousands of Légionnaires who have died before; to be worthy of the uniform that marks the foremost soldiers of the world.

To be a Légionnaire is to live grimly, and perhaps to die miserably; to suffer even after death insults and butchery, and then be fed to the jackals who laugh at the medals for *Honneur et Fidélité, Valeur et Discipline,* pinned on the carrion's chest.

Where else on earth is there a spirit, a self-sacrifice, like this? Where else are there men like these? They may be sunk up to their eyes in all the sins the devil ever dreamed of, but by the very gods they mock, I know that when at last an Arab bullet gets them, their souls, with the banners flying, the drums rolling, the fifes and bugles piercing the air, will go marching up into the blue African sky, straight through the gate of the land of the blest into the paradise of the brave.

CHAPTER IX

GULBEYAZ

If some one were to ask me to which foreign city I most wish to return, I would have a hard time answering. I would think of Rio de Janeiro, and Athens, and Peking. I would certainly think of Fez. This city, so proud and mellow and mediæval, never fails to captivate whoever visits it. My own capitulation, on my return with Moye from Rich, was immediate and complete.

Fez, we found, has entirely escaped the invasion from the West. France has built an ugly, sanitary modern community on the outskirts, and there the white man and the Christian carry on their tin-can trade. But the original city itself, wrapped in its dreaming sun-splashed walls, despises this upstart neighbour. Into its own narrow malodorous alleys, Western modernity gains no entrance. We heard there only the soft slow pad of camels and the scrape of sandals worn upon the feet of undistracted Moors . . . and a voice from the minaret that bade us linger in this *Arabian Nights* town, among the white domes and towers, the dim arched streets, the secluded gardens from which dark-eyed women, veiled and mysterious, smiled at us . . . and, for the time, forget the Flying Carpet.

We found an ancient Moorish house right in the middle of the native city. It was surrounded by a jumble of tortured lanes, tiny shops and cul-de-sacs, in which I was always, to my delight, getting lost. No one knew when our house was built—maybe in the eighteenth century, maybe in the eighth. It was of one storey and constructed around a court, with high blank walls on the outside, and a luxuriant garden inside enclosed by a gracefully arched colonnade. The tops of the arches were filled with lace-like arabesques once coloured bright, now faded by generations of sun. But even in its decrepitude the old house was beautiful still—what one could see of it beneath the masses of bougainvillea and geranium that rioted over every wall. The crumbling marble fountain cast its spray upon the blossoming pomegranate trees as gaily as it had done for countless seasons past. And now that early summer was flowering the land, the air in every court and corner seemed saturated with all the perfumes of Arabia.

We tried to make our house a refuge from the Philistines who inhabited the French city. To it only Arabs could come, and the few Europeans who enjoyed their company. Only the prettiest girls, only gay-spirited men, were welcome. The Foreign Legion had a pass-key, and the Spahi native cavalry, because they were devils and left fabulously beautiful white horses standing at our door. But no one who was solemn and severe was admitted.

Inside the garden, walled away from care, we slept by day in the shade of the lemon trees. By night, we hung the crescent moon of Islam in the sky and bathed in the pool and listened to our native orchestra . . . and the miseries of the world seemed very far away.

Every evening there was dancing and music—the exciting agonised music of the Arabs, their bagpipes wailing, their tambours thumping, their one-string violins squeaking frantically. The musicians sang as they played, sang with heads thrown back, mouths open wide, shrill nasal, delirious.

And how those Arab girls could dance! With this intoxicating rhythm vibrating in the courtyard, they would continue hour after hour—no wild leaps and bounds, but with stamping of feet and undulations of hips and *corps*, as they clinked and rippled the tiny silver cymbals, fastened to their finger-tips.

The prettiest girl who came to our parties, the most striking personality, and by all odds the most accomplished dancer, was an Arab damsel of about eighteen, with the name of Gulbeyaz. She wore six richly carved woollen dresses indicative of her wealth and station, and enough jewels and junk to adorn a dozen gipsies. Her supreme decorations were a frieze of olive leaves tattooed in blue across her forehead, and two stunning gold front teeth (carefully substituted for good white ones) which lit up her face when she laughed.

At first sight of her, Moye and I were both enslaved. Neither of us knew a word of Arabic, and Gulbeyaz knew no other language. That made things difficult. Moye—who usually depended on the tall tales of his flying exploits to break feminine hearts, and usually with complete success—got nowhere with this method. And I, who after long experimentation have found that I am most irresistible when reciting love-lyrics in a slightly quavering voice with a few telling gestures, made even less impression.

However, it was soon evident, to me at least, that Stephens' curly hair and reserved manner were accomplishing with Gulbeyaz what his words could not. When she danced she scarcely even looked my way, but would cast those great black eyes of hers upon Moye, and smile, with her radiant teeth, like August sunshine.

Chagrined, I looked over the rest of our ballet, but there was none other who could match Gulbeyaz. If I were to win her, I must act at once or suffer complete defeat. In this crisis I remembered that once in Italy I'd had notable success—in a similar contest over an Italian girl—by buying my way into her heart: silk stockings, cheap jewellery, pastry and such things so dear to women. I got hold of Frankie, the irresponsible, undismissible little cockney Foreign Légionnaire who was always on hand (and always drunk!), and gave him fifty francs with which to go out and buy for me the fanciest and pinkest frosted cake in Fez—one that would completely capture Gulbeyaz's heart.

Of course, I shouldn't have trusted Frankie with such a serious commission—or with fifty francs. He had joined the Legion—so he always said—to escape the penalty for having murdered three or four people; but I suspected he was just boasting and had joined because he was, like so many Légionnaires, too much of a dipsomaniac to thrive elsewhere. And so, as I should have anticipated, he spent thirty francs on brandy and only twenty on the love-cake. Thereupon, he returned reeling home to deliver my prize, but on trying to cross the court he tumbled with a yelp and a thundering splash into the fish pond, and sank to the bottom—still clutching the elegant pastry with which I was to lure the beauteous Gulbeyaz away from Moye's sinister toils.

To my great annoyance and disappointment, he did not drown.

78

This disaster was no doubt intended to make it clearly evident to me that Allah was on the side of Stephens. But Allah or no Allah, I wasn't going to give in just because a drunken fool of a Légionnaire fell in a fish pond. I was still determined to persevere.

Beyond our garden walls, Fez offered endless opportunities for exploration, and almost every day Moye and I would venture out. Frankie, who had appointed himself our permanent courier, made an excellent guide, since in his progress from bar to bar he had come to know the city well. Sometimes, when the afternoon had begun to wane, he would fetch Gulbeyaz and meet us before one of the mosques, and we would wander through the bazaars and twisted streets of the town. Donkeys and camels brushed past us, dogs and brats, veiled ladies, porters, princes, Arabs, Berbers, Jews, Negroes—all in one confused tangle of traffic milling through the narrow alleyways.

Moye and I would stalk manfully ahead through the crowd, in Arab fashion, shouting *"Balaak! Balaak!"*— Make way! Make way!—with Gulbeyaz, swathed in veil and burnoose, trotting behind. In this costume she looked just like everybody else, so we were forever losing her or speaking to the wrong outraged burnoose. Frankie brought up the rear, struggling to keep the procession intact.

We never grew tired of the bazaars. Of all the bazaars in the world, I'm sure those of Fez are first, in variety, in colour, in evil and fragrant odours, in richness and age. And what a stock they offered! Paltry and useless little mosaic ornaments, ostentatious nothings, enticing yellow *darioles*, idle delights that held infinite surprise. But it seemed as though we were the only ones who ever purchased anything. Indeed, Moye and I spent our *sous* rather recklessly, buying trifles with which to break the heart of the ravishing Gulbeyaz. Moye would give her perfume and embroidered leather slippers; I'd give her tin bangles, hashish, and stick candy. Moye's gifts she received with extravagant gratitude, mine with a polite smile of thanks—but I continued to compete, in the hope of ultimately finding some bauble that would absolutely slay her.

Alas, I couldn't.

Having exhausted the resources of Fez itself in this

fruitless pursuit, I thought perhaps some opportunity for me to outdo Moye might be found at the great fair then being held in the near-by town of Moulay Idris. For four days each year, some seventy-five thousand Moslems gather to barter and to pray at the tomb of Idris, the great saint who first brought the Koran to Morocco. If one wants to behold the unalloyed essence of Morocco, to see the Moors as they were in the days of their greatest glory, this occasion is unsurpassed. For then the true spirit of the land is revived, with its barbaric vitality, its splendour and fanaticism, its filth and beauty; and one is translated for these four days of grace back into anterior times.

Gulbeyaz didn't care anything about anterior times, but she was delighted when I suggested the fair—and promptly asked Moye to come too. Three being a crowd, particularly in this case, I decided to take Frankie also. All four of us managed to stow into the Flying Carpet—it was only a ten-minute flight, and we could endure discomfort that long. That is, I could—for Gulbeyaz, of course, sat in the double front cockpit with Moye, leaving Frankie and me to squeeze into the single rumble seat.

All the way there, I sulked over this latest frustration; but once the fair spread before us, with all its colour and excitement, I must confess I entirely forgot about my elaborate heartaches. Gulbeyaz would be lucky if she got even a tin whistle out of me to-day!

There were so many diversions it was difficult to know which way to turn. Most of the action of the fair takes place on a broad field above the city. Across this field our little band struggled through the dusty, surging, good-natured crowds.

Hearing the wild howling of Arab bagpipes, we moved in that direction and found two hundred men of all ages formed in a great circle, dancing a religious dance. They were leaping up and down at a signal given by the leader in the centre, yelling the name of Allah in chorus, swaying, stamping, and repeating the measures and invocations countless times, until each dancer had lashed himself into a trance, a delirium, that no longer felt exhaustion—only glory. Enchanted by the shrill savagery of the pipes, they had been leaping and shouting without a moment's pause since eight o'clock in the morning. It was now past noon. And not a single dancer, even among the oldest, had fallen dead!

Next we came to a troupe of Arab acrobats exhorting coins from spectators, but their feats seemed tame after the frantic dance, so we wandered on. Snake-charmers —glass-eaters—trained animals—magicians—and a hundred other forms of entertainment, each held a dense ring of pilgrims enthralled by the timeless and familiar tricks.

Gulbeyaz liked the snakes. We couldn't pull her away until she had seen the charmer swallow the cobra's head and suspend an adder by its fangs from his nose. She also fell in love with the man who removed one eyeball from its socket and placed it in fetching positions about his face. Moye liked best to loop-the-loop dizzily on the children's home-made Ferris wheel. Frankie kept wandering around looking for the only thing not to be found—a bar.

I soon discovered what was my own favourite amusement at the fair—the fantasias, the wild superb group-riding of the Arab horsemen.

From all over Morocco the best and most reckless riders had collected, bringing the finest Arab stallions. Wild riding is the national sport, the release, the joyous passion of the Moroccans. And here at Moulay Idris there were seventy-five thousand people ready and eager to applaud.

For each manœuvre the horsemen line up at the end of the race-course—twenty abreast and wave after wave. Each rider has striven to outdo his companions in brilliance of costume and trappings. The saddles and bridles are made of vivid-hued leather, studded with gold, and covered with green and salmon silk. The linings of the burnooses likewise flame with colour. The stallions, often pure white, rear and neigh and paw the ground in their impatience to be unleashed.

At a command the first riders drive their spurs into their horses' flanks. The beasts leap frantically forward. Down the course they flash, goaded on into a terrified frenzy of speed. The riders, shouting their war-cries, stand upright in their silver stirrups. White tails and manes, white burnooses, orange-coloured cloaks, red and purple sashes, yellow and scarlet draperies, loosened turbans, all stream, sweep, swirl behind upon the wind storm.

From out of this infernal gallop of twenty yelling demons, twenty strong bronze arms stretch forth, brandishing in the air twenty copper muskets. Upon a signal yell, at this mad career, they shout in unison, in unison twirl their guns, and in unison fire a deafening fusillade, fling their gleaming smoking weapons into the air, leap out to catch them, and thunderously plunge on in a tempest, a fury, of dust and colour and ferocity.

Wave after wave, each wave more abandoned, more savage, than the last; each superb rider fiercely handsome and graceful as a god. Saddles and bridles break—blood streams from the horses' flanks—the ground is shattered by the flying hoofs. The muskets explode—the insane yelling and the smell of powder fill the air—the riders and the horses go wild—and so do the spectators—and so did I!

It was late afternoon when we flew back to Fez. On our excursion, my suit for Gulbeyaz had not advanced one inch, but it had been a happy day just the same. While Frankie took the damsel home, Moye and I returned to our garden and went for a swim in the pool. Refreshed after the heat and dustiness of the day, we climbed to the terrace atop our house to watch the sun go down.

We always loved this hour. The city about us turned pale gold, and the snowy peaks of the Atlas, soaring mysteriously across the southern sky, burned with a conflagration of reflected fire. Everything seemed hushed, expectant. . . .

And then, just at sunset, it happened—a white flag fluttered up to the summit of the minaret of the Great Mosque, not far away, and on the balcony a muezzin appeared. Facing eastward, he wailed forth the evening chant, and from all the hundred other minarets of Fez a hundred voices took up the cry . . . Al-lah! Al-lah! Twelve hours before and half the world away, this call to prayers had started—in the Philippines, when it was sunset there. At a thousand miles an hour it had raced before the coming night to Java and Singapore. Then on to India, to Delhi, to be echoed from the minarets of that great Moslem capital . . . Al-lah! Through the Khyber Pass it swept, on to Isfahan, across Arabia to Mecca itself. Al-lah! On to Cairo. Al-lah! The cry rang over Tripoli—on to Tunis—into the Sahara. *Al-lah! haya il' al' falah!* now sang the muezzins from the towers of Fez, sending the invocation on toward the great ocean in the west, where, in a few moments more, the chanting would fade as the sun at length sank into the sea.

The darkness fell.   Moye and I continued to sit quietly on the terrace, enjoying the coolness of the wind.   At length, he broke the silence.

"Don't you think, Dick, it's time we were taking leave of Fez and travelling on?   There's the rest of the world—we shouldn't become too attached to just one place."

I didn't know, at first, what answer to make . . .   I had never wanted this little paradise we were living in to end . . . nor had I seen the sights of Fez half often enough . . . and Gulbeyaz—I didn't want to retreat so ignominiously while she was still scorning all my overtures, still languishing only for Stephens.

"I should say that your suggestion, Moye, shows a rank indifference on your part to Gulbeyaz's smiles."

"But it also shows a consideration for the Flying Carpet.   We've got to get to Paris soon for an overhaul if you expect to keep flying."

That was a point against which I had no argument.

"All right," I said reluctantly.   "But let's have one more party first."

The night before our departure we gave the party, asking into our secret garden, to say farewell, all those who had shared it with us.   To-morrow it would not be ours, but to-night . . . the Arab musicians played and sang their frantic best; and Frankie, dissipating with ambrosia his sorrow over the loss of us, fell for one last time into the fish pond.   All through the evening Gulbeyaz danced, danced as she had never danced before.   How truly beautiful she was that night, despite her tattoo and gold teeth, how lithe and young, and how shining those great black eyes whenever Moye noticed her!

In a lonely and defeated mood, I left the joyful gathering in the courtyard, and, well after midnight, climbed up by myself to the terrace to look, once more before my departure, upon the sleeping city—a city I felt at home in and had grown to love.   How still I found the sky at this half-enchanted hour.   Every star in the universe was shining down on Fez.   The minaret of the neighbouring mosque seemed cut out of slate and pasted against the dim horizon, and all about me the white ghosts of Moorish houses huddled and whispered together.

With so much loveliness, I should have been content to be alone.   But I was not content. . . .   Gulbeyaz—I heard her cymbals clinking down below.   Why must she like Moye so much, and never like me? . . . To-morrow at dawn I was going away, cheated and dejected. If I could only see her, here, for one brief moment, in this dimness and this starlight . . . to say good-bye. . . .

Were my prayers being answered? Some one was coming up the steps, slowly and hesitantly. . . . I listened for the cymbals, but the music had stopped and all was quiet below. Gulbeyaz—it could only be Gulbeyaz! She had caught the glance I gave her, had seen me climbing to the roof and was coming after me, to say she was sorry for her indifference, sorry to see me go. She would ask to be forgiven. . . . "Never!" I said to myself, "—at least, not at first. I wouldn't even look around. I'd be cold and aloof, adamantine, superior . . . I'd gaze out, with folded arms, into the sky, while she pleaded with me."

The footsteps had reached the roof—she was now quite near . . . but I was determined to let her wait a while before I looked or spoke.

And then, beside me, I heard—was it a sigh?

She was punished enough. Slowly, a little ashamed of my cruelty, I turned.

There—prostrate over the balustrade—was Frankie!

And Frankie was ill.

As soon as I had recovered my own composure, I saw that he was *very* ill—so ill, indeed, that he needed prompt assistance. I loosened his collar, eased him as best I could, and tried to remember the proper antidote for too much ambrosia.

Preoccupied with my first-aid efforts, I paid no attention when another person came noiselessly on to the dark terrace and stood waiting, apparently for me.

After a moment, since I did not look up, the newcomer spoke—in Arabic, caressingly. Not until then did I recognise—*Gulbeyaz!*

But she had come too late.

"Oh, go on home," I said to her, over my shoulder. "I'm busy!"

CHAPTER X

BACK in Paris, after a leisurely flight from Fez through Seville, Lisbon and Madrid, Moye and I found ourselves no less eager to continue our exploration of the world by air. The Flying Carpet, now thoroughly overhauled, was ready to take us anywhere we wished to go.

We spread the map of Europe before us. Moscow beckoned, Norway beckoned, Sicily beckoned. We chose the Alps.

Some years before I'd spent a month wandering among those ice-clad peaks. I'd gone up the valley of the Visp to Zermatt, and from there, with one of my schoolmates, climbed the bloodthirsty Matterhorn. It had been one of the great moments of my youth—that savage battle with the snow and the wind, the heights and the chasms. For experienced Alpinists the conquest of the Matterhorn is no longer considered a great climbing feat. It is by no means the highest of the Alps—there are five peaks higher, four of which literally look down upon the Matterhorn. But for me, who at that time had done no climbing at all, this first battle with a mountain in the clouds was a terrific struggle. I was violently seized with mountain nausea; my head almost burst from the rare atmosphere; my heart stopped beating from sheer fright when I lost my grip on the suspended chains and slithered down a five-thousand-foot precipice toward Switzerland—as far as the climbing-rope fastened to my waist allowed.

Even so, I had crawled on, and the summit was attained, and the world far below rolled away in homage from the foot of this iceberg throne.

But it had been a costly victory. My face was frost-bitten, my ankle was wrenched, and the seat of my pants was worn through.

Now for my revenge!

From the moment we turned south again from Paris I began to plot against the Matterhorn. Three miles high, was it? My Flying Carpet could climb higher. Wreathed in a barrage of mist and clouds? We could swoop over them and around them at will. The time before I had only unaccustomed legs and sea-level lungs to fight with. Now I had two hundred and twenty-five winged horses to draw my scarlet Carpet through the Alpine thunder, and Moye's relentless grip to hold the reins.

At Geneva we girded ourselves for the battle. Then up the lake we advanced—over Lausanne—over Montreux—over the Castle of Chillon—into the teeth of the sky-scraping barriers. The Rhone Valley closed in two miles below; the river trickled down, walled by the gleaming titans of the Alps. Vast flocks of clouds roamed beneath. Mont Blanc, thirty miles away, blocked out the sky with its white magnificence.

How unfamiliar, from the air, these mountains seemed! On the previous visit, one vista at a time had been revealed, beautiful but fixed. Now all Switzerland rolled by below, changing, towering, hiding, falling. The miracle of flying, long since a commonplace, gripped me anew. Flight! It *was* a miracle. One moment our Carpet almost touched a glittering mountain-top. The next, the whole world fell away, and only space, bottomless, infinite space, gaped hungrily beneath. Now the clouds blanketed our view; now the sun burst through against the glaciers and half-blinded with a dazzling light.

What was this apparition there below me? Surely not the earth on which I lived, but rather some strange, nameless, frozen star. I did not belong to it; I never saw it before. Tiny clusters of tiny houses inhabited by tiny specks could be seen in the valleys far beneath. But they were merely colonies of specks. Their existence was of no importance. Their life, their death, their happiness and wretchedness, their works and wars, were all reduced to complete insignificance beside these terrible peaks of ice. At moments during this journey above the summit of a continent, I felt as detached from the earth as from the moon. They seemed equally remote.

Captain Stephens suddenly gave our Flying Carpet a sharp right-angle turn. We had reached the tributary valley of the Visp. Here the mist came down like an angry ocean and half-filled our canyon corridor, but the towering giants all about us still marked the way.

Closer and closer pressed the spires, white as the mountains at the poles. Above them the sky had turned to a blue so deep that it was almost black. Under this indigo dome, across the jagged iceberg sea, the Flying Carpet, scarlet-bodied, black-cowled, wings and tail of polished gold, flashed and sparkled through the flood of sun.

The jaws of the canyon, at its narrowest point, now waited just ahead, the right flank guarded by the incomparable Weisshorn, the left flank by the pinnacle of the Dom. We rushed between them at full speed, fearful that these Alpine Symplegades would clash together across the chasm and destroy our Fire Bird before we could sail through.

We escaped, but the mountains marshalled themselves anew. The Dent Blanche, as if in league with the foe, loomed out of the clouds to hold the west; in the east, Monte Rosa, next to Mont Blanc, the highest of them all, blocked the way into Italy. Eight thousand feet below us, through a rift in the barrage of fog, we caught a glimpse of the village of Zermatt, shrinking deep into the valley as if in mortal dread of the terrible frozen monsters hanging over it.

And straight before us, with its head lifted in mighty isolation, the Matterhorn, the tiger of the Alps, awaited the onslaught of the Flying Carpet and its crew.

At a hundred miles an hour we rushed toward its soaring northern precipice. How appallingly sheer it looked! How did climbers ever scale it? How did God ever build it? But this was no time to soliloquise—for while we were still half a mile away, a great bank of clouds condensed right in front of us, and completely blocked our vision. Moye did a sudden wing-over, and we turned on our tracks. But the blinding fog was now behind us as well, and all about us. We must get out at once. This shifting mist might at any moment reveal—too late!—another fang of ice lifted in our path. Moye, noting through the rifts clear skies above, pulled us upward in a spiral, at the sharpest angle such thin air permitted. But we had to climb a thousand feet before we emerged completely from the clouds, which now rolled in vast waves below us.

The altimeter registered fourteen thousand feet—eight hundred feet more, and we could clear the Matterhorn.

But which one *was* the Matterhorn? All the mountain-tops, so easily identified from below in the valley, seemed to have shifted, and changed their appearance. An entire archipelago of islands swam below us in the white and tossing sea, all looking more or less alike. Their familiar aspects were so distorted from this height that we could no longer identify my old enemy among a dozen others.

It seemed impossible to believe. A moment before, the great peak had soared before us, distinct and challenging—and now we couldn't even find it!

We resorted to our maps.

"It should be that one," Moye indicated, pointing over the side.

Ridiculous!—that strange peak couldn't be it! As though I wouldn't recognise my mountain. Hadn't I sat on top of it long enough!

"It's *this* one," I insisted, none too sure myself, directing Moye to a peak whose sheer and savage bulk looked familiar.

Its summit still rose well above us. We climbed to fifteen thousand feet. This, I knew, was somewhat above the level of the Matterhorn's utmost point. But it was not high enough, for the winds were blowing a violent blast that warned us to go higher and farther out of reach of the treacherous spire.

Oh, those winds! The peak was now up in arms. What devilish contraption was this that came roaring defiantly over its head, bearing two men from earth? Winds! Assault them! Break them and destroy them, winds! And the winds rushed at us with a breath that froze and a fury that almost hurled us from our seats.

But Moye, at the helm, was undismayed. Into the very thick of the battle we climbed, yet another thousand feet—sixteen thousand now—got a running start, nosed downward and swooped exultantly right over the top of the outraged mountain.

I looked overboard, straining my eyes to recognise some distinguishing feature of the summit.

I recognised nothing. Perhaps this wasn't the Matterhorn at all. It was probably some other confounded peak.

I glanced back at Moye and shook my head, and cursed all the mountains in Switzerland.

We were now hopelessly confused. I knew that the Matterhorn had two vast precipices sliced from its northern and eastern slopes—but all the other mountains seemed just as precipitous. The Gorner Glacier would get us straightened out—but it was completely lost beneath the sea of clouds.

Fortunately, the clouds were not stationary. They shifted and rose and fell, hiding peaks here, disclosing others there, though the valleys remained always submerged. And every time a new pinnacle appeared, the Flying Carpet, colder and colder, and angrier and angrier, went charging after it. In this grim game of hide-and-seek, we probably flew over some of the mountains twice.

At the summit of one pinnacle, resting on the topmost rock, we noticed two figures of climbers . . . black dots against the snow. With what excitement they waved at us, and we back at them! How astonished they must have been, after spending perhaps a day and a night toiling upward to this needle's point, to behold our gold-and-scarlet Carpet appearing out of the cold thin void and diving *down* to have a look at them. But whether their mountain was the Matterhorn or Pike's Peak, we hadn't the slightest idea. We circled five hundred feet above them, and dropped a note, tied to a monkey-wrench: "*Where* is the Matterhorn?" But our aim was poor; the note missed the rock by a hundred feet and went bounding down into the abyss.

We took a photograph of this peak, as we had of a dozen others, and fled. We must get out of these increasingly ominous clouds. We were being forced higher and higher as the mist vapour climbed after us. All Switzerland was about to be submerged. But for one glorious moment, the tips of just the six highest of the Alps, armoured in plates of gleaming ice and drenched in sunshine, rose higher than the fog. Mont Blanc, the loftiest island, far in the west, was unmistakable. On billows of fleece floated the summit snows of the cluster below us, a cluster containing Monte Rosa and Lyskamm and the Weisshorn and the Dom—*and* the Matterhorn; but we still didn't know which was which—and by now we didn't give a damn.

Then as we looked, there came a great surge in the cold and rolling ocean. All five of the peaks sank beneath the veil, and only Mont Blanc beckoned across this boundless sea.

Three miles high, we fled over the clouds toward the one remaining beacon, *en route* to Geneva. What canyons, what glaciers, what crags and depths, were hidden below, we could not tell. Mont Blanc alone joined us to the earth.

Europe's highest mountain was now only a mile away. We shot forward through the freezing sky at our utmost speed. Fly, old Carpet, fly! There was not going to be any argument about this mountain! Half a mile remained—two hundred yards. Hep! Over we went!—found a hole in the fog above Lac Leman, and tumbled home.

Next day the manager of the Geneva airport came to see us.

"We've just had a phone call from Zermatt," he said. "Two German climbers were on top of the Matterhorn yesterday and saw a red-and-gold airplane fly right over their heads and try to drop a note. They wanted to report it, and to find where the plane came from. I told them you flew that way yesterday, and were undoubtedly over the Matterhorn——"

"Undoubtedly!" Moye and I exclaimed in unison.

CHAPTER XI

FOLLOWING an immemorial pathway, the Flying Carpet sped through the Simplon Pass in order to reach Italy. Safe over the Alps! Our orders to the Carpet were now sharp and clear. Like the wind our airplane bore us eastward. Milan slid by; Verona looked up in astonishment; Padua we hardly saw at all. Then, flying very high, we reached the Adriatic and beheld a city built on islands anchored several miles from shore, looking from a mile above like a bouquet of russet flowers floating on the waves.

I had been in love with this city since my picture-book days. And now, sailing over it, I recognised all the familiar features. There were St. Mark's and the great piazza; there the Campanile and the Doges' Palace; there the Rialto Bridge. The great winding river was, I knew, the Grand Canal, and the thousand tiny boats, gondolas. The Flying Carpet had brought us to Venice.

That night the band played in the piazza, and the great crowds of summer visitors strolled about beneath the stars, listening to the music and enjoying that special pleasure which Venice offers above all other cities—leisure. Moye and I joined in the parade, and within an hour encountered, as one always does, several acquaintances.

One of these was a young American idler whose extravagant and lively nature had won him the sobriquet of "Whoopee." He knew intimately every bar in town and all the countesses, squandering a fortune one day to be lost in debt the next, irresponsible, irrepressible and exceedingly likable.

Whoopee volunteered to be our guide. He was a bit vague on his Tintorettos and his Titians, but made up for this by his familiarity with the most curious and charming corners and the most extraordinary people.

His favourite rendezvous was Harry's Café, overlooking the entrance to the Grand Canal, and here we foregathered next day for luncheon. Out the windows we could see gondolas and *vaporetti* moving up and down the most diverting and most beautiful thoroughfare in the world. Pale and imposing, the Santa Maria della Salute church looked upon us from the opposite bank, and across a lagoon the campanile of brick and bronze commanding San Giorgio soared above the rich red sails of fishing boats. There were colour and loveliness on every side, all meeting together and flowing through the broad Canal between its walls of dreamy palaces.

Even without one of Harry's famous "Venetian Moonlight" cocktails this rainbow vision of past ages would have been magic and alluring. *With* "Venetian Moonlights" the vision became irresistible—so irresistible that I decided to go swimming in it. . . . I challenged Whoopee to a swimming race down the Grand Canal.

"I axshept," he promptly agreed. He had been drinking Moonlights, too.

Harry, the proprietor, made us a proposition. He promised that if we'd begin at the upper end, by the railroad station, two and a half miles away, and race to his café which marked the lower end, he'd reward the winner with the best and coldest bottle of champagne in all Venice—and the loser, too.

That settled it. We'd start right now.

Moye refused to take any active part in the forthcoming water pageant, since he was sure really nice people did not bathe in canals, but he agreed to go along as referee. In less than half an hour the three of us had reached the station aboard a *vaporetto*, and climbed into the first gondola that came by.

Thereupon Whoopee and I began to take off our clothes, ignoring the violent protestations from the gondolier— swimming in the *Canale Grande* was strictly *proibito*, especially as we'd forgotten all about bathing suits. A hundred people lined the *fondamenta* before the station to watch with astonishment the public removal of our pants. Moye tried to sink out of sight, fearful he'd be recognised, and the gondolier's pleadings were pitiful to hear. To pacify him Whoopee and I left on our linen shorts—and dived overboard with a shout to Antonio to keep up with us if he could.

To our surprise we found the water salt. The taste was very, very bad. Even so, we both started out bravely, pushing the tin cans out of our way and swallowing as little of the Grand Canal as possible.

It was like trying to race down Fifth Avenue. *Vaporetti* charged us from fore and aft; barges ran over us; launches tooted frantically for their right of way. Antonio was almost beside himself.

But on down the Grand Canal we splashed, undismayed. Palace after palace drifted by—pink ones and yellow ones, grey palaces and gold palaces, each one as proud as the great nobles who five hundred years ago, when Venice had become the richest and most dazzling city in the world, built them with stones brought back from the conquest of Byzantium and filled them with all the riches of the East.

Time, alas, has diminished their former glory. The merchants of Venice who fetched and carried for the fifteenth-century world have all departed. Where dukes and ambassadors reigned in imperial splendour, paupers have swarmed in to occupy marble tenements, and family wash now hangs where the purple banners of a prince once fluttered in the wind.

With it all, there's still nothing else on earth so lovely, so romantic, as these faded palaces. With half-closed eyes, or by the light of the stars, Venice is Venice still, a mirage from yesterday that refuses to vanish, a magic city one has dreamed, and waked to find the dream come true.

And though not recommended by Baedeker, a really diverting way to observe the splendours of the Grand Canal is to swim in it. Swimming allows one to become thoroughly saturated with the essence of the place. In one of these palaces Byron lived and loved; in another, Browning wrote much of his poetry:

> Open my heart and you will see
> Graved inside of it, Italy.

From a window farther down, Napoleon watched the water carnivals pass. In this palace Wagner first dreamed the glorious strains of *Tristan and Isolde*, and in that one passed on to the beyond.

I didn't know all this, but Whoopee, when not dodging

vaporetti and mortified cats, told me about it. We had both, long since, become too winded to keep up the racing strokes (except when passing the fish market) and had decided to reduce speed and enjoy the scenery. Harry had promised a bottle of champagne to the loser of our contest, anyway, as well as to the winner, and as there were no medals at stake, it didn't matter much who won.

Splashing on around a curve in the Canal, we caught sight of the Rialto Bridge some two hundred yards ahead. It was in the process of rebuilding when Shakespeare wrote *The Merchant of Venice*. Whoopee, though I hardly believed him, insisted *this* house, right beside the bridge, was where Shylock and Jessica had lived. Pushing wet hair out of my eyes I looked fondly up at that house. Had I not played a home-made version of Shylock myself, at age fourteen, on an improvised stage at one end of my primary school gymnasium? I'd worn a white beard dripping to my waist, and a sort of black mother-hubbard that my dramatic teacher supposed was a Venetian Jewish garment of the fifteen hundreds. .

So this was the house from which I'd lost my daughter and my ducats! Ah, that cursed Antonio—and that sly Doctor Portia—"The quality of mercy is not strained"— How well I remembered that schoolboy play! "How far that little candle throws its beams! So shines a good deed in a naughty world——"

At this point Shylock and Whoopee were pinched by the police.

We looked up to find a launch, manned by two patrolmen, right beside us. Their orders were unmistakable, but as they wore no uniforms, had no badges, no billies and no Irish brogue, we decided they couldn't possibly be the police. And even if they were, we decided not to be arrested anyway. It would be much funnier. Whoopee dived under water and tried to get away. It was no good. The patrolmen, angered by such disrespect, were right after him, and when he came up for air grabbed his linen shorts. Making a fearful splash in order to get his captors as wet as possible, and shouting that he was being murdered, he was dragged, despite his yells and struggles, into the half-capsized launch.

The law came after me next. I was swimming like mad for the Rialto Bridge, but laughing too hard at Whoopee standing up in the launch and cheering me on, to make much speed. I had not gone fifty feet before the *polizia* grabbed me too.

Needless to say, by this time the entire Canal was in an uproar.

Meanwhile Moye, instead of resisting these outrages, was bent double with glee at the sight of Whoopee, and then me, being hauled by our underpants out of the Grand Canal by two irate and dripping Venetian cops. But he stopped laughing at us very abruptly when the police, thoroughly annoyed, and thinking Moye was laughing at them, laid hands upon him with a curt order that sounded like "You, too, cocky!"

Properly squelched, the three of us, followed by the gondolier who had shared our disgrace, were then taken in the launch back up the Canal to the police station, and locked in a guard-room to await the arrival of the sergeant. Whoopee and I were still without our clothes, which were being withheld so the sergeant could see for himself in what scanty underwear the two criminals had been disporting themselves in a public place. This objection seemed particularly absurd in Venice where the natives bathe in the side-canals with nothing on at all, and where foreigners are encouraged, over on the Lido beaches, to array themselves in not much more. Evidently one could undress to swim in the ocean, but not along Main Street.

On the sergeant's return we were all marched before him—Moye elegantly attired in starch and waistcoat, Antonio in his gondolier's uniform, and Whoopee and I in a fetching little costume of wet and sadly misused sky-blue *caleçons*.

The sergeant made it clear that we were being prosecuted for *una contravvensione ai regolamenti municipali.*

We were fined fifty cents apiece.

CHAPTER XII

THE GHOSTS OF SANTA SOPHIA

WE spent a month in Venice. A month wasn't nearly long enough, but after that time we both began to feel the urge to fly again. Once more we unrolled our map of the world. Moye suggested Berlin. I voted for Malta. We compromised on Constantinople. A few hours later the Flying Carpet and its crew were in the air.

Our first stop was Vienna. Then to Budapest—to Belgrade—to Bucharest—through storms, across plains, over mountains—on to Constantinople and the Golden Horn.

As we approached, the sun was low in the west, beating against the vast land walls that stretch, with their hundred towers, straight across the peninsula on which Constantinople stands. Reflecting this fire rose a forest of minarets. The domes and the gardens, the castles and the seas, were suffused by the same violet haze that crowns Athens at the sunset hour. The Golden Horn mirrored the flaming clouds. The Bosporus, a deep blue ribbon, hewed its way between Asia and Europe, escaping from the Black Sea which stretched away to the north in deep dark gloom. Gold walls and violet light, blue waters and sunset sky, all were softened and harmonised by the fast fading afternoon. And this concentration point of history and of splendour, this stage of endless epic dramas, this imperial city which next to Rome longest shaped the destiny of the world, lay, five thousand feet below, in the hollow of my hand.

Jason and his Argonauts first came this way, more than three thousand years before. Constantine and Justinian made it the centre of civilisation. Mohammed the Conqueror and Suleiman the Magnificent adorned it and glorified it. But not even they ever saw their capital revealed as it was revealed to me. They did not know, as I knew, how truly magical it was, how fabulously beautiful. They had not soared into space above their palaces, to survey their domains from the Black Sea to the Hellespont. This was within the power only of the jinns, and the characters out of story-books who travelled miraculously across the skies aboard their flying carpets.

Long before we arrived at Constantinople I knew what most I wanted to see there—the Basilica of Santa Sophia. Pictures of this astonishing temple I had seen all my life; histories of it had filled me with an eagerness to enter its doors. Through those doors the ebb and flow of conquest, the emperors and the captains that ruled the earth, had passed for a thousand years before Michelangelo raised the dome of St. Peter's above the Eternal City.

There it was, a mile below, a monarch commanding two continents. Approached from the air the great Basilica seems to scorn all outward grace, relying on its enormous size and strength to capture one's eye. Instead of statues and lace-like stone, massive buttresses, solid and practical, ornament its heavy box-like walls. Even the four minarets added by Moslem conquerors, rising above the granite mountain, are too incongruous to add much charm. In fact, from the outside, Santa Sophia is a disappointment. One might mistake it for a fort—until one sees the interior.

The first evening of our visit to Constantinople, a half-moon rose in the sky. Even though we had flown six hundred miles that day and well deserved a night of rest, I chose not to take it—not with this moonlight shining through the windows of the most ancient and most storied cathedral in the world. On such a night what might one not see within?

Alone, about nine o'clock, I went to the courtyard before the mosque and found it cool and calm at this late hour. The enormous mass of masonry, confused and meaningless in the dark, towered above. At the side door, now used for the entrance, a guard stopped me—it was late—the last prayers were being said—he would soon be extinguishing the lamps—I could not enter . . . unless I cared to contribute a little backsheesh to him personally.

I contributed, took my shoes in my hand, plunged into the black emptiness, felt my way down a vaulted corridor, passed between two enormous marble columns, and there,

97

moved to the depths by the incredible picture, I stood and stared. . . . "The terrestrial paradise, the second firmament, the throne of the glory of God. It rises to the heavens. It is the marvel of the earth," exclaimed a chronicler eight hundred years ago.

I knew just how he felt.

Had I entered this Temple of Divine Wisdom first by day, I am certain it would have been an adventure astonishing enough; but to have been drawn through the darkness into its appalling expanse of space, illuminated by the shafts of moonlight that streamed down through the forty windows of the most audacious dome in history, made me feel that I beheld a vision of a temple too aspiring, too vast, to be the handiwork of man.

Fourteen hundred years old—the first of the great Christian temples. Many other have since risen to compete with it, but as I stood within its walls I felt this temple was still supreme among cathedrals, and would be always until the giants and angels who must have helped in building it came back to earth to build a greater one.

Once my eyes became used to the obscure light I began to move across the carpets, around the edge of the vault, past a row of marble columns—moving softly in order not to disturb the small group of Moslems bowed down toward Mecca. An imam led this late gathering of the faithful, and chanted forth his prayers to Allah, prayers repeated by the congregation as they knelt and stood and knelt and touched their foreheads to the floor in rhythmical, rustling unison.

The services were over, the last for the day. The worshippers, treading silently in their stockinged feet across the thick mats and carpets, flowed past my dark recess and out into the deep-shadowed corridor.

The priest alone remained, tiny and unreal in the presence of such soaring space, such huge dimensions, about him. And then he, too, without sound, without effort, in his long robes, seemed to float over the temple floor, and in slow and solitary dignity fade into the outer dark.

From out of this same dark, my friend the guard came in, extinguished the lamps, and disappeared, leaving only the beams of moonlight for illumination.

So utterly entranced had I been by the dim glory of my

surroundings I had not given a thought to my own departure; and the realisation that I was utterly alone within this haunted vastness strangely did not drive me out of it. Rather was I held, fascinated, by my nocturnal excursion into this moonlit and mysterious realm. There was no profanation here, no mock-heroic escapade, but reverence and wonder—reverence for the passion and the genius that built the temple, for the centuries that have consecrated it, for the millions of Christians and Moslems who have worshipped in it and approached nearer to their God. I was possessed by an irresistible desire to rest peacefully in the dark shadow of this mother of all cathedrals, to enjoy the dream of fourteen hundred years of history, to possess utterly, for my very own, these carpeted floors, these columns torn from pagan temples, these mountainous marble walls, this soaring sensational canopy nearly two hundred feet above me, through which the moonlight streamed.

For three enchanted hours I roamed about my marvellous domain, touching, through the shadow veil, the pillars and the walls, the rostrum and the urns. I leaned back against a marble column and looked up at the incredible dome, a dome such as no man ever dared to build before, or has been able to build since. The master architect who designed it defied every structural law. Gravity is apparently dismissed. It should have fallen before it was half built, so ethereal it is, so flat, so fearless. And yet the innumerable earthquakes that have shaken the city to pieces have not so much as cracked this earth-scorning canopy.

How still the great mosque had become with the midnight hour; how peaceful its deep gloom. The weariness from six hours spent that day flying through the skies crept over me. My lodging was far away and the carpets in my secluded corner deep, and very soft. Perhaps if I rested throughout the night in this ghostly place I'd hear the chorus of angels that sometimes chants when no Mohammedan is near, or like Jacob, see them mounting up one of the ladders of light that led to Paradise.

I made a pillow of my leather flying coat and stretched upon a carpet bed, still able to look out between the marble columns and up at the soaring canopy of dim stone sky. The moon continued to ride in the heavens, drifting around the circle of windows upon which the great dome spread its wings. That moon seemed determined to look through all the forty ancient panes; and as it wheeled, the angle of the shafts of light that fell upon the carpets at my feet wheeled too. I lay quite still, and watched the slow procession of these moonbeams, wondering if they were the ghosts of the emperors who once ruled Byzantium, the Christian kingswho had worshipped here, the sultans of the Saracens . . . convening in this dark and overtowering vault from which all living human beings but myself had been driven out.

The first and proudest of these spectral shafts, if they were ghosts, must have been Justinian—Justinian, whose giant spirit conceived this glorious temple, who commanded his architects to build these walls, in order that Byzantium might behold the supreme manifestation of the worship of the Christian God, and remember the power and the glory of the imperial builder.

Who better had the right to lead the march of the ghosts than Justinian? It was his lordly gesture, in the year 537, that swept away the acres of houses standing where he wished his great Basilica to rise. It was he who stopped all other works to marshal sixteen thousand builders under his authority, who scoured the empire for extravagant materials, who pillaged the colossal marble columns from the Temple of Diana at Ephesus, ransacked Baalbek for its riches, and levied from Athens, Delphi and Rome shiploads of treasures.

What matter if building costs soared into prodigious figures? Justinian was not the man to be dismayed. He merely seized the salaries of all the state officials, closed the schools and forced the army to fight without pay, thus providing forty thousand pounds of silver for the altar piece and half a million pearls for the sanctuary's curtain. Extortion, taxation, torture, robbery, played their part in the creation of this supreme monument to the Divine Wisdom of God.

Justinian's temple stood at last complete, faced inside with marble from a hundred lands, roofed (with the help of the dark and secret powers) by one miraculous, floating dome. This was the Emperor's triumphant hour. Surrounded by his glittering court, his generals and his ministers, accompanied by a thousand priests and a vast orchestra and choir, Justinian mounted to the silver altar and cried out for the multitudes to hear, "Oh, Solomon, I have surpassed thee!"

Yes—that foremost of the moonbeam ghosts—that was Justinian.

And the ghosts that followed—perhaps they were the other Byzantine kings; or perhaps Christian knights of the Crusades who had tarried here, bearing the cross and the sword with which to free the Holy Sepulchre.

And the final shaft but one, in the slow procession, was that Constantine XIII, the last Christian emperor of the Byzantines? Fate had forced him to watch his empire crumbling before the tidal wave of Saracens, until in 1453 the deluge came. Knowing his city was doomed and he about to die, he came into the imperial church to take the sacrament. He looked up at the huge mosaic figures upon the ceiling of the marvellous dome—Christ and the Virgin, the Saints and the Apostles. He knew they were soon to be flung from the thrones which they had graced nine hundred years. He kissed the great gold cross that hung suspended from the cupola. He knew that before the day was done a crescent would shine in its place.

And so it came to pass. Over the bodies of ten thousand Christian dead, Sultan Mohammed rode into the Basilica. The interior was packed with terrified citizens, praying for deliverance, but deliverance did not come. Mohammed mounted to the silver altar, knelt toward Mecca, and gave thanks to Allah for the victory.

That brightest shaft of moonlight—the very last of all—that, surely, was Mohammed, for was this not the great Sultan's mosque as well as Justinian's church? Had he not transformed it? Had he not stripped it of every Christian symbol, appropriated its most valuable treasures, gilded over the mosaics of Christ, removed the altars and the crosses? Had he not spread verses from the Koran across these ceilings from which the saints had looked down? Had he not erected minarets from whose balconies the muezzins might call a Moslem Byzantium to prayer? He had found Santa Sophia the greatest church in Christendom. He had renamed it Aya Sophia, and turned it into the greatest mosque in all the Moslem world —and no man has been able to dislodge him from that day to this. How proud and slow his ghost marched past; proud of possession, proud of Islam, proud of Sultan Mohammed.

And on and on the shadow figures moved, pacing, with the wheeling moon, their path across the temple floor where they had known their mortal glory; until the moonlight waned, and one by one the spectres faded back into their crumbling tombs. . . .

It was early dawn, and there was not a ghost in sight. The moon had entirely departed, and a pale grey light crept in through the windows of the dome. Cold, and a little apprehensive, I seized my flying coat and sought the door of the mosque. It was open, screened only by a heavy curtain of mats. The same guard of the evening before slept soundly on the floor of the stone porch outside, and I did not disturb him as I crept beneath the curtain and, shoes in hand, slipped past.

But I did not reach the street, for at that moment one of the muezzins was coming across the courtyard to ascend the minaret—and I stood still, seized by a fantastic idea. . . . The muezzin—the minaret of Aya Sophia— at dawn—the first call of the day . . . if only I could accompany him and hear him at close range summon Istanbul to prayer, my night's cup of adventure would be filled.

I spoke to him and indicated that I wanted to climb the minaret when he climbed. Never had I wanted anything so much. He looked at the guard. The guard slept soundly. He looked at the courtyard. Not a stir. He nodded assent. Oh, Islam, Islam, how has your fanaticism faded!

Behind the muezzin, in the blackness, I felt my way up the spiralling stairs. We emerged on the high balcony with the sun just ready to spring out of Asia, and all Istanbul, grey and misty, sleeping at our feet. Before us the dome of the mosque rose so close I felt that I could almost reach it with my hand. From the Marmora Sea the daybreak wind whispered past our minaret, blessing alike with its clear, cool touch the faithful and the infidel.

Allah' u' akbar—Allah' u' akbar. The muezzin leaned out to the east, out to the sun, and chanted in that weird, quavering whine always used, that sounds like mournful wolves a-howling. *Allah' u' akbar—God is great.*

Ashadu an la Ilah ill' Allah—I testify there is no god but God. There is no god but God.

The chanting priest now leaned to the north, toward the

Golden Horn, the swirling, awakening Bosporus, the vague Black Sea—*I testify that Mohammed is the Prophet of God—Come to prayer—Come to prayer.*

He moved to face the west, the myriads of domes and minarets, the hundred towers of the great land walls, all tinted brightly with the first colours of the sunrise—*Haya il' al' falah—falaaaaaaaah—Come to salvation—salvaaaaaaaa-shun—*

It was a futile call, an appeal in vain, apparently, for no one seemed to heed. The mosques are almost empty in Istanbul, the religious springs are dry. Mohammed's reign over Byzantium is tottering to a close. *Tout lasse, tout casse, tout passe.* Just how long until the crescent topples from Aya Sophia's dome, only a major prophet can foretell. But any minor prophet knows the time is not far off. Then bells will ring in the minarets, and back from exile will come the Christian saints to take their places on their thrones; and once more the doxology will fill the glorious Basilica as it did in the golden ages fourteen hundred years ago.

CHAPTER XIII

GALILEAN DAYS

THE armies of the First Crusade, fighting their way from Constantinople to Syria in the eleventh century, marched the eight hundred miles across what is now Asiatic Turkey in seven months. The Flying Carpet took just seven hours.

Moye and I left Istanbul behind one day at noon. We climbed and climbed above the minarets of Santa Sophia, waved good-bye to the Golden Horn, and sailed up the castled shores of the Bosporus. Then we turned east, found the trail of the Crusaders and sped on toward the Holy Land. Our immediate objective was the Sea of Galilee.

The Sea of Galilee! In all the world has any lake a more romantic, a more poetic, history than this? Wherever Christianity has prevailed, this little sea is known and loved. Since the beginning of our era a halo of immortality has crowned its name. Its shores were the scene of Jesus' ministry; its waters bore Him many times; from its people came Peter and Andrew, James and John. Whenever He journeyed into the neighbouring provinces it was to this haven He invariably returned. One can well imagine that when He hung upon the cross, slowly perishing from the torture and the thirst, His dying eyes saw the vision of the cool blue depths of Galilee.

And now, below us, the very lake appeared.

It is not a large basin, this so-called sea. From north to south it measures less than sixteen miles, and only seven miles across. But if it were larger, perhaps we should love it less. Mountains, treeless now and grey with stone, stand round about, broken only by the River Jordan, which flows in from the peaks of Lebanon and out to feed the insatiable Dead Sea.

We landed in a broad field beside the river, and remained for two weeks, held prisoner by the charm of this historic region. We climbed the mountains, tramped along the shore, and embarked on the lake in the tiny fishing boats.

The fishermen soon became our daily companions. I have never had companions I admired more, for, as is the case with fishermen everywhere, they had grown to be like the sea they continually contemplated—free, honest, natural, clean. It was not otherwise in Jesus' time. What greater tribute to a calling was ever made than this: that of the Twelve He chose for His disciples, seven were fishermen?

Among those following this profession, two Arab brothers, Akhmet and Ali, were my special friends. Like James and John they owned a boat together, and like those two disciples, observed the great tradition of their lake—the tradition of honesty, simplicity and fidelity. Ali was twenty, Akhmet twenty-one. The Galilean sun had burned into their dark skin a healthy ruddiness that found good company in their clear black eyes. They each wore a single white cotton costume made in the native style, and they were barefoot. They had no money—their sailboat was their only capital.

For several days, while Moye was occupied with the Flying Carpet, I accompanied these two brothers in their fishing boat when they set their nets or hauled in the catch collected the night before. Our verbal communication was limited to the dozen English words they had picked up from occasional tourists, but in pantomime they were eloquent, so we got along.

Despite their lack of worldly goods, or perhaps because of it, they had the most untroubled, untarnished hearts I've ever met. They sang and sang all day with shrill discordant voices—the way all Arabs sing. Akhmet, the elder brother, would chant out a line alone, and then the two of them would repeat the line in full-lunged duet. It was always of love they sang, for, like most young Arabs, they had incorrigibly romantic natures, responsive as the strings of a harp to any touch of sentiment.

> *Alhoub fi kalbi amanah, Kafia,*
> *Malakti kalbi bi ridayek*

was their favourite song, and Kafia the lady of their dreams.

Love in my heart is to be trusted, Kafia;
I can be trusted with your love.
Every shadow of my soul is yours, Kafia;
In your hands rests my destiny.

Tiberias, the once-royal city of Herod, was our harbour.
From there, in the late afternoon, we'd sail close inshore up
to the site of Capernaum, Jesus' adopted home, or across
the estuary of the Jordan to Bethsaida where Peter and
Andrew and Philip once lived. To-day only a few stones
and capitals strewn about among weeds mark the spots.

But before these ghost cities the fishermen cast with the
same type of net, from the same type of boat, in the same
free and hardy spirit, as two thousand years ago. At twilight Akhmet and Ali and I would fix one end of their net
upon the shore, and then drag the weighted line, to which
the mesh was attached, in a semicircle out into the sea
and back to shore again. We slept near by to guard the
line, and then, when it was dawn, we drew our catch to
land, gathering the larger fish into baskets, and casting
the very small away.

And upon me, always, was the consciousness that this
shore by Bethsaida had seen things strange and wonderful.
Here Jesus, standing in Simon Peter's boat, often taught
the people gathered on the beach. Here, it is recorded,
He said to Simon:

Launch out into the deep, and let down your nets for a
draught. And Simon answering said unto him, Master,
we have toiled all the night, and have taken nothing:
nevertheless at thy word I will let down the net. And
when they had done this, they enclosed a great multitude
of fishes: and their net brake.

Such a miraculous draught of fishes from the Sea of
Galilee has not, alas, been seen in many a day. The fish
of late years have become few and small. There were
several times when Akhmet and Ali and I toiled dili-
gently before Bethsaida and, like Simon, took nothing.
But, probably unlike Simon, we were not in the least
downhearted by a meagre catch, for it meant there would
be less marketing for the brothers to do and more time for
us to sail, or explore the hills.

One such morning, after a particularly lean haul, we
three stood on the pier at Tiberias looking about for new

amusements to fill the day. I noticed the high gold mountain wall that rose up abruptly from the eastern shore of the lake, seven miles away, and wondered what hidden ancient splendours might lie buried there. I had a sudden urge—the morning was so radiantly beautiful— I suggested to Ali and Akhmet that we sail across and spend the day on the other side, in "the country of the Gadarenes."

The two fishermen agreed, but on launching forth we found there was a dead calm. They took to the oars in a leisurely fashion, and I dived overboard and swam alongside. The water proved so cool and stimulating, I decided, after a mile or two of lazy paddling, that it might be amusing to swim all the way across.

From the centre of the lake I could look around at the barren shores. Upon those shores, in the time of Christ, a dozen busy cities had stood, offering anchorage to large fleets of fishing boats built from the timber that grew in deep forests upon the surrounding hills.

Of all this abundance, only Tiberias remains, now a squalid village. Except Capernaum and Bethsaida, even the locations of the other lake-side cities are lost. Gone are the fishing fleets. On the entire lake there are now less than twenty sails. I could scan the encircling mountains and not find one wooded spot to break their gauntness.

Among these mountains, the Mount of the immortal Sermon, above Capernaum, stood out most conspicuously. From Capernaum, Jesus and His disciples had climbed to this commanding altar and surveyed the entire sea spread below them, intensely blue amid the then green hills. Here was space for the crowds who flocked to hear Him speak in all His wisdom. . . . *Lay not up for yourselves treasures upon earth . . . for where your treasure is, there will your heart be also. . . . Take therefore no thought for the morrow: for the morrow shall take thought for the things of itself. . . .* No treasures upon earth, no thought for to-morrow—was that, after two thousand years, still the way to happiness? To look at my two Galilean companions, reared in the shadow of the Mount, one would think so.

All morning there had not been the faintest breeze. Not a single ripple disturbed the glazed surface of the lake. But Akhmet warned me that this quietude would not last;

that on these hot August days the calm always gave way to a violent squall. . . . And just as Akhmet had prophesied, the wind, shortly after the noon hour, sprang up with astonishing suddenness; the whitecaps began to break about us—and the yellow mountain wall still lay a mile away.

The lake has been famous since Biblical times for these sharp summer storms. Utter cloudless calm all morning, and then, in the early afternoon—swoop!—down comes a sudden vortex of wind, sucked into the basin by its sub-sea-level position; and in an instant the waters begin to foam.

It would have been the sensible thing for me to climb back into the boat and allow the fishermen to raise their sail and hasten to the shore. But having covered six of the seven miles, I naturally wanted to finish off the last remaining one, and so I stuck at it, through another half-hour of wind and waves.

Reaching the foaming rocky beach at last, I lay down, half-drowned, beneath the great mountain wall, while Ali and Akhmet, having anchored our boat in deep water, swam ashore, dragging our sodden clothes behind them.

We had no hope of getting back to Tiberias before the wind abated, so we made ourselves at home in a sheltered corner of the cliff. Our little excursion had left us ravenously hungry, but as we had set out that morning unexpectedly, we had brought no food. However, for my two Galilean fishermen, that was not a serious matter. They just took their small casting nets from the boat, stood among the rocks along the shore, and, fencing with the angry breakers, cast for fish.

The waves burst against them and over them, but they only laughed and braced themselves for the next assault. Their lithe and agile bodies, drenched with spray and sun, gleamed like polished copper as they swung their nets and wrestled with the sea.

Soon they had taken six fish—two for each of us—and proudly brought them back. Then while Akhmet built a fire from driftwood and dead reeds, Ali and I went to visit a small encampment of shepherds we had seen half a mile away. We returned with a basket of unleavened bread. By this time Akhmet had a grill of hot coal ready, and upon it he laid the fish. Never in my life have I dined more royally.

Twilight was approaching before we thought of going

home. But the wind still howled across the lake; and we did not dare start back until it blew less violently. However much the land of Galilee has changed since the time of the Apostles, the Sea of Galilee has remained the same—moody, tempestuous. Nineteen hundred years ago the first story of a Galilean storm, just such as this, was told. It has become one of the most familiar stories in the world:

> When the even was come, Jesus saith unto his disciples, Let us pass over unto the other side. And . . . they took him even as he was into the ship. . . . And there arose a great storm of wind, and the waves beat into the ship, so that it was now full. And he was in the hinder part of the ship, asleep on a pillow: and they awake him, and say unto him, Master, carest thou not that we perish? And he arose, and rebuked the wind, and said unto the sea, Peace, be still. And the wind ceased, and there was a great calm.

The stars were out before we were able to embark again aboard our fishing boat. Though the lake was no longer driven by the storm, it had not ceased to roll. Nor had the wind entirely subsided. Since it still blew fitfully against us, we had to use the oars, without the assistance of the sail. Akhmet sat at the rudder, and Ali and I each manned an oar, and stood as we rowed.

Alhoub fi kalbi amanah!

chanted Akhmet at the stern.

Alhoub fi kulbi amanah!

Ali sang after him, in rhythm with our oars.
Love in my heart is to be trusted . . . just an Arab love-song, so popular locally that even I knew the words; yet now, sent ringing over the Galilean waves by these two simple fishermen, it seemed almost like the faint, imperfect echo of another, older love-song—the divine love-song once spoken to the music of these waters. For is not the refrain of that song, too, only the same simple message in a higher, more spiritual key—Love is to be trusted? These words, with their universal truth, rising in a great tide from the shores of this insignificant little lake, have swept like spring upon the spiritual deserts of

the world, carrying the name of Galilee to the hearts of men.

During the second watch of the night the wind faded to a breeze, and then died away entirely. The Sea of Galilee slept, motionless, and on across it, guided by the outline of the hills, we rowed unto Tiberias.

CHAPTER XIV

THE HOLY SEPULCHRE

FROM the moment the Flying Carpet left Constantinople behind and turned toward the Holy Land, the Crusaders had become our guides. And as the Holy Sepulchre had been their goal, so likewise it now became our own. The Crusaders had crossed the Taurus mountain range in south-east Anatolia with the greatest difficulty, and so did we. We tarried before Antioch, as they had tarried, and still in their tracks, flew on along the coast of Syria to Tyre, and Sidon, and Acre.

After our excursion to the Sea of Galilee, we continued south down the valley of the winding Jordan until we came to Jericho, a modern village built upon the ruins of the trumpet-tumbled walls. Here we turned to the west, rose four thousand feet out of the walled-in valley, sailed twenty miles over the wilderness of Judea, over the Mount of Olives—and Jerusalem burst upon us.

The soldiers of the First Crusade had attained this goal more than eight centuries before. Or rather, their remnant had, for out of every ten who marched forth from the cities of Christendom, only one arrived, and these, after three years on the way, were starving and exhausted.

Even so, the fanatical zeal that had driven them to the deliverance of the Holy Land still burned bright, and they did not falter at sight of the huge stone ramparts behind which an equally fanatical Moslem army watched and waited. The soldiers of the Cross, gaunt and weary, but raised to a pitch of religious frenzy by their priests, hurled themselves against the walls, shouting their battle cry of *Deus vult!*—only to be hurled back with frightful losses.

Godfrey de Bouillon, greatest among their leaders,

then decided on less zeal and more science. His engineers built a movable siege-tower capable of overtopping the walls, and this was pushed forward. The Moslems flung fire and boulders against it, raised their rampart higher, and concentrated all their strength to meet the giant.

But the Crusaders grimly advanced. Only a foot remained between their tower and the wall. The tower's drawbridge was allowed to fall, and across it, led by the indomitable Godfrey, the Crusaders charged. *Deus vult!* God wills it! Seldom in history have soldiers been so fired by religious passion; seldom has any battle been so terrible. The Crusaders were fighting in the name of Christ. His sepulchre lay only a few hundred yards away. Nothing could withstand their frenzy. The Moslem ranks crumbled, the gates were opened from within, and the entire Christian army stormed exultantly into Jerusalem.

The soldiers went mad with joy. For this moment they had left their homes long months before. For this moment they had struggled three thousand miles through every obstacle. Their god and their dead comrades would be avenged, and the infidels who held Jerusalem swept from the sacred city they profaned.

The butchery was indescribable. Moslem families crowded for sanctuary into the Mosque of Omar—to be annihilated by the revengeful Christian sword. Not even the children were spared. The Via Dolorosa became a river of blood through which the conquerors waded to their goal. Upon a pavement of slaughtered bodies the Knights of the Cross knelt in pious prayer before the Holy Sepulchre.

And now from the Flying Carpet we could see below, amid the jumble of Jerusalem, the domes and towers of the church that marks this same historic spot—the spot where, so the holy legends say, Christ was crucified, and buried, and on the third day rose from the dead.

In wide circles we sailed back and forth over the city. The present walls, though of later construction, rise on the ruins of the walls assaulted by the Crusaders. I could follow their entire circumference at a glance. This was the Jaffa Gate—this the Damascus Gate—this Herod's Gate. Where the wall turned the north-east corner, the Christian armies had manœuvred their wooden tower.

Looming above all other things, from the centre of the great temple enclosure, rose the Mosque of Omar, which had served Godfrey's zealots for a slaughter house. Over thirty acres about the mosque spread the immense court, covering a sixth of the city—the same court that once supported the wonderful temple of Solomon. Eastward stood the Mount of Olives, crowned with churches; at its foot, Gethsemane. And over a ridge to the south the afternoon sun shone on Bethlehem.

It was already twilight when Stephens and I, on foot, penetrated the walls and entered the sacred city. Like all pilgrims to Jerusalem, the moment we had found a lodging and unburdened ourselves of our baggage we went straightway to the Church of the Holy Sepulchre. The route to the church led through the twisting crowded lane . . . past Jews and Arabs, priests and mullahs, Christians and infidels. Meeting every race and creed and costume in the world, we made our way down the narrow stair-stepped Street of David. Along this very street the Crusaders had hewn their way eight hundred years before.

The Church of the Holy Sepulchre is not the same as when Godfrey worshipped there—only the location. The present structure, restored behind a twelfth-century front, is not much more than a hundred years old.

Finding it, hidden away amid a labyrinth of lesser buildings, we entered a little door that penetrates the entirely unimposing Romanesque façade, walked through the cavernous gloom of an outer chapel into the main rotunda, and stood beside the hallowed Sepulchre.

Despite all previous warnings, I had hoped to find the church austere, simple, quiet—befitting the site it is supposed to honour. To make the pilgrimage and find miraculous peace and comforting at this shrine has been the lifelong dream of so many millions of people. Thousands and thousands, during fifteen centuries, have made great sacrifices and endured great hardships, merely to come and kneel upon this spot. To deliver it into the hands of those who would cherish it, two million Crusaders laid down their lives. If there is any sacredness in Christendom, surely it should be here.

But the astonishing, disillusioning reality! No Oriental festival was ever as blatant, as garish, as spurious, as the interior of this church at the present time. Decay and shocking disrepair are everywhere. Of the large sums given by the constant streams of visitors, no part ever manifests itself except in the form of gaudy tinsel ikons, soiled plaster saints, and dusty paper flowers. Rapacious "guides" dog one's heels. Moans and lamentations rise from the pitiful women who drag themselves on their knees to the Sepulchre and cover its marble slab with passionate kisses. Tourists are being photographed before the dilapidated altars. Wrangling priests of differing creeds glare at one another and grasp their holy candles like bludgeons, prepared to strike the enemy over his heretic head. These priests of rival Christian religions hate one another with an irreconcilable hatred. Actual fights among them are not infrequent, even at the Tomb itself.

At Easter, the high feast of all these brawling sects, the mobs of fanatics become hysterical and violent, their frenzies and antagonisms boiling over. Heads are broken, pitched battles occur, people have been beaten and trampled to death. At this season, lest too many of those who come for salvation should lose their lives, soldiers stand guard in the courtyard, trying to control the processions of turbulent pilgrims dancing and struggling around the Holy Sepulchre and shrieking "Christ is risen! Hallelujah!" If there were only a booth for red lemonade, a tin band, and fireworks at night through the dome, the Church of the Sepulchre at Jerusalem would be a complete sideshow of barbarism and buffooneries.

And this holy spot which has been the scene of such battle and bloodshed, such drama and sacrifice, for fifteen centuries, is without any proof whatsoever of authenticity. During the three hundred years following the death of Christ, Jerusalem was utterly destroyed, and completely rebuilt, several times. Not until 330, a lapse of time as long as that between the landing of the Pilgrims in America and the present day, was any thought given to the Sepulchre's location. Then Constantine ordered Calvary to be "found," and some one had a vision, and said, It is here! And that's all the proof we have.

These things I knew. Even so, respecting the overwhelming symbolism of the place, I came from far away to see it and entered reverently. I have recorded what I saw. And yet, despite the barbaric and unholy scenes,

I left the Sepulchre as I had come—reverently, knowing that while one can doubt the authenticity of the church's claim, one cannot doubt the authenticity of the faith of the millions and millions of devout people who have worshipped there. Their adoration is extravagant, but in the simple hearts of those who pray, it is desperately sincere.

Those weary-looking women with distraught eyes, crawling on their knees oblivious to the bickering priests, were realising the sweetest moment of their sorrow-filled lives. They pressed their lips to the dubious Sepulchre, and in their faces came a look that passed all understanding. They had brought their heartaches here; the touch of the Sepulchre opened the portals of their souls and healed the wretchedness. They *were* comforted. They *were* redeemed. The tinsel, the trash, the hocus-pocus, was distasteful to me; but for each person like myself there are a thousand others whom these things console and spiritualise. Even if the Crucifixion took place a hundred miles away, even if the Resurrection had not occurred at all, the faith of the countless worshippers who have *believed* has made this place as sacred as if it were truly the scene of the Redemption. "Peace I leave with you, my peace I give unto you: not as the world giveth . . . Let not your heart be troubled, neither let it be afraid." Peace—legions of the faithful have found it beside the Sepulchre. With all its falseness and its blatancy, this church is still the most blest of sanctuaries for half the people of an unhappy earth. In the face of such profound trust, such transcendent reality, who am I to scoff?

I burned a respectful candle where the mumbling pilgrims were burning theirs.

And when I had departed and reached the streets again, the night had descended, but the stars were shining in the sky.

CHAPTER XV

OUR Flying Carpet safely housed, Moye Stephens and I resided two months in Jerusalem. Every day and half the night we spent prowling through its ancient lanes, atop its walls, about its hills. Familiarity only made the city more interesting. We mixed with scholars, rabbis, priests, mullahs, eager to learn whatever we could about the inexhaustible subject of Jerusalem.

Of all the people we encountered, Dr. Jacob Spafford gave us the most enlightenment. For over sixty years, as a member of The American Colony, he has lived and studied in Palestine, and has come to be recognised as the final authority on local history and archæology.

Doctor Spafford's stories of the Holy City were always vivid and dramatic; but one of them, a story of the original Jerusalem, the original city of David, captured our imagination so completely that it sent Moye and me off on the strangest adventure that had befallen us since our Flying Carpet left California.

This, briefly, was Doctor Spafford's tale:

Three thousand years ago Jerusalem was called the City of the Jebusites, and was situated on top a steep-sloped ridge now well outside the present walls.* The founders chose this spot because it stood just above the Fountain of the Virgins, the only constant spring in all the neighbourhood. This spring flowed unprotected from a cavern at the base of the slope below the walls, and on into the Valley of Kidron. But the Jebusites, to assure their water supply in time of siege, drove an inclining irregular shaft from the summit of the ridge, one hundred feet down

---

* Known to-day as the Hill of Ophel.

through the solid rock, by which they could lower their buckets into the pool.

Thus they were able to defy even King David when, having subdued all Judea, he turned upon this last remaining unconquered fortress. As usual the Jebusites felt themselves invulnerable. They mocked the besiegers and cried down to them that blind men and cripples could defend so secure a city.*

But David was not easily discouraged. He doubled the intensity of his onslaught, and promised that he would make supreme captain of his host, the first man who set foot within the stubborn citadel.†

And then one night during a lull in the fighting, Joab, one of David's officers, resting near the outlet to the Virgins' Spring, thought he heard the clink of copper buckets against the rocky cavity from which the water flowed. He waded into the grotto. The sound was unmistakable. Undoubtedly the Jebusites had a shaft leading from their fortress to an inner chamber of the spring!

This explained their endurance against the siege. But it also gave Joab a desperate idea. He undressed, left his arms and armour behind, and plunged into the pool. There *must* be an inward-leading channel—and there was. With barely enough space to breathe above the water level, he crawled along an utterly dark passage, and was rewarded for his daring by emerging into the vaulted pool where the Jebusite buckets were lowered.

He could see the outlines of this pool, for it was dimly lighted by oil lamps from above. He noted the bucket shaft, opening just above his head, and saw that the shaft was not sheer but somewhat inclined. In fact, assisted by knobs and crevices, he was able to climb stealthily up the rock chimney to a point five times his own height. And there he found steps and a passage leading farther upward through the core of the hill.

With pounding pulse Joab slipped back into the pool, through the channel, and out again into the open night. Quickly he went to David's tent and revealed to the King what he had found, and asked for a small company to go with him in a daring attempt to reach the city by way of this newly discovered route.

---

* II Samuel v, 6.
† I Chronicles xi, 6.

At once David saw the possibilities of this plan.* In an hour Joab and his few chosen followers were dragging their swords behind them through the water-channel. The King, by prearrangement, crept up to the gates with his army.

As before, Joab climbed the shaft, and his men followed. They reached the rock staircase—the tunnel—more steps—another tunnel. On tiptoe, scarcely breathing, they crept up to the open entrance of the passage and emerged into the citadel.

Except for the guards on the walls all the Jebusites were sleeping soundly. Not even the watch-dogs gave the alarm. Joab rushed upon the sentinels before they could cry out. The gates were flung open, and David's army poured in upon the helpless city. From that night to this, Jerusalem has been the capital of Israel.

But that is by no means the end of the story about this Virgins' Fount. Three hundred years after David's capture of the Jebusite city, Hezekiah ruled as king. The site of the city had still not been changed from the Hill of Ophel. During Hezekiah's reign the Assyrians invaded Judea, overcoming every obstacle put in their path. Jerusalem was their goal, and it seemed that nothing could stop them from attaining it. In this desperate moment the king thought of the Virgins' Spring, still flowing as it had flowed in the days of Joab. Why should this spring be allowed to supply his enemies as well as himself? Might it not be possible for him to tunnel under his citadel from Joab's grotto clear to the centre of the city, and so divert the flow of the water entirely into Jerusalem?

Hezekiah was a man of action. He ordered such a tunnel dug. Immediately a gang of miners assaulted the solid rock at the source of the flow, and, directing their tunnel through the base of Joab's vertical shaft, pushed ever deeper into the granite hill. Steadily the tunnel lengthened—high as a man and half that wide. But, fast as they worked, it was not fast enough. The Assyrians, fired by their victories, were sweeping on to Jerusalem with alarming swiftness.

Hezekiah was beside himself. He ordered a second gang of stone-cutters to start at the point where the tunnel was to emerge into the cisterns within the city walls.

* II Samuel v, 8.

118

They too dug into the rock at top speed, pushing forward to meet the up-stream excavation. Every man, woman and child was forced to contribute to this labour.*

For some unaccountable reason the two groups did not even attempt to dig straight toward each other. Each worked forward on a winding uncertain course that turned and twisted in the most bewildering manner. The miners would suddenly abandon the forward thrust, and, retreating a few yards, strike off at another tangent. But by the grace of God, having cut a passage over seventeen hundred feet long, they actually did meet, and with such precision that the levels of the two floors were no farther apart than the span of a man's hand. And at the spot where they met, an inscription in ancient Hebrew was chiselled into the wall. It read:

The boring through is completed. And this is the story of the boring through: while yet they plied the drill, each toward his fellow, and while yet there were three cubits to be bored through, there was heard the voice of one calling unto another, for there was a crevice in the rock on the right hand. And on the day of the boring through the stone-cutters struck, each to meet his fellow, drill upon drill; and the water flowed from the source to the pool for a thousand and two hundred cubits, and a hundred cubits was the height of the rock above the heads of the stone-cutters.†

The moment the tunnel was completed, the old outlet of the spring was filled in with stones, and all evidence of it destroyed. And not one hour too soon—the Assyrians had reached Jerusalem. But as Hezekiah had planned, they found the neighbourhood utterly devoid of water, and, driven off by thirst, retreated without striking a blow.

Two thousand years passed, and Jerusalem moved completely away from the Hill of Ophel on which the city of the Jebusites had stood. Ophel became a barren mound, neglected and forgotten. But a hundred cubits below, the water from the hidden Virgins' Fount flowed

---

* II Chronicles xxxii, 1-4.

† This inscription was removed intact and is now in the Imperial Museum at Constantinople. The ancient measurement of the tunnel is given as twelve hundred "cubits." It also measures seventeen hundred feet. From these figures the hitherto unknown length of the cubit was fixed for the first time—seventeen inches.

on through the centuries of accumulated silt that almost choked the tunnel, emerging into the Pool of Siloam, which became, in its turn, the only constant spring for miles around.

Not until modern times was the Fount of the Virgins reopened and Hezekiah's tunnel rediscovered. As a small boy, fifty years ago, Doctor Spafford was one of the first to crawl through. Only a child could have done this, so filled was the gallery with silt, and so near the ceiling was the water. A schoolmate of his, on a similar adventure, found the famous inscription.

In 1907 a society of English archæologists cleared out the entire passage, and restored the Fount to general use. Once again the water flowed freely through the rock as in Hezekiah's time, and what is more, the vertical shaft near the upper end, through which Joab had climbed to capture the city of the Jebusites three thousand years ago, was found intact.

Moye and I listened, deeply interested, to this story one afternoon at tea—and from his glance, I knew that the plan which had occurred to me had also occurred to him.

That night we left Jerusalem by the Zion Gate, and following a rocky path, stumbled down into the steep wadi of the Kidron, with the vast walls of the Temple enclosure rearing above. We meant to explore for ourselves the scene of Doctor Spafford's fascinating chapter from Jerusalem's ancient history.

A lantern lighted us on our way to the Pool of Siloam. At this midnight hour the pool, so busy with water-carriers by day, was entirely deserted. Descending fifty feet of stone steps we reached the stream, and by the light of our lantern looked closely at the large fissure from which the water flowed. It seemed much like the source of a hundred other rock springs we had seen, there being not the slightest indication of the dramatic tunnel within. But we knew its secret, and were determined to penetrate as far as might be possible.

Hiding our clothes and wearing only canvas shoes, we plunged through waist-high water into the inky cavity. This was the spot at which the second gang of miners had begun to excavate.

By the light of our single lantern, we could see quite

clearly the chisel marks on the walls, marks there since 700 B.C., but fresh and clear as the day they were cut. Underfoot, the silt, twelve inches deep, made a soft cushion upon which to tread. The splash of water as we forced our way forward echoed down the black and hollow gallery, as if the ghosts of Hezekiah and his hard-pressed miners were crying out against this visitation, fearful that we were the Assyrians learning at last the vital secret of the city.

At first there was ample room for our heads and shoulders, for the tunnel near its exit was ten feet high. But shortly the roof descended and the walls closed in, so that Moye, who was well over six feet tall and proportionately broad, had to bend his head and walk sidewise.

The passage wound and writhed. Why was it not cut straight? Why this mole-like burrowing? At six hundred cubits we came to the intersection where the two gangs had met. Here the level of the floor rose about seven inches; and the dimensions of the tunnel and its workmanship changed abruptly. The two groups must have had entirely different tools and different specifications. But that they ever met at all, with each group blindly chiselling its own aimless course through the solid rock, will always remain one of the marvels of ancient engineering. That they did meet, the ancient inscription proved. We thrust our lantern into the gash in the rock wall where Hezekiah's tablet had rested—the tablet that had remained in darkness, unread by human eyes, for twenty-seven hundred years.

Another six hundred cubits of waist-deep water, of grotesque shadows and eerie echoes, of bumped heads and skinned shoulders, and a vaulted pool suddenly opened up at the left. This we knew must be the entrance to Joab's shaft, for by pushing on a few yards farther, we emerged into the grotto of the Virgins' Fount and saw the stars again.

This was the place where Joab had first entered the cavern. We followed his course back to the vaulted pool, and turned our lantern full upon it.

For some reason the 1907 excavators had blocked access into the shaft from the main tunnel by a masonry wall, six feet high, but with an opening of several inches left between the top of the wall and the rock roof above. Moye, with his large stature, could not hope to pass this barrier; but, being of a more slender build, I was able, by smearing my body with wet mud, to squeeze over the partition and drop in a heap into the three feet of silt and water on the other side. Reaching back through the gap I seized the lantern from Moye and, ignoring his protestations, left him in the dripping darkness, seated none too comfortably upon the very floor of the tunnel, with the waist-deep stream of the Virgins' Fount flowing calmly past his ears.

"No loitering, now," he growled across the wall, knowing I meant to climb Joab's shaft if I could. "This is not my idea of a place to spend the night."

"Oh, stop grumbling," I exclaimed. "I may find a couple of Jewish princesses up there, imprisoned in an underground dungeon. If I don't come back you'll know I have."

"If you don't come back, and damned soon, I'm going home!"

But with no light and no clothes, this did not seem likely.

Standing in the shallow water, I looked about me. This was the very pool into which the Jebusite women had lowered their buckets in the time of David. I listened, almost expectantly, for the clink of the descending copper. Complete silence. I raised the lantern overhead. There was the shaft, four feet square, just above me. If Joab could climb that shaft with his company of men, I could climb it too! Taking the handle of the lantern in my teeth I laboriously began to raise myself, an inch at a time, up the rock, taking advantage of every knob and digging my toes into every crevice—the same knobs and crevices to which Joab had clung a thousand years B.C. In a few moments the top of the vertical shaft was reached —it wasn't more than thirty feet in height—and there began the steps, hewed out of the same rock, leading farther upward. I crept on, crouching to avoid the low rock ceiling. But I did not crouch low enough. My head struck a hard and heavy object. Startled, I turned my lantern upon the ceiling. There, almost rusted away, hung an iron ring, eight inches in diameter and three thousand years old, from which undoubtedly the Jebusites had hung their lanterns to illuminate this passage to the well. It may have been the glimmer from a lantern hanging on this very ring which had first guided Joab up the shaft to the capture of a city.

The capture of a city! I wondered what lay ahead of me. . . . . What would I find deeper in this ancient and almost forgotten gallery? Might not some turning lead secretly to the tomb of Solomon—to the legendary treasure stored beneath the Mosque of Omar—to the True Sepulchre itself? With increasing tenseness I moved forward, hands and lantern extended, antenna-like, before me.

But at this moment a faint, faint, far-off cry, coming from the other side of the spirit world, from across the land of the dead, floated out of the darkness below. In sudden alarm, I started backward, slipped on the treacherous wet rock, and fell with a crash upon the hard steps. And as I fell, the lantern struck against the wall and instantly went out.

The cry was only Moye's voice, calling out in impatience from the bottom of the pit. But in this tomb-like place the twisting of the sound, over the masonry barrier and upward through the tortuous channels, distorted it into the most inhuman cry I've ever heard.

Realising this though I soon did, I still sat huddled against the clammy and invisible rock wall for several seconds in complete panic. Then at the top of my lungs I called back down the black shaft, "Moye! Moye!" The sound of my own voice shouting through this evil place only exaggerated my alarm . . . until from far away came an answer—that same ghostly cry. The words echoed and rolled and faded as they ascended. But I could distinguish them. I was not abandoned. There was another living human being in this stygian labyrinth.

I forgot all about the Jebusites, all about Solomon's treasure. My only thought now was to get out. With caution increased ten times over, on hands and knees, I felt my way downward—down to the rock steps—down the sloping tunnel—more steps—more tunnel—groping blindly, feeling ahead for security before I moved. And then after what seemed miles I reached a place where there were no more steps—only a drop—and I knew that this was the brink of the thirty-foot pit.

There was no hope, without light, of ever finding my way down the pit by way of the crevices that had helped me up. They were too scattered, too hard to locate. Nor was there any hope of immediate help from Moye, who because of his height and girth could never climb through the opening over the masonry barrier. I could wait until he had found his way, without light and without clothes, at two o'clock in the morning, back to our hotel, and waked the porter and hired an assistant small enough to squeeze through the opening to rescue me with a lantern. But even if Moye were able to find some one unsuperstitious enough to enter the tunnel at night, they could not return before I had endured hours of waiting.

Yet there was only one other alternative—to jump.

I decided to jump.

This would be unpleasant enough, though not, I knew, really dangerous. It was almost certain that the three-foot cushion of mud and water below would break my fall; but for some moments I still hesitated on the brink, summoning up sufficient courage to launch into the blind chasm. There was no point in waiting . . . I must get down . . . I lowered myself over the rim, kicked away from the rough wall—and dropped.

It probably didn't take me long to fall twenty-five feet, but that blank instant in which I could neither feel nor see was one of the longest moments I have ever lived.

The jolt, when I banged into the shallow pool, sent me sprawling across the mud floor. And there I sat, too stunned and faint and knocked about to move.

"Well, Brother Joab," came Moye's ironic voice over the barrier through the murk, "did you find your Jewish princesses?"

"No," I answered, sick and shaking.

.   .   .   .   .   .

We later found out that the Joab shaft no longer has an upper exit, for the entire surface of the Hill of Ophel, where it formerly emerged, is buried deep under twenty-five centuries of accumulated débris. Solomon's treasures may indeed be somewhere in that shaft, and the mummies of all the mighty Hebrew kings . . . or perhaps those lovely Jewish princesses, languishing in a dungeon and waiting to be rescued, far below the citadel of the Jebusites. I still do not know—but Doctor Spafford says it's most unlikely.

CHAPTER XVI

MATILDA'S MARRIAGE

JERUSALEM, with all its solemnity, is not without a comic side. The very intensity of its sacredness has caused the city to lose its balance and become a little mad. Set apart by three of the world's four great religions as a holy city, it naturally attracts many visitors with whom religion is a mania. In fact one finds here more mental and emotional freaks, unhinged by too great a concern with their immortal souls, than in any other spot on earth. The streets and temples teem with sanctimonious lunatics and militant fanatics, Messiahs in long hair and tacky robes, saints with a new Revelation, glory-eyed women mumbling out strange visions, penitents swooning automatically before the holy Tomb, prayer-dancing epileptics, professional self-deniers, from every creed and country.

But Jerusalem does not judge the merits or demerits of these warped and fanciful pilgrims. The Holy City is concerned with eternal salvation rather than with temporal mental accidents. It offers asylum alike to the rational and the irrational, and with benign and patient grace allows them all to live unconstrained within its walls, devoting their lives to saving one another from perdition.

Sometimes among these more or less disordered minds one meets a case that is truly tragic. But usually their sanctity is painless, and from time to time there appears some harmless pilgrim whose delusion is so absurd even the most sympathetic observer must give in to laughter.

The reader can best decide to which class my friend, Mrs. Wales,* belonged—the tragic or the ludicrous.

This good lady enjoyed as kindly and gentle a nature as

---

* I've changed her name.

was ever bestowed upon a woman. And though it was evident, after the briefest acquaintance, that she was mentally somewhat deranged, the expressions of this derangement were so innocent—and so original—that they were not only tolerated by those who knew her, but frequently, as in this story, worth encouraging.

I met her on my second visit to the Holy Sepulchre. Her grey hair and sweet face commanded an immediate deference on my part when, carrying a beautiful cat in her arms, she introduced herself to me. I told her my name. We found we were living in the same hotel.

"It's barbaric, isn't it?" I remarked, gazing across the church, "—and yet impressive in a way."

"I think it's too beautiful," she exclaimed with a look of ecstasy. "I've travelled all the way from England for this moment."

"You are making a pilgrimage, then?"

"Yes. But the pilgrimage is not for myself. It is for Matilda here," she said, stroking the cat who at that moment was yawning vigorously. "I have brought Matilda to Jerusalem to arrange for her wedding."

"Her wedding!" I exclaimed faintly.

"Yes, her wedding," she continued. "You see, I am a Christian, and Matilda is a Christian too. She was born in a convent, and the sisters trusted her to my care. I baptised her myself, and she has grown up in the Christian atmosphere of my home, protected from all impure contacts with other cats. But she is no longer a child——"

Matilda squirmed and tried to get down.

"You see how restless she is. I'm afraid the time has come when I must consider finding her a husband. But I almost wish I didn't have such a responsibility. The male cats in London are so shockingly dissipated and irreligious—I never saw one I'd dare introduce into our home. Doctor Taylor, my husband's cousin, did have a really nice Manx cat, but even it seemed to lack something. . . . I finally prayed for guidance—and the thought of Jerusalem came to me. I knew that if I brought Matilda here, to the very fountain-head of her religion, she would be sanctified by a visit to the Holy Sepulchre—and that would prepare her for marriage to a good Christian husband living right in the Holy City."

I stared at the woman. She was in dead earnest.

"Have you found the proper mate?" I asked solemnly.

"No. I must admit I haven't. But I only arrived this morning. The proprietor of our hotel has promised to help me."

"I'd like to help you too," I offered, as gravely as possible. "I suppose you'll prefer a High Church Episcopal cat for Matilda's husband."

"Oh, yes," Mrs. Wales agreed. "That would be lovely. Poor Colonel Wales himself was always inclined towards the High Church. . . ."

"But you would accept a Methodist?"

"As second choice."

"Of course no Mohammedan."

"Oh, mercy, no!" she exclaimed in alarm.

I promised to get busy at once, to turn myself into a matrimonial bureau for Matilda.

And I did.

Jerusalem is absolutely alive with cats, of the wildest, most unregenerate breed on earth. At night they hymn from every housetop and every alley. My problem was not finding them but catching them.

Two Arab urchins solved this difficulty. I promised them backsheesh for every tom-cat they would bring to my hotel—and I agreed to ask no questions as to where they came from. Giving my young assistants a huge basket, I sent them forth to collect husbands for Matilda.

In less than an hour they were back with six cats—four males and two females, not having stopped in the general round-up to note the difference. With one exception all six of the cats were the very dregs of the city, scarred, battered, savage, wild as tigers. Inside the basket there was pandemonium.

I paid off my Arabs, and liberated the two females. They were poaching on Matilda's preserves. And then I looked over the field. One huge grey devil stood out among them. He was a perfect monster, sleek and beautiful, but with a temper like Beelzebub's. Even so, I picked on him as Matilda's fate.

Then Mrs. Wales and the maiden came in to meet the suitors.

From Mrs. Wales' anxious glance, it was obvious that these cats were not the gentle male tabbies she had hoped for. But Matilda herself seemed to find them by no means without interest, for she at once fluffed up her hair and assumed an arch attitude. To soothe Mrs. Wales' alarm, I insisted all four of the gentlemen had come from the most respectable of Christian institutions.

"This one," I said, pointing to a yellow lynx-like beast, "is straight from the Methodist Mission. His faith is unquestioned, and his nature as God-fearing as Matilda's. *That* one is owned by the sexton of St. George's chapel, and absolutely *lives* in church. Simon Peter here grew up with the vicar's niece, and has led a life of the holiest celibacy. Matilda would not make a mistake with any one of them. But personally I would recommend Saint Thomas," I said, pointing to the big grey villain. "He is High Church—the very archbishop of cats."

Mrs. Wales still hesitated. She still was unconvinced. Somehow none of these suitors, despite my recommendations, had quite the proper Christian mien.

"Remember what Saint Paul said to the Corinthians, Mrs. Wales—'It is better to marry than to burn.' "

"Yes, of course," she admitted, trying hard to smile, "—but there are so many—how am I to know which is the right one?"

"Why not let Matilda decide?" I suggested. "You want her to be happy—in love with her husband. It's hard to regulate such things, you know. Let's leave her to interrogate her suitors."

Uneasily, reluctantly, Mrs. Wales relinquished Matilda, and allowed her to be deposited for the night, alone with the four toms, in the hotel store-room.

By this time the entire hotel (a very small family affair) had been informed by the manager of the extraordinary procedure going on within its walls. At dinner it was the talk of the dining-room—Matilda's marriage. One British spinster expressed doubt that such an international alliance could be happy, but the general opinion was that nothing mattered except to be in love—and of the same religion. "One fold and one shepherd," as Mrs. Wales said. She and I were urged to give the other breathless guests the latest developments.

The developments were rapid. All night from the store-room came the most magnificent yowling. Matilda's shrieks simply rent the building. One might have thought Saint Ursula's eleven thousand virgins were being overtaken by the Huns. Never in cat history had there been such a noisy, disorderly, bust-up of a wedding.

Next morning I scarcely dared look into the bridal

chamber, fearful I should find the little bride scattered all over the place. But Matilda, apparently, had the strength of her convictions—or else she was just an extraordinarily tough little animal. She appeared, sadly battered but in one piece, and looking, as a matter of fact, not a little coy.

Mrs. Wales, when she had taken Matilda into her arms and wept happy tears for an appropriate time, announced that Saint Thomas, the prosperous-looking High Church cat, had been Matilda's only chosen consort. Saint Thomas hadn't—but never mind. There was a wedding breakfast just the same for the bride and the grey demon, at which Mrs. Wales said grace and asked the Lord to bless this holy union. The bridal pair had fish and waffles, and all the cream and chicken they could eat. Then everybody consoled our hostess for the loss of her beloved pet, who, it was understood, would now live on in Jerusalem with her husband.

Mrs. Wales soon after prepared to take leave of us, saying with a sad smile that she was no longer needed. She had accomplished her purpose—Matilda was happily married to one of the leading Christian cats (had I not assured her?) from the very heart of the Holy City. With prayers of thanksgiving the good woman gave her blessings to Matilda and Saint Thomas, and left a fat deposit with the hotel to pay for the ample feeding of the young couple, and for the baptism of their babies. Then, her eyes shining over this triumph of godliness, Mrs. Wales departed.

There is, unfortunately, a scandalous sequel to my story. Matilda, whose marriage had been—as nearly as this earth permits—made in Heaven, turned out to be a perfect minx. No sooner was Mrs. Wales out of sight than Matilda boxed the ears of her lawful husband, and in defiance of her careful Christian upbringing, eloped with the ugliest, sportiest, most disreputable Mohammedan alley-cat in all Jerusalem.

CHAPTER XVII

THE ENCHANTED CITY

ONCE upon a time in the far-off ancient days there was a great king living in Arabia, who by means of a magic talisman had been able to gain dominion over the jinns. With the assistance of these jinns he built for himself a capital that became one of the wonders of the Arab world. It was a city grander and more beautiful even than Thebes —a magic and mysterious city such as one encounters only in myth and fairy-tale. He called his city Petra.

Now in no sense was Petra like other cities. It was located in the wildest mountains in the middle of a barren wilderness in the land of Edom, south of the Dead Sea. Unless one knew the country well, one might not have found it, for the main entrance was just a crack in the mountain wall. This crack led into a deep sunless canyon, and the canyon into the city.

But once one had reached Petra itself, no sight could have been more wonderful. All about were vast palaces and tombs, beautiful and noble beyond belief, carved with hammer and chisel out of the solid rock.

But the king of Petra did not spend all his time building tombs and temples. Besides being the Lord over the jinns, he was also the most dreaded robber in Arabia. Sallying forth from the hidden canyon in the rock, his robber bands would drive the passing caravans into the impregnable fortress, nor could any revengeful army pursue them, for so narrow was the single canyon corridor that four soldiers could block it against four thousand. The city became a vast fortified storehouse where gold and pearls and silk were piled in fabulous array.

Gorged with wealth and power, the arrogance of the people of Petra knew no bounds. They conquered all the neighbouring nations, and driving their prisoners of war up to the great altar built on top the High Place overlooking the city, they slaughtered thousands of these living victims as sacrifices to their gods. To Petra its rulers dragged captive artists and sculptors from Athens. Grander and grander grew their temples, conceived in gigantic scale and executed with miraculous perfection by Greek genius . . . all in the solid sandstone cliffs.

Proud as they were in life, the Petrans became prouder still in death. The construction of their tombs became their great concern. Each noble set himself to carve from the glowing rock a tomb more stupendous and more magnificent than his neighbour's. To hew burial chambers in the solid rock as wide and deep and tall as a palace of King Solomon's was the task of the jinns . . . but only the sensitive hands of the Greeks could carve the graceful colonnades and cornices and statues across the façades, all in one superlatively beautiful piece.

To what length might not this bold and beauty-loving race, with their slaves the giants, have gone to rival the glory of the gods, had not their king, the source of their power, at last brought about their destruction through his own vanity and pride!

He saw the tombs of his nobles rising higher and more regal every day. More and more envious he became of their display, and more and more resentful, until, in a passionate and violent mood, he commanded his enslaved jinns and his artists to carve for him a temple-tomb such as the world had never seen, nor would ever see again—a temple that must overshadow the efforts of the nobles as the moon outshone the stars. And it must be so beautiful in form and colour and ornament that whoever looked upon it, no matter in what age to come, would fall in love with it, and remember it until the end of his days.

So the king commanded, and he was obeyed. From out of the living rock the temple-tomb appeared, in one miraculous piece, colossal, and yet delicate, perfect, classic in its beauty, a poem in burning stone, a vision of the glowing sunset reproduced by the hand of a Phidias out of the rose-red rock.

The king looked upon this perfect thing—and loved it no less than other men. Then, fearful lest a rival try to build a fairer monument than this, he made a sacrifice to the gods of the architect who had conceived it, and decreed that no more rock tombs should be built.

All the people of the subject nations flocked to Petra to see this masterpiece. It became the city's crowning glory. But it soon proved to be a fatal passion for the king. The nobles, envious of their ruler's over-towering monument—a monument so completely obscuring their own—plotted against him, and murdered him.

What madness was in that act! With the king, the power of the Petrans over the jinns departed. He alone had known the secret charm that held them in thrall.

When the last heart-beat of their master had ceased, the jinns found themselves free. With one accord, these terrible spirits burst the bonds that had bound them to their hated overlords, and with a single magic word enchanted the whole of the glorious rock city they had helped to build.

This was centuries ago. But Petra is enchanted still, unchanged, in all this time—its tombs, its monuments, the proud and lovely burial palace of the vainglorious king—all, all standing as on the day when the revengeful giants cast their magic spell. The sunset glow that bathed the city at that moment was captured and enchanted too. It still shines in undiminished glory on the temple walls. And, as the king commanded, to this hour whosoever looks upon the unearthly beauty of his temple falls in love with it, and remembers it to the end of his days.

This is a true story.* I know—because I've seen Petra with my own eyes. I've stood before the enchanted temple, face to face. . . .

Stephens and I flew to Petra in our Flying Carpet. And what a beautiful and romantic journey it was! From Jerusalem, we had sailed on south toward Egypt—over the oldest trail of travel in the history of the world. We had seen the wonders of Egypt from the air—and marvelled. But when we heard of Petra we said farewell to the Pharaohs to seek a rarer prize.

Petra! The Flying Carpet was given its sailing orders. We rose above the housetops of Cairo, soared out over the

* Those who wish a less fanciful version of the rise and decline of this extraordinary city may find numerous literal records concerning it written by archæologists and historians. But to me, as to any one who has actually stood in the midst of its strange stony silence, any literal account of the place is more difficult to believe than the tales of enchantment which the neighbouring tribesmen tell as truth. In the face of Petra's riddles, reason becomes unreasonable, but magic grows commonplace.

gardens of the Nile, circled the Sphinx and zoomed the Pyramids.

And then the Carpet, flashing gold and scarlet in the burning sun, headed for Arabia.

Cairo was soon out of sight. Once more the wastes of sand stretched to all sides. The Suez Canal, dotted with tiny ships, appeared below—and disappeared behind; and desert without end, scarified and gutted by the sun, rolled on.

For three hours we flew straight east, across the base of the Sinai Peninsula, on through the land of Edom. Petra was too well hidden among a maze of rocky canyons for the Carpet's crew to find it from the air, but we located the oasis of Maan which we knew to be near by, and spiralled down to earth.

Two Bedouins, who said they had no fear of Petra's jinns, offered themselves as guides to the enchanted city. At dawn next morning Moye and I stood before the hidden entrance of the secret canyon corridor. Here the guides were left behind. I wanted no conducted tour through this magic realm.

Amid the wild and tumbled country on all sides, we could have passed by the canyon and never noticed it. Only the Stream of Moses, the same stream the prophet brought forth with his miraculous rod, betrayed the entrance, for the rivulet suddenly turned from the open valley and struck straight into the mountain wall.

We followed the stream and found ourselves at the bottom of a tremendous split in the rock, overhung on either side by black precipices three hundred feet high that shut out the sky and the sun. These evil cliffs seemed only to be waiting for a human being to enter there, in order to close in upon the ribbon of space that separated them and grind to bits their helpless victim.

Uneasy and hesitant, we moved deeper and deeper into this appalling gorge. We could stretch forth our arms and touch both walls. At times the daylight almost disappeared. This was not a corridor for the passage of mortal men, but for the efrits and the demons who shunned the sunshine and moved, with the bats, always in the gloom. This was the enchanted entrance to the enchanted city. No wind stirred: no flower bloomed . . . a world petrified and deserted centuries ago.

But I knew it had not always been like this. The

canyon floor was still paved with well-worn blocks of quarried stone; the walls were lined with altar-niches where statues of the gods had stood. Along this corridor the wealth of Arabia had ebbed and flowed; the caravans, laden with silk and pearls, had passed, musical and slow, in never-ending streams; the retinue of a king, returning from Jerusalem, had filled the living canyon with the clatter of their cavalcade; and the charioteers, driving forth their thundering vehicles, had cracked their whips, and shouted, for all the seething throngs to hear—Make way!

For over a mile we crept along the tortuous abyss. Gloomier and gloomier it grew, more overhanging, darker and more sinister.

And then we turned a corner in the canyon, and, suddenly, out of the gloom, a glorious burning pool of carved rose light sprang from the cliff of a transverse gorge running at right angles, and smote down upon our two tiny figures in the canyon like a blow from the mace of the Sun God.

We could only stand and stare, believing we beheld a vision, a miracle of immaterial light and loveliness, appearing at the end of this sunless chasm. The vision took shape, and became reality . . . a cameo temple carved from the coral-red rock, lifting its radiant and exquisite face high up the towering cliff. For the first few moments we made no effort to understand the heavenly apparition. We only let ourselves be flooded by the sunrise glory that fell in splendour from its walls.

Surely, I thought, this great jewel must be the temple-tomb raised by the genius of Greek art, with the power of the jinns, at the order of the king of ancient Petra . . . "a temple-tomb that was to overshadow the monuments of the nobles as the moon outshone the stars, a temple such as the world had never seen nor would ever see again." So the king had commanded, and the artists and the jinns had obeyed . . . thus had the legend run . . . and from out of the living rose-red rock the temple-tomb appeared in one miraculous piece, colossal, and yet flawless, a poem in burning stone, a magic moment of the glowing sunset reproduced by the hand of a Phidias . . . "and whosoever shall look upon it, no matter in what age to come, shall fall in love with it, and remember it to the end of his days."

I looked upon it, and in that moment, as the king would have desired, felt all the powerful, magical attraction of its sheer beauty.

Moye much less so. Moye was the artisan, not the dreamer. He noted that the façade was one hundred and fifty feet high, and a hundred feet across; that the great rock chamber within was forty feet square and forty high; that the temple was supported by graceful Corinthian columns; that cornice and architrave, capital and cupola were adorned with the most exquisite and elaborate carving—garlands and flowers, angels and goddesses, standing forth in delicate relief; and all, all, in the solid rock.

But I did not analyse these things. To me this was a true work of enchantment. How else could one explain the way the sunshine turned the temple walls to sculptured flame? What else but the magic of the jinns could have painted so glowing, so vibrant, a coral colour into the sandstone precipice? I accepted it utterly, unquestioningly, as one accepts a rainbow arched across the castled clouds, or moonlight on the sea.

Reluctantly we left the royal temple-tomb behind, and moved on.

The transverse gorge in which the temple stood now led us into Petra proper. But whereas the first canyon had been almost a tunnel in the rock, this second one was two hundred feet across, opening wide to the sunshine and the sky, and lined with temples, temples, in endless procession, all cut, like the royal tomb, from the solid rock. Here too the sandstone dazzled one with its brilliant and varying hues. In the interiors, the stone-carvers had taken full advantage of this painted rock, and produced effects in natural colour on wall and altar and ceiling that the greatest artist in the world would have been proud to achieve. Obviously these were the tombs of the nobles. No wonder the king had feared their marvellous display and needed all his riches and authority to surpass them.

But Petra is not all gorges and tomb-flanked canyons. The valley soon opened into an enormous amphitheatre two miles across, walled in by towering and fantastic precipices utterly barren, utterly untraversable. In this amphitheatre, before the time of the enchantment, had lived the people who had spent their lives robbing caravans, hoarding riches and building stupendous rock mausoleums. In the midst of all this majesty and this magnificence, Moye and I spent several days, crawling about the tomb-studded cliffs, climbing to the holy High Places where stood the great rock altars down which blood in oceans, pouring from slaughtered prisoners of war, had flowed in sacrifice.

There was not one corner of Petra which we did not explore. But all the time the coral miracle of the king's tomb had been foremost in my thoughts. This beckoned to me continually across all the other wonders of the enchanted city. Each day I had wandered back for a secret tryst with the radiant temple, and now that a full moon was shining down upon the sandstone wonderland, I slipped away, for the first time at night, from the cave where we had pitched our camp, and walked alone up the gallery of noble tombs that led to the great jewel.

How pale and beautiful these tombs appeared in the soft, silver night and yet how sinister. Created to shelter Death, they seemed like phantom dwellings for the evil spirits of the nether world—shadow-spirits which even now moved and peered at me as I strode past.

But as I pushed on through the enchanted vale, between the high rock-monster walls, skirting the black lakes of darkness that alternated with moonlight along the way, I tried to whistle a bit, to drive the ghosts out of my path and announce to the ambushed demons that I was not afraid.

Whistling, but faint-hearted, I went to keep my moonlit rendezvous.

How changed I found my temple—yet not less beautiful. If its burning beauty of the day had disappeared, a softer, gentler glow had come into its face. I had believed nothing could be lovelier than its coral colour inflamed by the sun. I now saw that there *was* something lovelier —its coral colour subdued by the moon. Had a perfume come from the place, or swelling radiant music, with such magic and mystery already suffusing the temple, I would not have thought it strange.

Better to behold this overwhelming vision of beauty, I backed against the cliff wall opposite. I could picture to myself the day when the king of Petra, with envy of his nobles burning in his soul, rode to this spot where the narrow entrance chasm opened into the sunlit gorge, and pointing to the glowing rose cliff opposite, commanded his Greek sculptor to carve there the royal temple-tomb, beautiful and proud beyond all other mausoleums in the world. I saw the Greek sculptor bow in obedience and summon the enslaved jinns. Terrible and roaring in their chains these giants attacked the solid rock with drill and mallet. Thousands upon thousands of cubic feet of red sandstone were chiselled from the face; and the streams of jinns carrying away the huge rock fragments on their backs were never-ending. Beneath the furious bombardment, the cliff took shape—the columns and the capitals appeared, the statues grew in beauty on the walls.

The rough façade stood ready for the Greek sculptor's final touch, and from his hands it re-emerged, smooth and delicate. The interior chambers were hewn clean, the great entrance door framed in fragile decoration, and the sun invited to drench the finished temple with his fire.

And then the sculptor bade the king look upon his tomb. I could imagine the king returning, borne on his litter of gold, and stopping, speechless, before the miraculous mausoleum—"so beautiful in form and colour that whosoever looked upon it should fall in love with it and remember it to the end of his days" . . . and every one who stood before it fell in love with it—the king, who most loved beauty, most of all.

But did the king's mummy ever rest within that great black vault opening wide its framed portals behind the shining colonnade? . . . did not the jinns at the very moment of his death enchant the city? Indeed, they must have, else this pink and silver dream beckoning to me in the moonlight would have been in ruins, and desolate, a thousand years ago.

Grateful, I looked up at the temple's sublime face with humility and worship. I had not worshipped anything in such a long, long time. It was as if I had been saving all my homage for this vision of beauty, for this enchanted hour. . . . "Eternal, silent, beautiful, alone . . . eternal, silent, beautiful, alone"—a line from the poem this temple had inspired in a poet's heart, but I meant it to be from my own heart, a tribute and a dedication. . . .

The months have passed since that memorable night. I have encountered other things and other faces I have loved. But until the end of my days, I shall remember, as one of the great loves of my life, the enchanted coral temple, alone and beautiful, in the moonlight.

CHAPTER XVIII

BRIEF LANDINGS

As Stephens and I rode from Petra back to the oasis of
Maan to rejoin our Flying Carpet, we agreed that all the
high hopes we had entertained in California of seeing
the world by air had not been too extravagant. We had
not had a single mishap, nor failed to reach a single place
we had set our hearts on. With every new flight our
plane became more truly a magic vehicle. Sky-high
and happy, we were enjoying our adventure in full.
Our self-confidence was growing every day. In fact,
we had now begun to dream of India.

But we had chosen no definite route to the East—
routes were difficult to choose, when between Petra and
the Himalayas a hundred places, widely scattered,
beckoned to the Flying Carpeteers. We decided to
drift. Perhaps we'd get there some day.

The first direction we happened to drift was toward the
Dead Sea.

Flying north from Petra, we beheld this celebrated sea
thirty miles away and three thousand feet below, shining
like a lake of molten sapphires in the midst of lifeless
hills. Both Moye and I were curious to visit it, for we
had been speculating about flying conditions at such an
extraordinary sub-sea-level . . . how would our plane, so
responsive in the upper air, perform at thirteen hundred
feet *below* ocean level—at the lowest spot on earth—where
even the birds, according to folklore, drop stricken and
lifeless into the baleful sea below?

As we flew over the rim, we began to drive the Carpet
downward into the great sink—down until the altimeter
registered one thousand feet—five hundred feet—zero—
and we were still thirteen hundred feet above the surface
of the water. We continued to descend until our wheels

all but touched the waves. Then having opened the throttle wide, Pilot Stephens pulled the Carpet's nose suddenly upward, and we shot out of the dense atmosphere of the pit at such a steep angle and at such violent speed that my head swam. But to the complete destruction of my idea that we had performed a spectacular experiment, Moye insisted the low altitude was not low enough to make any appreciable difference in the airplane's performance.

Somewhat disappointed, we gave up the pursuit of science and turned our attention to the wild and compelling scenes about us. I had expected, because of its name, to find the Dead Sea dismal and depressing. Instead I found it—at least from the air—incredibly beautiful. The water is of a deep dazzling blue, contrasting vividly with the dull gold shades of the towering shores. Far from being sombre, this lake is one of the most brilliant in the world—brilliant in its lifelessness as some huge blue-winged beetle set in a tarnished ring.

It has also one of the most colourful histories. At the south-eastern corner Sodom and Gomorrah, now buried beneath the waves, once stood. How different the Dead Sea must have been in Old Testament days, when on its banks could flourish two luxurious cities so iniquitous as to incur the wrath of Heaven! Up which of these mountains rising from the sea had Lot climbed to escape the fire and brimstone that rained down to destroy them? Which of those rocky spires on the hillside was his sodium chloride wife?

Atop a precipice on the western slope, we could see the ruins of the fortress of Masada where, in 70 A.D., four thousand Hebrews, besieged by the Roman army which had pursued them from Jerusalem, fought bravely for months and then slew themselves to the last man rather than suffer captivity. Circling several hundred feet above the precipice, we looked down upon the remains of the tragic citadel, and observed, at the base of the cliff, the elaborate military camp constructed by the Roman besiegers. Preserved by the extreme dryness of the air, it appeared at this distance so perfectly intact that one might have thought it still garrisoned.

Flying over to the other side of the sea, and somewhat inland, we located the hilltop site of Machaerus, where King Herod held the famous birthday party at which

Salome danced to entertain his guests—and received the head of John the Baptist in reward.

Clear in the sunshine, near the north end of the sea, rose Mount Nebo. Here Moses, wandering in the wilderness with the Israelites, beheld Palestine—the Promised Land. But the cruel panorama that met our eyes seemed more like a threat than a promise. We decided that if it were this barren in Moses' day, the Children of Israel had been sadly swindled.

As Mount Nebo fell behind, we turned north-east out of the valley of the Jordan and sped on to Damascus.

Charming though it was, Damascus offered little that Fez and Cairo had not already made familiar, so we took to the air again, looking for Baalbek, fifty miles farther on.

Baalbek burst upon us unexpectedly. The first glimpse of those colossal tumbled temples brought us swooping earthward in wonderment. And each day that we remained the wonder grew. What giants in heart were those third-century Syrians who held the East in fealty to Rome, yet arrogantly planned Baalbek greater than Rome itself! How confident they were of perpetual dominion—building their city with granite blocks some of which weighed eight hundred tons apiece, and then adorning those titanic stones with the most delicate and fragile beauty, and with inscriptions which boasted that these monuments might perhaps last as long as the Roman reign endured. Now the race is gone, but the temples they raised still commemorate their power and their genius. When its mighty columns stood, Baalbek must have been impressive as Egypt and fair as Greece, for even to-day, shattered and prostrated by earthquakes though it is, the ruins still present one of the grandest, and most overpowering pictures of architectural achievement to be found on earth.

Still wandering, we now turned east and flew across the uninhabited plains of Syria, until after two hours in the air we saw, rising right out of the barren wastes, unexpectedly, like a mirage, a classic city . . . classic courts and columned avenues, graceful palaces, forums, theatres. These we knew were the glorious remains of what was once, after the fall of Petra, the most queenly city in the East—Palmyra, mistress along with Baalbek of all the lands from the Nile to Byzantium—destroyed by the jealousy of Rome and left utterly to the mercy of the sands. The Flying Carpet, coming upon this wraith of imperial grandeur lost in the wilderness, paused to rest, while Moye and I wandered about the beautiful and tragic ruins.

And then we drifted on—toward India.

The next air harbour to the east lay across a desert as flat and hot and barren as the Sahara. But we had no fear of deserts now—not after our flight to Timbuctoo. A hundred miles of the old familiar sands sped past —three hundred—four. Then when the desert weariness was beginning to lie heavily upon us, we caught sight, miles away, of a great gold dome and gold minarets floating on the horizon and shining like fire against the sunset.

With our spirits revived by this vision in our path, we rushed to greet it. Nearer and nearer it came. We soon saw that the gold dome crowned a superb turquoise mosque lifting its glittering minarets high above a great cluster of pale white houses. The houses, bowered in gardens, stretched along the banks of a broad, deep-flowing river. Compressing this river and this city and this verdure, the desert rolled in from every side to break upon the dense groves of palms that held the enemy at bay.

This beautiful and welcome oasis was—Bagdad.

Even had the map not told us, we would have known that this was the city of the *Arabian Nights*. From the air, it looked the part completely. Nor were we disappointed from the ground. Some of the new streets and suburbs Harun al-Rashid would not recognise; but the old town, the bazaars, the river banks, were just like the romantic Arabian city we had hoped for.

On our very first day we met a hundred characters from the famous tales. We sat in coffee-shops and watched for veiled princesses to go by. Some of the ladies were lovely enough to be princesses—at least judging from their eyes, which were all we could see. We followed more than one mysterious face through dark streets and into ancient courts, hoping they would lead us into a rich merchant's neglected harem or some such indiscreet adventure. But we had no luck. The ladies just reached a door in the wall, and banged it behind them, and turned the bolt . . . and we found ourselves so lost it took us half the night to get back through the twisting lanes to our hotel.

The crowds of people, struggling through the streets, delighted us—students and mendicants, venders and soldiers and porters. We watched the silversmiths carving delicate little bottles to hold love philtres, and heard the coppersmiths burrowing like gnomes in their dark shops and pounding out huge jars big enough to hold one of Ali Baba's forty thieves. The merchants looked just as we had seen pictures of them in our childhood copies of the *Arabian Nights* . . . There was a certain merchant of Bagdad of an excessively jealous disposition, having a wife endowed with perfect beauty—that's the way the stories often began; and there would be a picture of a merchant, ample of waist, turbaned, bearded and colourfully gowned, seated cross-legged in his booth, surrounded by piles of flaming silk and scarlet leather shoes, and flowers and perfumes and Persian carpets. That's just how they looked to us now, and just how they sat in their booths.

We made only one purchase from a merchant. He was a carpet vendor and came crying his wares in our ears as we sat in a coffee-shop. I asked him, through an Arab friend, if he had any flying carpets. Immediately he laughed and said yes, and extracted from his bale a most perfect silk carpet from Samarkand. The design was intricate and original . . . he held it up for me to see. "Here is a flying carpet," he said.

I bought the carpet at once. It measured twelve inches long and eight inches wide. It would be the mascot for its big brother, in which we had now decided, definitely, to fly on around the world.

CHAPTER XIX

THE PRINCE OF BAGDAD

In the city of Bagdad, at the time of the flight of the Flying Carpet, the king, Feisal al Husain, was much in the public eye, for he was endeavouring with his whole heart to administer his country wisely and generously, and to maintain the loyalty of the people of Iraq.

In return for these good offices, Fortune had played kindly with the king. He possessed, in the words of the *Arabian Nights*, "numerous troops and guards and servants, and beautiful palaces on the banks of the Tigris." He had three devoted children, two of them daughters of exceptional comeliness, and a son, young Prince Ghazi, whom the king loved above all other things. Indeed, the king's affection for the charming and handsome crown prince endeared them both to the entire nation.

In his own family affairs, as in the affairs of state, Feisal had proved himself a man of foresight and sound judgment. He loved his children wisely, as well as deeply. For example, he withheld from Prince Ghazi most of the riches and luxuries usually accorded a prince, lest the boy grow to manhood soft and self-indulgent. In keeping with this hardy policy the royal father sent the boy to a school for soldiers instead of a school for princes. Here he was subject to the hard food, the hard beds and the hard discipline imposed upon his comrades. Only on holy days, when the school closed, was he allowed to leave this military life and return to the royal palace, where, amid the palm groves and rose gardens by the river bank, he could lay aside his simple uniform and don the purple garments of a prince.

On those rare days the king relaxed from his severe attitude toward his son, and stood ready to grant whatever wish the Prince of Bagdad cared to make.

On one such day, Ghazi asked for a beautiful Arabian horse he had seen at t   race-course. The purchase of the horse was promptly made, and the prince, with shining eyes, mounted the spirited half-tamed steed, and rode him away with all the natural ease of his wild-riding Bedouin forebears. The king watched with pride and admiration. His son was growing properly—graceful and straight and strong.

By the time of his next holiday, Ghazi had heard about a wonderful new model of a phonograph which reproduced music that was indistinguishable from the original. Ghazi asked for one of these, and records to go with it, especially those that made the music loud and rhythmical. Immediately the king sent out his ministers to bring in such a machine as the prince described. Then all day long and all night the rose garden rang with the outpourings from the royal phonograph.

Another season passed, and once more Ghazi returned home for his holiday. "What is your wish this time, my son?" asked the father.

"I want to be king for a while," answered the prince.

Feisal did not think this request as extraordinary as his ministers thought it. Why shouldn't the boy try his hand at government! After all, he was sixteen. The experience of rulership should be useful to one who must some day be ruler in his own right. Indeed, Ghazi's request would be granted. The king had pressing affairs that would take him away from Bagdad for a day and night. During his absence he resolved to leave the fate of the nation entirely in the hands of his young son—for twenty-four hours. The king's ministers would remain behind to counsel and assist the prince; but the boy's wishes were to be law. He was to be the absolute ruler of Bagdad.

According to his plan, Feisal departed and Prince Ghazi sat upon the throne.

❧ With such a sudden embarrassment of power in his hands Ghazi hardly knew what orders to give first. After much thought he commanded five cartloads of fresh-cut clover to be purchased and fed to his beautiful Arabian horse. The order was promptly executed by the proper vizier, even though it seemed that five cartloads were rather excessive.

Prince Ghazi now considered what he would do next.

He recalled his new phonograph. "Go into the bazaars," he ordered his ministers, "and buy me *all* the records in Bagdad, and bring them to me in the garden." This instruction, too, was obeyed. It took four porters to carry Ghazi's wholesale order to the palace. There he piled his treasures mountain high on the garden benches and set about to amuse himself with several hundred pounds of music. Not a record remained in Bagdad, but Ghazi was radiant. Here was something worth being king for! His concert lasted the rest of his twenty-four-hour reign, during which time he turned over the boring responsibilities of his royal office to a regent whose tastes were practical rather than artistic.

King Feisal, on his return, decided his experiment with Ghazi had been entirely satisfactory. True, no outstanding blessings had resulted to the nation from Ghazi's administration, but neither had there been any invasions, plagues or revolutions. Consequently when another holiday came around the king was still inclined to continue fulfilling the boy's seasonal requests, especially as his latest demand was so simple—and so inexpensive:

"I have heard, father, that three days ago a Flying Carpet with two foreigners aboard landed here in Bagdad, coming from the other side of the world. I want to meet the Flying Carpet's crew."

And so it happened that Moye Stephens and I were brought into the presence of the young prince and introduced.

Ghazi looked at his guests, and we at him, with curiosity. The prince had never before met people who travelled about the continents on flying carpets, and we had never before met a real Arabian prince. We found him decidedly likable-looking, and charmingly boyish—a rather little fellow but of perfect proportions and as graceful as a deer. There was spirit in his dark face, and intelligence in his proud and sensitive eyes.

"You are welcome to Bagdad," said the prince in perfect English, which was the language he spoke in his military school. "I hope you will like our city."

"It is unusually beautiful," I replied, "—especially from the air."

"Tell me about your Flying Carpet," the boy requested with an eagerness only half concealed. "I hear it is scarlet and gold and shining. Have you flown over all the world? Has it been a wonderful adventure? Are there other cities as beautiful as Bagdad? Have you met other princes like me?"

Now that I had taken it upon myself to act as spokesman, I hardly knew how to answer such a flood of questions. "No, Prince Ghazi," I said, answering the last question first, "we've not had the privilege of meeting any other prince like you. We had not even hoped to make your acquaintance when we came to Bagdad. So we think our visit to your city is well begun. . . . You asked about our Flying Carpet. We think it is the most beautiful airplane in the world—and the most faithful. Moye Stephens, here, should receive entire credit for its faithfulness. He is the captain, and has taught it strict obedience. But in return he gives it constant and expert attention. Wherever he commands, the Carpet flies, higher than the clouds and faster than the jinns."

"I was told," exclaimed the prince, "that you have come all the way from America."

"That is true," I admitted. "We started in California, almost a year ago. For a year we have travelled over land and ocean, following our inspirations of the moment, sometimes north, sometimes south, but never forgetting that some day we intended to reach Arabia and Bagdad."

Briefly I outlined our flight from Hollywood to the Tigris.

"And now that you are here," said the prince, "what are your plans?"

Moye and I exchanged glances. . . . "To take the Prince of Bagdad aboard the Flying Carpet, if he will but command us," I replied, "and show him his kingdom from the air."

The boy's eyes simply danced. "Oh, *will* you?" he exclaimed.

Before many hours had passed I had communicated with the king, and had received permission to take young Ghazi flying in the Carpet. This favour was granted on the solemn promise that Ghazi would be deposited, safe and sound, back in his military school before nightfall. By my eyes, by my beard, by my prophet, I swore that this promise would be fulfilled.

The next morning the Flying Carpet with Moye and Ghazi and me aboard rose up above the highest palms, and sailed—a gold and scarlet streak—over the domes and minarets of Bagdad.

Prince Ghazi was in ecstasy. From the air he could identify his school, and the pontoon bridges, and the emerald dome of the Haider-Khana, and the turquoise Midan mosque, and all the other familiar landmarks of his father's capital.

Then on down the Tigris the Flying Carpet sailed. Looming like a great cloud on the horizon, ten miles away, the crumbling palace of Ctesiphon soon came into view. For fourteen hundred years this palace has remained an architectural marvel, spreading its world-famous arch over the banqueting hall nearly a hundred feet high and a hundred broad.

The Carpet flew low about the palace walls. The wings of the main building were falling away. But the miraculous arch, still floating like a rainbow over the vast hall of audience, stood defiantly in the face of quakes and battles and time and the vandalism of man.

Ghazi, leaning overboard, suggested by gestures that we fly through the arch and astonish the shades of King Chosroes and his ten thousand lords who nightly banquet— so Bagdad legend goes—within the hall. But the opening at the far end looked dangerously narrow, and Moye would not risk the safety of our royal passenger in such a delicate manœuvre, so we flew on.

In thirty minutes more the Flying Carpet, having crossed the strip of land that separates the Tigris from the Euphrates, circled over Babylon.

Eagerly we three passengers looked down upon the ruins of the "glory of the kingdoms," the centre of the universe for two thousand years—now a tossing sea of desolation. . . . "It shall never be inhabited, never shall it be dwelt in from generation to generation: neither shall the Arabians pitch their tents there; neither shall the shepherds make their fold there. But wild beasts of the desert shall lie there; . . . and the owls shall dwell there, and the satyrs shall dance there" . . . So Isaiah had thundered his dire prophecy at the iniquitous city. And how completely Isaiah's prophecies had come to pass. Not even grass grew upon the huge mounds of brick where once stood the royal palaces and the Hanging Gardens and the Tower of Babel. "Babylon is fallen, is fallen, that great city."

Even so, "every one that goeth by Babylon shall be astonished"—and no less so because one was aboard a

Flying Carpet. For miles and miles along the yellow Euphrates stretched the corpse of Babylon, of her topless towers, of her walls two hundred cubits high, her hundred gates, her fiery furnaces through which the Old Testament heroes passed, her imperial avenues down which the chariots of Darius had fled before the flaming sword of Alexander . . . a desert wilderness, where only the owls break the silence that broods over the grave-mounds of a mighty city which, though struck down by the hand of God and buried by time, still testifies even in ruin to the grandeur of its ancient pride.

The Flying Carpet floated lower down. Excavated temple walls appeared from amid the pitched and tumbled hillocks of *débris*. The sun was shining on these walls, and we could see the bulls and lions moulded in bas-relief upon the brick façades. This great central group was the Palace of Nebuchadnezzar, where Alexander, home from the conquest of the world, had breathed his last, and where Belshazzar, two hundred years before, worshipping false gods, gave his historic feast . . . MENE, MENE, TEKEL UPHARSIN—the hand-writing on the wall—"God hath numbered thy kingdom, and finished it, Belshazzar. Thou art weighed in the balance, and art found wanting. Thy kingdom is divided, and given to the Medes and Persians. . . . In that night was Belshazzar the king of the Chaldeans slain." . . . The Carpet's passengers looked down with straining eyes. Upon one of those sculptured walls below, Jehovah's vengeful hand had moved.

Having seen Babylon from the air, Prince Ghazi now wished to see Samarra, which for a century after Harun al-Rashid's reign had been the capital of the Kings of Bagdad. Samarra lay as far above Bagdad on the Tigris as Babylon lay on the Euphrates. So the Flying Carpet turned upon its course, and flying a mile high, once more sped over Prince Ghazi's city.

> How many miles to Babylon?
> Three score miles and ten.
> Can I get there by candle-light?
> Yes and back again.

The prince got there and back again by *morning* light-It was not yet noon when King Feisal looked up from his palace garden and saw the gold-and-scarlet Carpet, bearing his adored son, winging its way up the Tigris to Samarra.

As in the case of Ctesiphon, we could see Samarra from afar. There was no soaring arch this time, but an extraordinary ninth-century mosque standing well outside the modern city, with ruined walls a quarter of a mile square and a crumbling ziggurat-shaped minaret encircled by a spiral roadway that climbed two hundred feet above the plain. In this same style, the Tower of Babel had been designed before the wrath of Heaven struck it to the ground.

Prince Ghazi noted the minaret's corkscrew path. "I want to land and climb it," he shouted to me above the whistle of the wind.

In compliance with this request, the Flying Carpet landed in a desert-stretch near by. Immediately crowds of curious natives came running up to examine the flashing Carpet—and whom should they see climbing out of it but their own crown prince! It is hard to know which caused the more excitement—the Flying Carpet or Prince Ghazi. Soldiers gathered and saluted; officials knelt and kissed the hem of his coat. Ghazi was only embarrassed by such ceremony. He bade the officials stand and talk to him.

Followed by mobs of Samarra's excited citizens—especially the youths of Ghazi's own age, who were almost beside themselves with joy over his visit—the Carpet's three passengers reached the ruins of the great mosque, and slowly and cautiously began to ascend the path winding up the towering minaret. The structure was a thousand years old, and the paving of the path decayed and crumbling at the edge. Only by clinging to the wall could one climb in safety. The constant circling to the left, and the ever-increasing precipice to the right, soon made our heads swim with dizziness. We had to stop to regain our composure—climb—rest—climb—until the final wind-swept platform was attained. Ghazi insisted he was going to return and ride up the incline on his Arab horse—even though he knew that the only man who ever tried fell off and broke his own and his horse's neck.

The tower stood in the midst of what had once been a great metropolis. For miles around lay the ruins of several Samarras, a city-site that had risen to great eminence in 2000 B.C., and faded, and risen again to enthrone the Caliphs. But they too departed in time back to

Bagdad, and the glory of Samarra departed with them.

Ghazi decided it was time—long past time indeed—for lunch. The king's own steward had supplied a provision basket, and perched on the top of the world, we opened it. Out came roast fowl wrapped in fine-woven napkins from Mosul, and a quantity of olives, and a vessel of wine; Othmani quinces, peaches from Oman and melons from Isfahan. The city of Samarra had also prepared a feast. An army of city-fathers came struggling up the dizzy minaret laden with vast platters of rice and curried sheep and unleavened bread and purple grapes. The royal prince was soon bulging with these delights.

The afternoon, occupied with further explorations, passed rapidly. The sun hung low in the west before I thought of my sacred promise to King Feisal to have Ghazi safe and sound back in his school by dark.

There was no time to lose. Once more seated in the Flying Carpet, the prince waved good-bye to a thousand people. With a rush and a roar the Carpet, like a scarlet rocket, soared into the sky, leaving all Samarra gasping down below.

On the flight up the Tigris from Babylon, Moye had flown at an altitude of five thousand feet in order that Ghazi might look down on Bagdad from a mile above. On the return journey, to vary the scene, the Carpet flew so low it almost touched the palm-tops. Over hedges it hurdled—over farms—scattering sheep—frightening shepherds—skimming the Tigris—two miles a minute home to Bagdad. Once more the dazzling gold-plated domes of the Kadimain mosque, lifted high amid the forest of palms, rose up before the fliers, and catching the direct rays of the setting sun, burned like great bubbles of fire. In the courtyard of the mosque (where no infidel may set foot) several hundred of the faithful stood and stared up at the scarlet arrow that came streaking overhead.

In a moment more the Carpet was seen approaching Prince Ghazi's military school. Ghazi had begged us to loop-the-loop, and roll, and spin, and fly upside down over these barracks, so that the other young soldiers would look up at him and marvel, and Moye had agreed.

The Flying Carpet was put through a few gyrations— right over the school's courtyard. Ghazi, hanging by his belt upside down, only cried aloud from excitement and delight, and asked for more. He could see that all the students were pouring out-of-doors to gaze open-mouthed at him, at Ghazi, their death-defying, earth-scorning, loop-the-looping prince. He would have had Moye flying right through the barracks dormitory had not I, fearing the king's wrath, been unwilling to take further risks with Ghazi's valuable young neck.

Prince Ghazi came down to earth in love with flying carpets. This stunting over his schoolmates' heads gave him the proudest moment he had ever known in all his sixteen years. Not only was he their prince by right of birth—he had now become their hero by right of bravery and audacity. His face was flushed; his dark eyes shone. At that moment, with all his hundred and ten pounds, he would have attacked whole armies of Bagdad's enemies single-handed out of sheer inspiration and self-confidence.

The boy was still up in the clouds when Moye and I deposited him at his barracks door.

"Did your enjoy you travels aboard the Flying Carpet, Ghazi?" I asked the prince as he bade us farewell.

"Oh, yes, yes!" the boy exclaimed. "It was just like a dream, wasn't it—just like the story-book."

Just like the story-book! For one whole day the pages of the *Arabian Nights* had come to life. For one day the Prince of Bagdad had sailed over the dreaming minarets aboard his flying carpet and looked down to find that his capital was filled with beauty, and that there was peace and poetry in the land.

CHAPTER XX

ON Thanksgiving morning I woke up in gaol. It was a Persian gaol. The Flying Carpet had reached Teheran, and *this* was the result.

Moye and I had come to the Persian capital straight from Bagdad—five hundred miles away—in one long flight. Wrapped in warm sheepskin coats we had climbed to thirteen thousand feet, up from the flat plains of the Tigris and Euphrates, and over the spectacular mountain ridges into Persia. More convulsed, more desolate, mountains we had never seen. Persia to me had always meant lutes and poetry—Shiraz—Isfahan. To find this harsh and unfriendly aspect, on our very first encounter, came as a complete surprise.

To climax this scene, after four hours in the freezing November air, we saw to the north, across the bleak brown wastes, the heaven-piercing ice-clad vision of Mount Demavend, soaring nineteen thousand feet into the sky . . . one hundred and fifty miles ahead.

At its foot, we knew, lay Teheran.

No sooner had the Flying Carpet come to earth at the landing field than a gesticulating stranger, about thirty-five years old and apparently American, ran up to greet us. I recognised him at once, from his photographs. He was William McGovern of Tibetan fame. The Legation had told him we were coming.

"Thought you might want a good guide," he said with a smile.

"We do want one," I replied, "—if it's you."

McGovern was a peregrinating author I had been trying to overtake for years, ever since reading his remarkable book *To Lhassa in Disguise*. Explorer, scientist, scholar, teacher, linguist extraordinary, he aroused interest wherever he went. Six weeks in Teheran—and he had already become the most popular personage in the capital, for he had flung himself with infectious enthusiasm into the life about him, eager to be a part of all he met.

As we motored into town from the field, McGovern expanded on the charms of Persia. "Oh, you'll like it," he assured us, "—and the people. They are hospitable to a fault—particularly the bandits. . . . A little backward, if you insist on Progress. There are no paved streets here, as you see. The hotels are an abomination. You'll probably freeze from lack of heat. But no Persian seems to need these things. They live on love and poetry instead—and opium—and past glories. And I must say they are happier and more beautiful than we.

"There's so much in Teheran itself that's colourful—such fantastic wealth and such armies of beggars. To visit the eighty-million-dollar Peacock Throne you have to wade through mud up to your neck. It's a place of contrasts."

"But I find that the contrasts in a city most reveal its character to me," I interrupted.

"Exactly! I'm trying to learn the character of Teheran—and I've thought of a contrast that should reveal a great deal, and might be considerable fun too. I've just come away from a visit in the Imperial Palace. Now, to complete the picture, I want to live a while in the Imperial Prison. All the aristocrats in town seem to be there. In fact the prison has become *so* exclusive they absolutely refuse to let me in. Perhaps if you or Stephens will come with me we can crash the gates."

Moye asked to be excused—this wasn't his idea of entertainment.

"But I'll go," I said, very much amused. "I am afraid gate-crashing a prison may be difficult, though. Have you tried to have the criminal court sentence you?"

"Yes. The judge thinks I'm crazy."

"If he thinks we're both crazy, maybe we can get into the asylum instead!"

"They'd probably never let us out. The prison is safer."

"Let's try the War Office. Maybe they will sentence us as spies or something."

We tried, without success. They were suspicious we *were* spies, but wouldn't commit us until they had more proof of our sinister motives.

"We'll have to appeal to the Shah," I said impatiently.

By means of a letter of introduction I possessed, addressed to the Shah's chamberlain, we reached His Majesty's ear. We stated our case clearly: We wanted to visit the Imperial Prison and live as prisoners, without favour, for several days. "We were making a survey of the Persian scene, and prisons were an important feature." We asked only three special privileges: no one but the warden was to know we were not legally sentenced, our heads were not to be shaved, and we were to be "pardoned" when we felt sufficiently punished.

The reply came back—"Granted!"

We returned to the "Grand Hotel" to await arrest. Shivering in my dismal and squalid apartment, we began to wonder if perhaps we had not plunged over-impetuously into our criminal career. If the most modern hotel in town were no better than this, how much worse might the prison be! But the Throne itself had sentenced us. There was no escape now.

When everything was ready, two police appeared, accompanied by the scandalised proprietor, with orders to seize us. They were armed to the teeth in case we resisted arrest. But arrest had resisted us too long; we followed promptly, looking as meek as possible, and were led up the hill to the prison. The door opened for us with a grinding of steel, and closed behind with a clang.

In the warden's room a sergeant took note of our criminal histories. Our offence was put down as "political"—the usual crime at present in Persia where the new autocratic government, maintaining its position with a high hand, has cast many of the leaders of the old régime into gaol. We were stripped, weighed and measured. The sergeant then thrust toward us two bundles containing the regulation cloth shoes, skull-cap and striped cotton uniform. Our disgrace was now complete.

Arrayed in these clumsy clothes we were taken out into the courtyard and told to lockstep toward the cell blocks. We stepped! We had to, for right behind us walked a guard with a gleaming bayonet pointed at the bulge in our prison pants.

The door to the cell blocks opened mechanically, and we were led down a well-lighted, scrupulously clean corridor of steel and concrete, lined with large sunny compartments. Could this possibly be a house of punishment?—it was unquestionably the most delightful prison we were ever in. Suppose—this apprehension grew upon us—suppose with all this comfort and efficiency, we were reformed before we could get out!

We "political prisoners" occupied a wing apart. McGovern and I were each given a cell, eight by ten feet, well heated and furnished with a cot, a table and chair, all new and all well made. Our barred windows looked out on a walled garden filled with evergreens, and dominated by the glorious peak of Demavend, soaring and shining in the Persian-blue sky.

There were no locks whatsoever on our doors, and we soon found that the guards took no notice of prisoners wandering in and out of the cells, making social calls upon their neighbours at any hour. Grills at the end of the corridor prevented one from wandering too far. I called upon McGovern to inquire after his health. He said he felt rested already. Tea was brought in. Then two of the guards joined us, with cigarettes and a deck of cards, and we four spent half an hour playing the local variety of blackjack. This was much finer than the Gibraltar gaol where, some years before, in similar circumstances, I'd had to play solitaire.

By dinner-time the news of our arrival in the cell block had spread around, and neighbours began to come in to greet us. We found ourselves in most distinguished company—ex-ministers, ex-tribal-chieftains, ex-governors, ex-generals—all enemies, proved or suspect, of the present administration. Some of them were nattily attired in striped suits specially fitted by the finest local tailors, and several had their cells furnished with rugs and pictures from their own palaces. No restraint was placed upon "seditious" speech. We could call all the mass meetings we liked and damn the government to our hearts' content —as far as the iron bars at the end of the corridor.

Fortunately these prison-mates of ours, being mostly from the educated families, nearly all spoke French or English as well as Persian. McGovern, of course, spoke everything, and even Fazlullah, our friendly blackjack-playing guard, had been with the South Persia English

Rifles long enough during the war to have acquired a perfect command of cockney . . . so in conversation I got along.

The more I heard of these prisoners' tales the more divided my sympathy became between the prisoners and the dictator who had sent them here. This dictator, besides having superior force on his side, probably had superior justice too. From the mélange of abuse directed at his head I pieced together his history:

Shortly after the war Persia found herself politically, financially and socially in ruins. Various tribal states had completely seceded from the central "government." The hereditary Shah was a weakling and a waster, living abroad, entirely unconcerned with the wretchedness at home. Violence scourged the land. Trade and transportation stood still, paralysed by bandits. Foreign powers, seeing the utter anarchy prevailing, had decided to partition Persia among themselves.

And then a miracle took place. From the Persian army emerged a towering giant, named Riza Khan, who through sheer ability, character and ruthlessness had forced his way up the ranks until, amid such civil and military chaos, he found himself a general. In 1925, with a few faithful soldiers, he marched on Teheran, captured it without opposition, formed a military dictatorship and set to work to end the prevailing anarchy. The legitimate ruler, absent as usual in Europe, was dethroned, and his brother, the crown prince, deported. Parliament became a rubber stamp for the dictator, who in 1926 crowned himself Shah of Persia.

The new ruler, having built our Imperial Prison to house all his deposed political opponents, next turned his attention to the defiant tribal tribes. These lawless tribes, which for years had been living by raiding caravans, learned with outraged astonishment that the new Shah meant to suppress their ancient means of livelihood. When the government at Teheran forbade further importation of arms and ammunition into those states, and declared that every young tribesman would be conscripted for the imperial army, it was too much—all the tribes exploded in wild rebellion.

The Shah promptly marched against their defiant chiefs, and in two years had subdued or captured every one.

Many of these had come to join the little house-party in our prison.

The next day passed quickly. It seemed to me we were eating half the time. The food was preposterously good and served in a much better fashion than in our hotel. During the morning an ex-general and McGovern and I took soap and towels and wandered off to the baths. Twenty showers of hot water lined the walls, and twenty jets of steam. McGovern and I, thoroughly cooked, sat around the dressing-room and smoked, while the general had his head shaved by the bath barber. In contrast to all this luxury I remembered the cracked bowl-and-pitcher bath at the "Grand" and resolved to advise all the readers of this book who may be contemplating a visit to Teheran, to wire ahead for reservations at the gaol.

On the return journey to our cells we loitered and looked about. We passed rug-weaving looms, carpentry benches—long rows of rooms devoted to the artistic crafts at which Persians excel. Evidently a convict was turned loose among coloured wool, and brass, and silver, and paints, and told to take his choice—a sort of Montessori method of keeping ex-prime ministers happy. As for ourselves, we got hold of our cameras and went in for photography.

That afternoon Fazlullah took us calling on some of the prison celebrities in the neighbouring wings. The most famous prisoner—and he had reasons—was little Mahmud. On introducing us to him, Fazlullah explained that he was fourteen years old, and had murdered his mistress.

"*Murdered his mistress!*" I exclaimed in amazement, looking at the child's chubby face and mild manner,—"he doesn't look as if he would hurt a kitten."

"Is this true, Mahmud?" McGovern asked the boy.

The little prisoner hung his head, but nodded assent. "*Bali—bali, sa'b,*"—Yes, it is, sir.

"Can you tell us about it?"

Again he cast down his eyes and refused to speak. He looked so unhappy at being asked to recite his painful tale that we did not press him further.

But Fazlullah told us later the details of Mahmud's case. It was true that he was only fourteen, and that he had murdered his inamorata, a designing older girl, in a jealous rage. From the time of the poet Hafiz, the

Persians have managed to suffer beyond other men from the agonies of love, even at fourteen.

"Will you release him later on?" McGovern asked.

"Most likely—as soon as he has learned a trade. He has been a good boy here—a sort of prison mascot who does as he likes. But I'm glad we haven't more of them on our conscience."

We walked on into the next wing. "Old Babadul lives in here," said Fazlullah. "He's almost as much of a celebrity as Mahmud."

"What did *he* do?" I asked, "—murder his mistress at ninety-five?"

"Probably several of them," said Fazlullah. "He's the biggest rogue in Persia, and just about the oldest."

Old Babadul seemed to be twins, for in his cell we met not one but two tall, lean old men, around seventy years old, with dark Arab faces half hidden behind huge white beards. We stopped to have a cigarette with these two fierce-looking Santa Clauses, hoping we might find out what indiscretion had brought them to this Persian garden.

"Been in long?" McGovern asked the more imposing of the beards."

"One year."

One year! We thought they were both serving at least the last lap of a life-term sentence.

"Couple of bandits," Fazlullah informed us.

"And at your age!" exclaimed McGovern, handing Old Babadul a light.

But in Persia there seems to be no age limit for bandits, up or down—at least judging from Babadul's record.

He had started as a youth, in his mountains of Luristan, in southern Persia. Then, along with his father who was a bandit before him, he had taken part in attacks on caravans, and on the neighbouring villages of other tribes, in which encounters (according to Babadul) he had always shown the greatest dash and courage.

The first big haul he could remember resulted from the attack he and his companions made on a caravan of a hundred camels carrying corpses to Kerbela, the holy city in Iraq, to be buried in its sacred confines. An armed guard escorted the pilgrims, but it was the first to flee when Babadul and his wild troop charged into their midst. The camel drivers scattered in all directions—only to be rounded up and systematically plundered. With the pack-animals appropriated by the bandits, the coffins were left beside the road, and there they remained until the hyenas and vultures disposed of their contents.

For the next forty years Old Babadul continued to live by banditry, emerging unscathed from every fight, surviving all his companions, who perished one by one. In 1920, when the war clouds had cleared, motor-cars and trucks appeared, and proved even more profitable to rob than the caravans. The passengers were sometimes Europeans who were sure to be rich. One such victim turned out to be an English missionary. Old Babadul stripped him of everything—and he laughed merrily as he told it—except for a black cloth coat with two long tails in the back, and very short in front. This the otherwise naked missionary put on hindside before, and, thus clad, walked a smajestically as possible into Shiraz.

Meanwhile Babadul was growing rather old for the exhausting demands of banditry, but he still enjoyed it and seemed to keep up with the youngest. He might have been at liberty yet, had his band not made one fatal blunder. They had lain in ambush for the tax collector who had robbed their village unmercifully (or so Babadul, wailing over such an outrage, expressed it), and had murdered him and recovered the tax loot he had taken.

In Shiraz there was a roar of indignation—the murdered man was well-born and rich—and the roar reached the ears of the iron-fisted new Shah. He dispatched a swarm of troops into Luristan and forced the people of Babadul's village, in order to prevent its complete destruction, to reveal the names of the guilty men and the spot where they were hiding. The soldiers surrounded the entire band in a mountain valley, and after a long and bitter battle captured those that were left alive. Nine Lurs were marched into the village, and publicly hung. Only Babadul and his equally antique companion, because of their age and flowing white beards, were spared the gallows, and sent to Teheran for life imprisonment. Judging from their tough and hardy appearance, with all their seventy years, I hadn't a doubt they were going to be guests of the government for many years to come.

"But your beards!" exclaimed McGovern at the end of the narrative. "You two are the only prisoners allowed to wear them."

"That is true," Babadul replied proudly. "We have

always worn them—and are they not splendid? When we came here the warden ordered us to cut them off, but we refused. 'You may kill us,' we said. 'That is nothing. But we will not shave off our beards. That disgrace would be too terrible, for who would respect us then?' So the warden made an exception—and our beards were saved."

Next day was Friday—the Sabbath Day in Mohammedan Persia.

During the morning all four hundred of the prisoners streamed out into one of the big sun-flooded courtyards. There they crouched on the ground in a semicircle about the benign and portly prison mullah, who sat amid his flowing robes upon a chair and read in a clear sonorous voice passages from the Koran. All our friends from the political ward were there, and little Mahmud and Old Babadul. McGovern and I, in our stripes, sat in the midst of the group, indistinguishable from the other men.

Rarely have I seen so strange, so moving, a picture—four hundred prisoners, among them murderers, bandits, wild mountain rebels, looking up with rapt attention and dark transfigured faces at the teacher of God's word, and listening, motionless and quiet, like children hearing for the first time a romantic and heroic tale. Even Old Babadul seemed entranced. I should not have believed my eyes had I seen such a sight in an American prison, or a European prison. But this was Persia, where, generally speaking, men have passions in their hearts, but little venom, and where the lowliest camel driver, even in these hateful stripes, is tuned to any voice that speaks forth music and poetry.

A most extraordinary interruption cut short this Sabbath morning idyll. A bugle was blown; the inner gates swung wide, and a general of the Shah's army marched into the prison courtyard. We judged from his distinguished air, his spurs and sword, his blazing insignia, and his retinue of brilliantly uniformed aides, that he must be at least the commander-in-chief. When he advanced and asked for McGovern and myself, there was almost a panic among the prisoners, who seemed to think a new sort of holiday-execution was about to take place. The mullah rose to his feet, and stood with open mouth as we two foreign convicts emerged from the striped congregation and shook hands with the general, who greeted us cordially.

"It was His Majesty's wish that I call to inquire if you have been comfortable," he said in French.

"Very comfortable, thank you," McGovern replied. "We have never been happier in a prison."

"And do you like the food?"

"It's excellent. . . . Perhaps you'll stay for lunch with us, and see for yourself. We can introduce you to very superior company."

"That's kind of you," the general said, with a smile. "But I have an appointment at the Palace; and besides, I've already met most of your table-mates—in a business way."

Even though he would not stay for lunch, he insisted on showing us—as the Shah had requested him—through every department of the prison which he thought we might not already have seen. Up one corridor and down another we marched—the general and his magnificent aides and two lowly prisoners in stripes—leaving a trail of gasping, goggle-eyed prison attendants in our wake.

In two minutes the news was all over the place . . . the Shah's number-one general was making a social call on a couple of convicts.

For those two convicts it was a disastrous call. No sooner had our distinguished visitor departed than McGovern and I, having returned to our cells, were met on every side with hostile glances, and whisperings behind our backs. . . . So! We were bosom friends of the Shah, were we!—hobnobbing with his generals . . . probably spies and certainly traitors to Persian freedom—*that's* what we were. Every one of our friends in the political ward cut us dead. Even Fazlullah didn't dare be seen in our company any more.

In vain we remonstrated against this injustice . . . we were *not* pro-Shah or anti-Shah. We had no political interests whatsoever. We were just a couple of visiting Americans who wanted to meet some of the best people in Teheran, and had come here to do it. Our only offence—if any—was social climbing.

But nothing could discount the glaring evidence against us—the Shah's general, calling out for us, and shaking hands right before everybody.

After this strange twist of Fate, there was no longer any

joy left in our little adventure. Henceforth, it was obvious, we would be ostracised from all the best prison society. There was nothing else for us to do but retire—and leave behind this warmth, this comfort, this cuisine, this palace of a prison, for the tumbledown icebox of the Grand Hotel. . . .

The great steel doors ground open. Deprived of our stripes, we stood for a moment at the threshold, looking back wistfully at the beautiful garden in the courtyard where several happy convicts were wandering among the trees—and then, realising there was no help for it, we went forth to face the cold cruel world.

CHAPTER XXI

THE PRINCESSES

ALL my life I've wanted to meet a real princess. Princes haven't mattered quite as much; they are not so rare and wonderful; they get about, and mix with people. And kings have always seemed too formal, too detached. But a princess . . . since the days of my childhood when I first read about the sort that had golden hair and wore jewelled girdles and were imprisoned in high towers and guarded by dragons—I've dreamed of meeting—perhaps even rescuing—a princess.

From the moment the Flying Carpet came into my possession, I was convinced that I now had the proper equipment for this rescuing. True, damsels of royal birth were becoming more and more rare in these drab republican days, and fewer still were likely to be in need of my assistance. Nevertheless, I had hopes, for my range was wide and the whole world lay before me.

My definition of princess was strictly limited. No Hollywood cinema star who had married a "prince" qualified. Side-show "princesses" at fairs and circuses were absolutely out. I did not insist on their golden hair, but I did insist on their being daughters of royal blood.

While flying about France, Moye Stephens and I encountered two royal ladies who, though not in jeopardy, agreed to adorn the Flying Carpet. One—a very pretty one—claimed to be Russian. We started out calling her "Your Highness," until we found that she and her husband came from Georgia in the Caucasus where every one who owned an estate was known as "prince."

The other princess, we were sure, would not disappoint us. She was one of the smartest women in Paris, with a manner that commanded homage and dissipated all doubt as to her royal birth. Her husband, who never appeared, she said was Italian, exiled by politics. But her accent, when she spoke English, was so suspiciously American that we were puzzled. We inquired further about the lady and learned that she had been born and bred in Brooklyn.

Shaken but undismayed, Stephens and I continued our quest for princesses. In Spain we found that they had all fled for their lives before the rampant revolutionaries, but had already been rescued by the newsreels. In Morocco they were confined so closely by their Mohammedan families we couldn't get a peep at them. In Timbuctoo they wore brass hoops around their necks and criss-cross tattoo scars upon their ebon faces. In Venice and Budapest we met legions of countesses, but all the princesses escaped. In Republican Turkey not one could we discover. Surely, Bagdad would offer a large supply. Had not Bagdad always been their favourite place of abode? But even there the king, who was willing enough to have his son Prince Ghazi accept our friendship, seemed horrified at the idea of his two daughters, who were never allowed outside their palace, even being seen in the company of two foreign infidels, much less flying around with them in the air.

We had borne with these endless disappointments patiently, for were we not, after all, on our way to Persia, and would not a Persian princess be the best in the world? Had not Persia been considered from the time of Harun al-Rashid the home of the loveliest women in the East, the most ravishing, the most inspiring? . . . "Tall of stature, with large hips, and a forehead like the bright new moon of Ramadan, eyes like those of gazelles, cheeks resembling anemones, a mouth like the seal of Suleiman, and bosoms resembling two pomegranates of equal size."

So had the princesses of Persia been described.

Once safe in Teheran—and out of gaol—I again put my mind seriously on princesses. Having made the acquaintance of a Persian gentleman, Mr. Jamshid Khan, educated in England and well connected with all the royal families in the capital, I confided in him my heart's desire—to take a real princess beside me aboard the Flying Carpet, and show her Persia from the air. He shook his head gravely. Princes, yes. There were several who would be delighted to go. But princesses! Most of them still wore veils and were kept in strictest seclusion.

"I do have two princesses in mind—cousins," continued my friend, "who would fit beautifully into your scheme—if only it weren't for their family's objections. Their names in English mean Flower-of-the-Morning and Queen-of-the-Stars. They are related to our last Shah. The father of Flower-of-the-Morning is Mohammed Kuli, one of the highest ranking noblemen in Persia. The two princesses are young and beautiful—*famous* beauties in fact. They have magnificent black eyes, and the finest hips in Teheran. But they'll never go—they'll never go," my friend lamented. "It would be unheard of—*unless*, perhaps, you got the approval of old Mohammed. He's a good sport—the most inveterate hunter in Persia. Perhaps—if you show some interest in the wild asses he's shot—he *may* contribute his princesses to your Flying Carpet."

"Lead me to him," I asked.

Mohammed Kuli received us hospitably—a fine-looking elderly man with white hair and beard, but tough and enduring enough still to be the terror of all the wild asses in Persia. Having drunk the inevitable tea, we started talking, both in broken French, about hunting his favourite animal, and from that to polo and flying. He seemed so liberal in his ideas I soon worked around to princesses, and finally got up nerve enough to tell him I wanted Flower-of-the-Morning and Queen-of-the-Stars to go riding with Stephens and me aboard the Flying Carpet.

"Certainly," he said, "they'd love it."

Jamshid Khan almost collapsed—three thousand years of precedent felled with a word.

I rushed back to Stephens with the good news, but checked myself in order to announce my conquest with the proper grand air. "I've a couple of girl-friends I want to take up for a ride to-morrow," I said casually, "—two princesses."

Moye did not seem in the least impressed.

"They're famous Persian beauties," I continued, looking down my nose. "I would be obliged if you'd go on ahead of me to the field early to-morrow morning and have the Flying Carpet washed and polished, and two bouquets of roses waiting in the front seat. I'll be coming out in the royal motor with Their Graces about noon."

Moye's comments about my sudden elegant airs were most unkind. Even so, I knew he would oblige me.

Next morning I spent hours before the mirror . . . **a** princess, a princess—at last . . . *two* princesses. . . . I wondered if they would like me. . . . I put more oil on my hair. . . . They spoke a little French, so I had been told . . . but what would I talk about? I'd take them up one at a time . . . there was room for only one beside me in my cockpit . . . me, aboard the Flying Carpet, with a Persian princess . . . and another looking up, watching, waiting. . . . I made a third change in my necktie.

And drove up grandly to their palace door.

A small army of people greeted me, all dressed to go to the flying field. Burning with curiosity I was escorted into the drawing-room, and there sat Flower-of-the-Morning and Queen-of-the-Stars.

For a moment I was too overcome to look at them. Then I lifted my eyes toward the exalted ladies. No wonder they were celebrated—in Persia. From every aspect, they filled all the requirements for Persian beauty. Their eyes were like those of gazelles, their foreheads like the bright new moon of Ramadan, and as for their figures—these were as ample as the most exacting Persian lover of plumpness could possibly have desired.

I bowed and tried to express in French my appreciation for their willingness to go with me aboard the Flying Carpet, and to assure them that as the first American airmen to come to Teheran, Mr. Stephens and I were proud to take aloft the first Persian princesses ever to fly. Flower-of-the-Morning made an equally pretty speech, though I missed most of it trying to remember the exact lifting power of my little plane.

It took half the motor-cars in town to transport our retinue, for it was composed of fully a hundred people— servants, children, friends, relatives, photographers, reporters and military bodyguard . . . as much excitement as the traditional balloon ascension at the country fair. Indeed, looking at my princesses . . .

The Flying Carpet stood ready, all gleaming after the scrubbing Moye had given it. Even the flowers were there. Without a word of comment Moye helped me guide the two leading ladies out of their car and over to the Carpet, but from the corner of my eye I saw him sizing up my regal girl-friends. With some difficulty we got Flower-of-the-Morning into the front cockpit.

I tried to crawl in beside her . . . but there wasn't room.

As I climbed back on to the ground, with all my royal plans in pieces, I didn't dare look at Stephens, seated at the controls in the rear seat. I knew what expression would be on his face—glee, slyness, suppressed laughter, mock pompousness . . . after all my grand airs and imperial orders . . . my Persian beauty princesses . . . my oiled hair . . . my snobbery—and I must remain behind with the servants and relatives, and watch Flower-of-the-Morning fly off without her Lochinvar.

She was gone, and soon became a gold-and-scarlet speck in the sky—while I sat on the ground in the shade of her cousin and talked to old Mohammed about wild asses.

After this sad adventure with princesses I decided to retire from the pursuit of the daughters of kings. Evidently I was not destined to come into the life of any one of these lofty beings. My ambitions along this line were folded up and tucked away on the top shelf beside a number of other brave ideals I had dreamed about—but found too large for me to encompass.

Resigned, I learned to be happy with common-clay playmates, and with them dined and danced away a fortnight in Teheran.

Meanwhile Moye (McGovern, to our deep regret, had departed) was being even more social than I, and attending more parties, and having more success with the local ladies generally, both native and foreign born.

One evening he came home to our hotel reporting still another girl he had met and particularly liked—"Persian," he had said in a manner quite offhand. He suggested taking her for a ride in the Flying Carpet.

"Of course—take her," I insisted. "Who is she?"

"Oh—just someone. You might come along with us. I thought of flying around Mount Demavend." And then he added with the familiar sly twinkle in his eyes: "There'll be room for you both in the front cockpit this time."

Next morning, chaperoned by a distinguished-looking Persian matron, Moye appeared at the field with his "date," the prettiest, daintiest, most charming girl I ever hope to see. Her luxuriantly lashed black eyes shone like torches from above a black silk veil held carelessly across her pale aristocratic face. Every movement she made was graceful, and every word, spoken in perfect French, refined. She wore the *izzar*, the black all-enveloping mantle worn by Persian women of position, but beneath its many folds a delicate and slender figure was indicated.

" *Mon camarade, Monsieur Halliburton,*" was all the introduction Moye made.

She smiled delightfully, and extended a slim and beautiful hand.

We buttoned up her fur coat, adjusted her goggles and lifted her, as one might lift a child, into the Flying Carpet. Having said good-bye to the chaperon and promised to bring the damsel back soon and safely, I climbed into the front seat beside the girl, Moye into the rear.

Our companion showed no fear as we sailed up into the sky, but looked overboard at the housetops of Teheran with the most intense interest. We climbed to ten thousand feet, and sailed up close to the gleaming slopes of Demavend rising like a vast iceberg above us. The wind from the snow stung our faces. The girl beside me snuggled into her coat, and hid her glowing cheeks. But there was no anxiety—only excitement and stimulation.

Finding the wild blasts from the peak too violent to attempt encircling it, we turned east to the Caspian Gates through which Alexander pursued the fleeing Darius nearly twenty-three hundred years ago.

Back over Teheran we sailed—over the bazaars—over the Peacock Throne—over the jumble of mud and jewels that makes up the hodgepodge capital. The girl beside me seemed to recognise every house and street, and to rejoice in this recognition from a mile above. Never had the Flying Carpet carried a more delightful passenger. I motioned to Moye to fly on to India—or some place it took hours and hours to reach. But the gasoline was getting low, and so, reluctantly, he brought us down to earth.

I helped our charming guest out of the Flying Carpet. With her hair blown into curls by the wind, her face flushed by the cold, and her enormous eyes alight, she made an astonishingly beautiful picture . . . and when she said good-bye and invited Moye and me to tea next day—my heart stood still.

The moment Stephens returned from escorting her home, I pounced upon him. "Moye!" I exclaimed, "who was that marvellous girl?"

"Oh—didn't you know?" said Stephens—and the old sly-and-gleeful twinkle came back into the corners of his eyes. "That girl, my lad—but for the present dictator—is the Queen of Persia."

CHAPTER XXII

THE STORY OF GABRIEL

In the clear dawn, before the east was red,
Before the rose had torn her veil in two,
A nightingale through Hafiz' garden flew,
Stayed but to fill its song with tears, and fled. *

THIS is the story of Gabriel, my Persian nightingale. It is a story of the capture and the bondage of a bird that yearned for freedom, and gained it, in the garden of Hafiz. If the story of a nightingale held prisoner in a cage distresses you, remember, there is the happy ending. But let us go back some months and begin with the beginning of this tale, not with the end.

It was spring in Persia. In no country in the world, save the Valley of Kashmir, is spring as soft, as flower-filled, as is this semi-desert land. From the icy slopes of Mount Demavend the melted snow pours down its cold streams into the orchards on the plain where the pear trees, blossoming white, dance exultantly in the wind. In a hundred thousand gardens the fountains, no longer frozen by the winter's cold, play again, and the roses, tearing their veils in two, emerge with a lushness that is famous over all the world. Even the poppies that furnish the infamous opium, for a month in spring paint the Persian fields and farms with a blood-red hue, and their wilder, brighter brothers frolic in countless legions across the wilderness. The iris and narcissus, the plum tree and wild rose, march up from the south in waves of colour. For these few brief weeks the whole land becomes a lyric

* This, and all the other poems quoted in this chapter, are taken from *Poems from the Divan of Hafiz*, translated by Gertrude L. Bell, and published by William Heinemann, London.

poem, a paradise, beautiful and passionate, and utterly occupied with love. Such is Persia in the spring.

Where else then but in Persia should the nightingales convene to sing their love-songs to the rose, and to fill the moonlight nights with the story of their ecstasy and their pain?

Of all the glories of a Persian spring, the music of these nightingales is the most glorious, the most haunting. In whatever garden a nightingale builds his nest, that garden is blessed and made beautiful; every tree from which he sings falls in love with the delirious singer, and not a bush or garden-bed but bursts into flower when, in the dawn, before the east is red, he pours forth the magic of his madrigal.

From the winter gardens of Arabia, from across the Persian Gulf, the nightingales, knowing it was spring, were flying north. They tarried in Shiraz to flood the tomb of Hafiz with their song. In Isfahan they found a rose garden belonging to a prince, and sang the whole night through.

But even Isfahan was not far enough to the north. The singers wanted to live in sight of the gleaming poem of Mount Demavend. So on and on they flew, until they found the city of Teheran, and close by, in the aromatic hedges, beside streams that flowed down from the great mountain, the male nightingales built nests for their brides and each night serenaded them with overflowing rhapsodies.

But one night several of the most joyous singers did not return to their nests, nor the next night, nor the next. Their hedges stood silent, except for the subdued cries from their mates. Had some misfortune come to them?

Alas, it was misfortune, bitter, cruel misfortune. They had been caught in a snare set by a nightingale merchant, and dragged, despite their desperate struggles, into a bag where they found a dozen other captives as unhappy as themselves.

Deep into the bazaars of Teheran the merchant carried his catch of despairing nightingales. There he owned a shop where he sold these song-birds at a price. Here the nightingales, torn from their mates, from their nests, from their rose bowers and moonlight nights, were thrust alone into rude wood cages which hung upon the wall. And then the merchant commanded them—to sing!

But for days they could not sing. Anguish lay too heavy upon them. And yet the spring breeze continued to drift into the bazaar, and to bring to them the perfume of the blossoming plum tree . . . and on a shelf near by, a pot of red geraniums stood—red like the roses that used to bloom to the music of their voices. Softly, haltingly, one of the braver spirits spoke to the scarlet flower, a sad little song. It was good to hear himself speak again, to surrender to the instinct that bade him sing, even if it were only to tell a story of his despair. One by one, the other nightingales, taking heart, joined in the lay, and soon the bird bazaar was bursting with the choral song. Crowds of people came and stood before the open shop, and listened to the concert of a hundred nightingales, of a hundred voices filled with melody—and tears.

. The spring had given way to summer, and the summer turned to early winter, when Moye and I reached Teheran aboard our Flying Carpet. Already flurries of snow were falling. There was no hangar in which to house the airplane, and consequently Moye, soon after our sky-riding with the three princesses, decided to fly on south to the shores of the Persian Gulf, where he would wait till I caught up with him, travelling overland.

Left alone in Teheran I amused myself each day by rambling through the byways of Persia's curious capital.

One morning I watched the miniature-artists painting their delicate and beautiful little pictures.

Another day I visited the rug mart, and saw new carpets worth a thousand pounds spread out on the ground of the open courtyard where they were being aged by the rain and the droppings from the mules.

Another day I entered the Gulistan Palace to see the greatest single treasure in the world, the famous Peacock Throne, and stood bedazzled before the enormous precious jewels with which the throne is set.

Another morning, moving on through the spice bazaar, through the silks, past the silver, I came at length, not caring where my ramblings led, to a shop where only nightingales were sold.

I stopped and looked within. A hundred wooden cages lined the wall. Most of them were now empty, but a few still imprisoned grey-brown little birds that pecked at the seed and lettuce leaves the bird merchant fed to them. I was fascinated by such a picture. I'd never seen a nightingale before, and so to encounter a whole flock all at once struck me as a great discovery. I entered the shop and held a living nightingale in my hand. With what modest inconspicuous plumage is that golden voice invested! The head and back and wings are reddish brown, with a shade of lighter grey upon the breast. No one would ever notice the sombre nightingale were all the birds to pass by in review, but who would notice any other bird once this supreme singer began his serenade?

Nightingales for sale! I could buy and possess one of these divine voices all for my own. This seemed to me like being able to buy an angel, or a rainbow, or a beam of sunlight, or a star—something too ethereal to be touched by the avarice of man. And buy one I would, if only to give him back his liberty.

As I went from one cage to another examining all the birds, a sharp burst of chirping came from the cage hanging in the doorway. I looked up and found there the finest, largest bird of all. I told the merchant I would buy *that* one. I paid the price, and proudly bore my nightingale home.

I named him Gabriel.

That night, though I built a special fire for him and fed him bountifully, Gabriel would not sing. Nor the next day, nor the next. Out the window, snow was falling; a cold wind howled about the eaves; and this no doubt explained his melancholy mien. He was the messenger of spring, of sunlight, of blossoming tree and flower. How could I expect him to rejoice over the arctic gloom that gripped the world outside! Give him a flowering rose-bush and a moonlit night in spring, and he would sing rapturously till dawn.

Very well, he should have his rose-bush! I was going south to Shiraz and the sunny Persian Gulf to rejoin the Flying Carpet, and Gabriel was going with me.

To travel in a motor-truck across eight hundred miles oi Persia, with a nightingale for a companion, was an adventure as difficult as it was unusual. The weather on this six-thousand-foot plateau had not relaxed its rigour, and I had to be ever alert to see that Gabriel did not freeze to death.

Shall I write about the Persian countryside we motored through, about its bleakness and desolation, and the snow that piled in drifts across the passes? Shall I tell about the glorious amethyst glow that falls at sunset upon Persia's ice-covered mountains? Shall I write about the caravans of pilgrims we met, marching slowly to Meshed, pushing forward with their wives and children through the wintry wind, and sleeping at night in the ancient caravansaries?

I think not. This is the story of Gabriel. Let's get him safely to Isfahan before he perishes.

Whatever hope I may have had that the sight of beautiful and romantic Isfahan would cheer my nightingale, was soon cast down. Gabriel would not sing. Did he remember the prince's rose garden here, in which, the spring before, beside his bride, he had brought a thousand flowers into blossom with his song? Did he remember the sea of snowy pear trees spreading through the green valley—trees that danced in the breeze when he flew past?—and the Zuyanda Rud River flowing between the gardens of iris and almond where, in the month of May, lovers strolled at sunset?

Gabriel would not sing. To be in Isfahan—in winter—in a cage, was more than his passionate little heart could bear. . . . Isfahan, the city of his dreams, where man and maid and tree and flower had surrendered utterly to love at the rhapsodic commands he issued from his moonlit throne in the top of a cypress tree!

But to give him his liberty now would be fatal, for he would perish. I meant to tarry only a week in Isfahan—and then we'd be on our way.

Isfahan! Where are the words to describe this lovely, lovely place? . . . the great Square where three hundred years ago Shah Abbas played polo with his courtiers . . . the turquoise glory of the Royal Mosque lifting its sea-green dome and minarets above a city submerged in trees. . . .

Isfahan should be blessed by all the poets of the present, as it has been blessed by the poets of the past. Its artistic consciousness, the incomparable charm of its flower-garden site, the beauty of its pleasure-loving people who apparently spend their days among the roses reciting verses from Hafiz, all go to make this place a refuge from the dreary moralists of the West—a heaven where one may sing without self-consciousness, and live freed from a sense of sin, and open wide one's heart to receive the gifts of beauty. No wonder the Persians say that *Isfahan nisf-i-jahan*—"Isfahan is half the world."

We had, as yet, by no means escaped the cold of Teheran. But I knew I would find sunshine and roses, even in December, three hundred miles farther to the south, in Shiraz. And so I again climbed aboard a truck with my knapsack and my nightingale, and travelled on.

Hafiz penning his odes half a thousand years before exclaimed:

> All hail, Shiraz, hail! oh site without peer!
> May God be the Watchman before thy gate,
> That the feet of Misfortune enter not here!

To Gabriel and me, remembering the snows of the north, Shiraz, bathed in warmth and sunshine, seemed like the very homeland of spring.

At once I found my way to the tomb of Hafiz, set apart in a crowded cemetery and guarded by a single beautiful pine. To this tomb thousands upon thousands of Persians have made pilgrimages since the fourteenth century, for in Persia Hafiz occupies the position held by Shakespeare in England. Perhaps he holds an even greater position, since it is not only to the enlightened Persians he appeals but equally as much to the peasant class, who know and love his poetry even though they may not be able to read or write one word of it. In an age of prudishness and asceticism in Persia, Hafiz preached personal liberty, and never ceased his praise of wine and love and boon companionship. He prophesied that his grave would became a Mecca for all the drunkards in the world, and in so far as he meant the Persian world, his prophecy has come to pass. But however much his heresies may shock the puritans, there must be truth and wisdom in his philosophy, for year after year the very nightingales, who comprehend no religion but liberty and no morality but love, come to the pine tree leaning over Hafiz' grave, and sing his praises all night long.

My Persian friends and I sung Hafiz' praises, too, all night long in our own manner, soon after my arrival in Shiraz. We had a Hafiz festival, in the most beautiful Persian garden in the valley. A wall of stately cypresses closed out the world; the orange trees, heavy laden, supplied the decoration and the fruit, and down between the beds of roses the streams of water curled. In the middle of this little Eden a fountain splashed melodiously, watched, through the branches of the trees, by a low-hanging moon.

From the garden's summer-house an orchestra seated on the floor poured forth its rhythm. A troupe of dancers whirled and swayed, men and girls, lithe and laughing. The cup-bearer set each glass afire with his red wine. A minstrel sang his Hafiz song:

> The rose has flushed red, the bud has burst,
> And drunk with joy is the nightingale—
> Hail, Sufis! lovers of wine, all hail!
> For wine is proclaimed to a world athirst.

Deliriously the tambourines thumped and jingled. The moon, curious as a child, rose clear above the cypress tops, to observe from her balcony in the sky the increasing tempo of the dervish-like ballet. And bolder and bolder grew the minstrel's song:

> Mirth, Spring, to linger in a garden fair,
> What more has earth to give? All ye that wait,
> Where is the Cup-bearer, the flagon where?
> When pleasant hours slip from the hand of Fate,
> Reckon each hour as a certain gain;
> Who seeks to know the end of mortal care
> Shall question his experience in vain.

The wine-bearer passed by, refilling each emptied cup; the music swelled, and the fountain danced to the melody. . . . Beside the fountain pool the minstrel clutched his glass, and standing in the moonlight, half-sang, half-shouted out, his revelling song:

> Bring, bring the cup! drink we while yet we may
> To our soul's ruin the forbidden draught;
> Like Hafiz, drain the goblet cheerfully
> While minstrels touch the lute and sweetly sing,
> For all that makes thy heart rejoice in thee
> Hangs on Life's single, slender, silken string.

Midnight had long since come and gone, but the musicians, to whom the flagon had not failed to find its way, only scraped their one-string violins the harder, and with swaying bodies and increasing ecstasy beat their fingers on their rhythmic drums. All the guests were turning minstrel now. One, a Shiraz poet, and a

favourite, took the floor amid loud applause, and, as the
music played, chanted a Hafiz love-song written five
hundred years ago:

> Hast thou forgotten when thy stolen glance
> Was turned to me, when on my happy face
> Clearly thy love was writ, which doth enhance
> All happiness? or when my sore disgrace
> (Hast thou forgot?) drew from thine eyes reproof,
> And made thee hold thy sweet red lips aloof? . . .
>
> Hast thou forgotten how the glorious
> Swift nights flew past, the cup of dawn brimmed high?
> My love and I alone, God favouring us!
> And when she like a waning moon did lie,
> And sleep had drawn his coif about her brow,
> Hast thou forgot?   Heaven's crescent moon would bow
> The head, and in her service pace the sky.

And other singers sang, and other poets read, from the
inexhaustible fountain of Hafiz, and the flagon passed and
passed. The tireless music, echoing from the summer-
house, pursued the guests straying down the flowered
paths and whispering in the shadow of the cypresses.
And so the night rolled on until the moon went down and
the wind of morning, slipping coldly through the trees,
began to disenchant the magic garden.

Homeward, through the coming dawn, we trooped, gay
as Hafiz ever hoped to be. I had not understood the
words of the Persian poetry that had been sung, but no
one had been more moved by it than I. I knew the
poems in translation; I knew the spirit of the songs; I
knew the theme, the argument; I heard the rhythm and
the music. . . . It had been a glorious night . . . the
flagons had never missed my cup . . . and now the
rhythm of the songs kept ringing in my head, the music,
was in my blood. . . . "Bring, bring the cup! drink
while we may to our soul's ruin the forbidden
draught. . . ." Hafiz had come to life for me.

In this happy and reckless mood I went home to Gabriel.
Neglected and forgotten, all night long he had sat caged
behind his hateful bars, while I had sung of overflowing
life and liberty, of red roses and joyous nightingales . . .
"drunk with joy is the nightingale—Hail, Sufis! lovers
of wine, all hail!" . . . What a mockery! . . . drunk
with joy is the nightingale! No—dying from grief

rather—mute with pain—desolate and alone. . . . I had meant, from the moment I bought Gabriel, to set him free when the proper time had come. By heaven, this was the proper time!—now—this very dawn. . . . He would thrive in the sunshine of Shiraz, safe from the northern cold. He should have his roses and his cypress trees, and in the spring find his bride, and there would be joy once again over all the land.

But his liberty would not be given him in this ugly room. . . . I knew a far better place.

Seizing his cage with a vehemence that completely upset the poor little prisoner, I tumbled down the stairs and out into the dawn-lighted streets. The tomb of Hafiz stood less than a mile away—deserted, I knew, and peaceful, at this early hour. Lacking a vehicle, I walked—ran—the distance . . . a crazy foreigner, carrying a bird-cage and consumed with an idea, flying up the deserted road toward the cemetery. . . .

I reached the tomb, feeling, with the Hafiz poetry festival just behind me, that I stood before a holy sepulchre. With a jerk I pulled wide the door of Gabriel's prison cell. A quick hop and a cry and he flew out . . . a whirl of wings . . . he was free, free—back into God's open air again—back into the pine-tree branches swaying over Hafiz' tomb—free to pour forth his madrigals, free to sing his love-songs to the rose, free to proclaim in rhapsodic measures his philosophy of love, love, love, to man and maid and tree and flower, from his high throne. I heard him up in the boughs above, half-singing, half-crying, his first song of liberty—a song from the heart of the poet whose soul, haunting this pine, was there to welcome Gabriel's return. . . .

In the clear dawn, before the east was red,
Before the rose had torn her veil in two,
A nightingale through Hafiz' garden flew,
Stayed but to fill its song with joy . . . and fled.

And that is the story of Gabriel, my Persian nightingale. It is the story of the capture and the bondage of a bird that yearned for freedom, and gained it, in the garden of Hafiz. If stories of nightingales held prisoner in a cage distress you, remember, this had a happy ending.

CHAPTER XXIII

THE FLYING FRÄULEIN

MOYE STEPHENS, during my overland travels across Persia with a nightingale, was having an adventure of his own, in Bushire, on the Persian Gulf.

The first chapter of Moye's adventure began in Timbuctoo.

About three weeks before our arrival in Timbuctoo with the Flying Carpet, that town had been greatly surprised one day to behold a German girl, about twenty-three years old, riding on the back of a camel into the market place. She was wearing a flying helmet and a flying costume. She was Elly Beinhorn. Her miniature Klemm, in which she had flown alone all the way from Berlin, had crashed in a swamp twenty miles away.

This air-traveller had taken the roundabout route to Timbuctoo. From Gibraltar she had flown down the west coast of Africa to Dakar, and from there inland along the Senegal River and the Niger, until she could almost see the mud minarets of her destination.

And then her oil ceased to flow: the engine "froze," and down came the little Klemm, Elly and all. She emerged from the wreckage unharmed, but the ship, inaccessible to pack-animals, had to be left behind.

Père Yakouba had talked to us at length about her.... She had great charm—a most courageous spirit—spoke excellent French and English—she was *very* pretty . . . the entire town had lamented her departure. Moye and I had expressed the hope that we might meet this unusual Fräulein some day and form a club of the three civilian fliers who had flown to Timbuctoo.

Months passed, and Moye found himself in Bushire, waiting impatiently for me to arrive from Teheran. One morning, while he was working on the Flying Carpet, a rickety Ford appeared from out of the desert and drove up to the hangar. In it was a pretty European girl half-buried under dust and half-dead from exhaustion.

"Had a motor failure and a forced landing—hundred kilometres up the coast," she said faintly. "I'm looking for a mechanic to help me repair my broken under-carriage."

"There's no mechanic here—except me," said Moye, "—but I'll do what I can. . . . I'm an American pilot flying to India with a friend. My name's Moye Stephens."

"I'm a German pilot on my way from Berlin to Australia. I'm alone. My name's Elly Beinhorn."

Moye greeted her with cheers—from Timbuctoo to the Persian Gulf! The moment she had rested a bit the two of them took off in the Flying Carpet, and landed in the desert beside Elly's stricken ship.

With Moye's help she was able to get started again, and the two airplanes flew back to Bushire side by side.

So Elly, as well as Moye, was on hand to greet me when I finally rolled into Bushire on a truck. We promptly organised our Timbuctoo club, and made Elly president. Her duties were to darn the socks and mend the threadbare pants of the other two members.

Elly possessed a combination of qualities so very rarely found—she was lovable and yet she was efficient, positive, self-reliant. Every one she met fell before her smile, her warmth, her youth, her winsomeness; but at the same time she was unquestionably the most skilful, most fearless woman pilot in Germany. Indeed, there were very few men pilots who could compare with her. That flight of hers all alone from Berlin to Timbuctoo, over a route nearly twice as long as our own, was one that demanded, for a solitary woman, extraordinary courage. The crash so near her goal was due to a broken oil pipe, and not to any inexpertness on her part. Again, the forced landing with a new Klemm in Persia was the result of an engine befouled by a sand-storm.

Not only could Elly pilot. She was a good mechanic too. Motor machinery for her was never the black magic it always remained for me. She could navigate like a sea captain. Her air acrobatics were as intricate and as daring as I have ever watched. And then when she had stowed away the brave little plane (her "husband" she called it), Elly would drop monkey-wrenches and coveralls, and appear for dinner, so fresh, so fragrant, so lovely, so feminine, one was filled with admiration for her all over again.

How many things we three had to talk about—Timbuctoo and Père Yakouba and our friends the storks and bats. Elly told us how it felt, having flown four thousand miles, to have to crash only twenty miles from Timbuctoo—and in a swamp. We told her how it felt, after having been free agents all our lives, to become the slaves of two naked piccaninnies we'd bought from the Tuareg on a rash impulse. In the Flying Carpet's tracks Elly had visited Vienna and Budapest and Constantinople. At Konia, in the heart of Asia Minor, we had both been rescued from Turkish officialdom by the same Shell Oil agent. We had both made dangerous landings at Aleppo in the dark. In Bagdad, preparing to enter Persia, we had all three been forced to submit to inoculations against typhus and cholera and plague, and been as sick as if we'd had these diseases.

Like ourselves, Elly was carrying a phonograph and a score or so of records. She was tired of hers—we were tired of ours. We exchanged—sight unseen. Elly on examining our set insisted she had been absolutely *swindled*. In fact she took back the one record we wanted most, *Falling In Love Again*, in German, and Moye had to clean her spark plugs as extra payment before we finally got it. To retaliate we wouldn't deliver our *St. Louis Blues* until she had given us both a much-needed haircut—with a pair of nail scissors—and not a German haircut either, mind you!

Though both Moye and I spent hours each day, in Bushire, trying to break Elly's heart (shades of Gulbeyaz!), she never decided which one of us she thought was the nicer—or the more trouble. In conversation, Moye ran away with the honours, because he could out-talk me about flying, without even trying . . . the Mount Tabor airline crash and the headless bodies—and the time he went over on his back making a trick landing for *Hell's Angels*. But after about five hours of this, I'd put *What Good Am I Without You?* on the phonograph, with a loud needle, and she'd get right up, and leave Moye flat, and dance with me in four languages.

And didn't I cheer when we went swimming together in

the bay! Moye, who was on the water-polo team at Leland Stanford, always said, and properly, that I, with my antiquated side-strokes, was a swimming disgrace. But beside Elly, Moyne was a *worse* disgrace. Lord!—how that girl could swim—and how she could ride—and how she could fly! In fact there was hardly anything Moye and I could do that Elly Beinhorn couldn't do better.

In a very short time we had come to love this young German Diana of the air, and she responded by adopting both of us as her foster papas. United we stood—and together we left Bushire behind, one grey plane, one red and gold, to fly on down the desolate Persian Gulf to India, and together seek new adventures in the East.

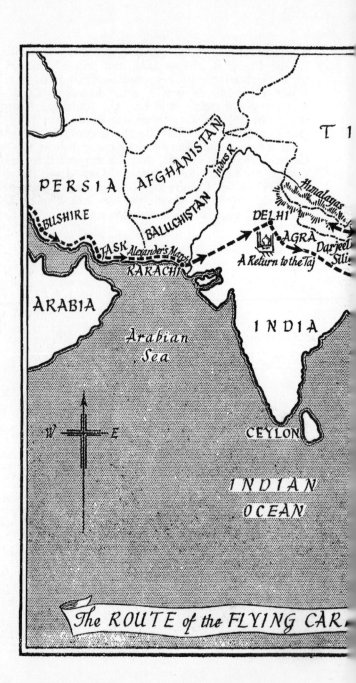

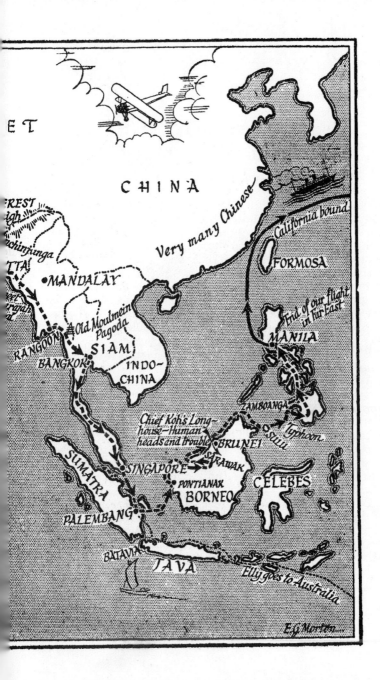

E T

CHINA

Very many Chinese

California bound

FORMOSA

EREST
igh
chinjunga

TTA

•MANDALAY

End of our flight
in far East

eet
nga
d

#Old Moulmein
Pagoda

MANILA

RANGOON

BANGKOK

SIAM

INDO-
CHINA

ZAMBOANGA

Typhoon
SULU

Chief Koh's Long-
house—Human
heads and trouble

BRUNEI

SUMATRA

SINGAPORE→

SARAWAK

•PONTIANAK

CELEBES

PALEMBANG•

BORNEO

BATAVIA

JAVA

Elly goes to Australia

E.G. Morton

CHAPTER XXIV

IN THE TRACKS OF ALEXANDER

KARACHI, the great air terminal at the western edge of India, was twelve hundred miles away—twelve hundred miles of sandstone wastes on our left, of indigo sea on our right. From time to time the white sail of an Arab dhow flecked the blue expanse, carrying pearls or opium, perhaps—a not infrequent cargo for the native traders in the Persian Gulf. Occasionally we sped over a starved-looking oasis which clung to the beach as if seeking to be delivered from the heat-scorched mountain wall that rose abruptly behind. And then we would pass another fifty or a hundred miles and see no form of life.

Elly flew close beside us, seeming to float forward, at the same speed as ourselves.

When not taking a turn at the stick, I spent the long hot hours reading the books I had with me in my cockpit-library—a volume of the *Arabian Nights*; *Hajji Baba*; a translation of Hafiz; and half a dozen biographies of Alexander the Great. The books on Alexander were of particular interest at the moment—along this very beach below, with the remnants of his army, Alexander had marched homeward from India after his conquest of the world.

But this interest in the great Macedonian was not only of the moment. It had been growing for months, as the flight of the Flying Carpet continued to parallel, more or less by chance, the trail of his campaigns—through Asia Minor, Syria, Phœnicia, Egypt, Mesopotamia and Persia.

Since starting in Constantinople we had never been very far from his path. On our flight to Galilee we had flown through the defile in the Taurus Mountains, just north of the Gulf of Alexandretta, where he fought the celebrated battle of Issus, sending Darius and his Persian army in wild disorder back to the East.

From Issus, Alexander had gone on his way to occupy Phœnicia—and the Flying Carpet had followed. "But the conquest of the Phœnician coast," so my wind-whipped pages recorded, "was not to be altogether easy, for Tyre, which owed allegiance to Persia, shut its gates, and for seven months fought off all assaults. The eventual subjugation of this island-city was achieved largely by building a mole out to the island, across which the Greeks were able to propel their siege engines."

With the Flying Carpet, we had gone to Tyre. There are no longer any walls; there is no longer any island, for the drifting sands have changed the mole into a broad isthmus that has claimed Tyre for the mainland. But we were able to climb a tower in the modern town at the tip of the peninsula, and with a little imagination reconstruct the celebrated city as it used to be. We could picture in our mind's eye the mole, topped with siege towers, being pushed out toward the battlemented island, and the rafts with battering-rams beating against the sea-walls below.

Later in our journey, we had continued, from Jerusalem, along Alexander's path into Egypt; flown over the Pyramids before which he reviewed his troops; over Alexandria, the seaport he founded in his own honour, and over the ruins of Memphis, where he had tarried and ruled as king.

But even Egypt at that time was only one province gained from Persia. Alexander was determined to conquer Persia itself. He turned north to Damascus, and striking east through Palmyra, fought his way with his invincible army straight to Babylon.

And over this same vast stretch of wilderness the Flying Carpet had flown—through Damascus and Palmyra, to Babylon.

Back and forth over Babylon, with Prince Ghazi as our passenger, we had wheeled, noting the avenues along which Alexander had made his triumphant entry into the greatest city of that day; over the excavated ruins of the palace in which he had been enthroned, and from which at twenty-five, having conquered all the world that was known to him, he had gone forth to conquer the lands he did not know.

I was called back from these thoughts by a signal from

Pilot Moye. He wanted me to take the stick so that he could eat his lunch and smile at Elly sailing along a hundred feet away. But within an hour, I was back at my books again:

From Babylon, Alexander ascended to the Iranian plateau [modern Persia] and marched upon Persepolis [just north of Shiraz], the summer residence of the Persian kings. There he found a citadel surmounted by halls and palaces grander than he had ever seen before. Having seized the city, he uncovered treasure that staggered even his imagination. Drunk on treasure and on wine, the Conqueror gave a feast in the colossal black marble Hall of a Hundred Columns, and as a gesture to strike terror into the Persians, flung a torch into the rafters and watched the most beautiful and most wonderful edifice of the ancient Persian empire tumble to the earth in flames.

I had wandered among the ruins of this hall, atop the citadel at Persepolis, on my way from Isfahan to Shiraz with Gabriel, and marvelled at the dimensions and magnificence of its remains. A number of the towering columns still stand, seventy feet high, topped by bull's-head capitals upon which the painted cedar rafters rested. Signs of the fire, after twenty-two hundred years, are still evident on the fallen stones; but great numbers of sculptured cornices, walls and doorways, fresh and flawless as the day Alexander first beheld them, remain to "astonish everyone that goeth by,"—even more than Babylon.

And another page:

Some thirty miles from Persepolis, in the centre of a wheat field that covers the site of the ancient Persian capital of Pasargadæ, rises the tomb of Cyrus the Great. The almighty Cyrus, founder of his line, had been one of Alexander's boyhood idols. To possess what Cyrus had possessed became a leading impulse behind his invasion of Persia. It was a moving moment for him when, with Cyrus' empire enslaved, with Cyrus' marble halls cast down, the young Macedonian—he was still only twenty-six at this time, still filled with romantic dreams—came and stood reverently before the tomb of his inspiration. Later, Alexander's anger knew no bounds on finding that his own soldiers had broken into the tomb to pillage it, and had dragged the mummy of the heroic Persian king across the floor. Alexander replaced the body, walled up the entrance again, and stamped his own seal upon the masonry.

This tomb was one of the things I had most wanted to see in Persia. It was inaccessible to the Flying Carpet, but I had been able to reach it on horseback from Persepolis. Arriving there I found that Pasargadæ had completely disappeared, annihilated by the numerous invasions which have swept across this part of Persia. But the tomb itself, as if protected by the wrath of the godlike Alexander, has remained intact, though the sarcophagus of the Great King is gone.

It gave me a strange feeling of close proximity to those fabulous days, to enter the stone chamber where Alexander, burning with rage against the desecration of the tomb, had lifted Cyrus' crumbling mummy back into its marble coffin, and sealed his own earth-shaking name across the re-barricaded door.

The stones of the tomb—a sort of ark built on top a tiered foundation twenty feet high—are of enormous size. But decay and earthquakes have allowed soil and seed to find their way into the chinks between the blocks; and consequently, at the time of my visit, a small forest of shrubs and weeds was growing out of the stone roof. With a heavy pocket-knife I spent all day clearing away the disrespectful growth, hoping that the spirit of Cyrus, and Alexander too, would appreciate my humble gesture of homage.

By now our two planes were approaching the village of Jask, huddled on the shore. This village, with its Imperial Airways landing field, was our first day's destination. Elly's Klemm, and then our Carpet, spiralled down and came to earth beside the sea. Next morning at dawn we were off again . . . more barren coast, more Persian Gulf . . . and I returned to my histories:

From Persepolis, Alexander pursued the fugitive Darius to his capital at Ecbatana, and on to Rhagae [Teheran], and eastward through the Caspian Gates. It was a spectacular race, king pursuing king, each accompanied by only a handful of followers . . . goading their horses, with life at stake, across the sandy wastes of northern Persia.

From Teheran, with Princess Mahin Banu aboard the Flying Carpet, we had flown over that same Caspian pass, over the sandy plain beyond, "where Darius' own escorts, in terror of the relentless Greek rapidly overtaking them, had stabbed the King of Kings, and allowed Alexander to rush upon the abandoned royal wagon and find, within, the ruler of the mighty Persian empire—dead."

With Persia completely at his mercy, Alexander, now planning the conquest of India, marched his Macedonians farther eastward, to Samarkand and Kandahar and Kabul and the Khyber—places where the Flying Carpet was prevented by military restrictions from following. Reaching the Indus River, Alexander and his army sailed down it on rafts until they came to the Persian Gulf, disembarking near the site of present-day Karachi—the city which was our own immediate goal.

Westward, back up this gulf, half the Greek army—led by their king and laden with the loot of India—had marched, homeward bound. The other half had taken to ships and sailed along the coast, later rejoining what was left of the forces which had returned by land.

That any one *could* be left after that march seemed impossible to believe, for week after week the Greeks had to follow this waterless rock wilderness of a shore below, the cruel desolation of which I could comprehend to some extent just by looking overboard.

. . . But Alexander endured, and managed to reach Babylon again. Hardly had he arrived when a fever came upon him. At first his attendants were not alarmed, but on the tenth day his speech was gone, and he sank rapidly. He himself, realising that he had not long to live, suffered the officers of his army to pass, man by man, through his chamber to bid him farewell. Next day the most romantic military figure of the ancient world was dead.

I put my history books away. We were in sight of Karachi, beyond which Alexander had never gone.

CHAPTER XXV

A RETURN TO THE TAJ

THE domes and minarets of the Taj Mahal—a mile below and several miles away—rose through the tree-tops. To visit it we had flown our two planes eight hundred miles on eastward from Karachi across the barren plains of western India.

This was not the first time I had seen the Taj Mahal. On a previous visit to Agra, some years before, this indescribably ethereal tomb had stirred me profoundly, as it stirs every one who visits it. In midsummer I had tramped through the parched suburbs of the city, along the dusty road that led to the grounds, and passed beneath the arched gateway opening upon the gardens. My first sight of the Taj, rising from a sea of fresh luxurious green, seemed like the sudden and supreme realisation of all the dreams of beauty in the world. The aspirations, the eternal quest, for one perfect thing—they were attained in that vision floating against the blue sky at the end of the avenue of cypresses. For me, all ugliness, all evil, vanished during that first moment when I stood in the presence of such overpowering loveliness.

In the shadow of this Taj, I had spent the entire day, and watched the sunset beat upon the soaring dome. I wanted to know every aspect, every mood, of this spirit of a woman made manifest in marble. I had even eluded the guards when at midnight the garden gates were closed, and had stayed on to possess for myself alone the starlit wraith of mystery encircled by the fragrant muted garden. When the moon came up I had dropped into the raised marble lily pool, half-way down the cypress avenue, and swum back and forth. I had sat by the pool and seen strange things reflected there, and felt myself transported to another mystic age considerably nearer paradise.

And there, seen from the Flying Carpet, beyond the crowded city, the Taj, cool and peaceful as the river that flowed beside it, appeared once more. . . . I was returning to an old, old friend.

The two planes flew nearer and nearer the marble minarets. We sailed low over the river, past the great Agra Fort, to mark the Jasmine Tower from which the Emperor Shah Jehan, who had built the Taj as a mausoleum for Arjemand his wife, had last looked toward that symbol of his love for her.

In another moment, having descended to a thousand feet, we reached the tomb itself, and could look straight down upon the domes, upon the broad dais, upon every corner of the gardens and the pools. We could see the miles of thirsty country surrounding this walled park of brilliant green that embowered the great pale pearl; and the winding Jumna flowing in a sweeping curve past the marble throne, as if proud to lend its waters to the adornment of this sublime memorial to a Queen.

Later, as I approached the gardens, again on foot, I wondered if it were wise of me to tempt disillusionment by revisiting a place about which I had such extravagant memories. Most attempts to recapture the emotions, the happiness, of the past, fail so lamentably. . . .

But with the very first glimpse through the gateway, the old spell of the Taj was upon me. Its magical appeal was as compelling as ever. It was still the one perfect thing on earth—still the ethereal Spirit. Not by one faint shadow had it changed. It seemed to possess an architectural immortality—eternally unblemished, incapable of growing old. The other marble poems that adorn the world become more time-worn with the years. Not so the Taj Mahal. After three centuries it still appears as fresh, as fair, as a temple built of clouds. Time leaves no mark upon its face. The weariness of the world, the decay, stand aside, disarmed before this embodiment of beauty.

My previous visit to the Taj Mahal was recorded as a chapter in a book of vagabond travels—*The Royal Road to Romance*. In this chapter I wrote, among other things, about my solitary moonlight swim in the lily pond. It was a minor incident, written in the romantic vein, but in no way deviating from the essential truth.

My surprise was considerable, therefore, when after the

appearance of the book a reviewer discovered that this particular story was a fabrication. He had, it seems, once visited the Taj himself, or at least read about it in a better book; and the pool in the gardens, he well remembered, is only three inches deep. So I could not possibly have swum in it. Here was a glaring imposture, which he need only expose in order to bring the whole book tumbling. He even went so far as to take my fable for a text, and sum up the whole field of travel writing as corrupting to literary integrity, advising that since travel writers would not balk at even the most obvious discrepancies, their works should be reviewed under the head of "Fiction" or not at all!

Naturally I laughed over this pother about my midnight bath, over this tempest in a lily pond, even when other comments on the same tale began to appear, always drawing attention to the shallowness of the pool.

For all this dwelling on the shadows apparently prevented any notice being taken of the depths. There *is* a long reflecting-pool ten feet wide, adorned with fountains, stretching down the Taj gardens from the gate to the tomb, which is three inches deep. But in the exact centre of the garden one not only finds a lily pool five feet deep and twenty feet square, but actually has to mount up to it and walk around it, in order to pass from the entrance of the gardens to the Taj itself. Moreover, lest some visitor pass blindly by this gem of Mogul landscaping, there are marble benches at the sides, where for three centuries lovers of beauty have sat, and looked down into the dark depths of the pool, and forgotten everything else—even books—in the contemplation of beauty, which is poetically the same as truth.

And so, just for the amusement of doing once more what had been so thoroughly disproved—and to celebrate New Year's Eve—I decided, on our first evening in Agra, to return to the gardens of the Taj and go swimming in the lily pond again.

This being a holiday, the gardens were open to the public all night, and even at two in the morning I found people strolling up and down the walks. But a protecting tree with low-hanging branches stood quite near, and I used this as an undressing room. The gardens were unlighted, and fortunately there were few stars and no moon. Waiting in the enveloping darkness for a momentary

193

ebb of visitors, I was able to reach the pool, drop into the five feet of water, and start to swim across.

Not until this moment had I felt any resentment against my discrediting critics. But now resentment rose within me, for had I not heard their pronouncements on the subject of the lily-pond story, I would have been spared the discomfort of swimming in this pool again. The first time, it had been clean and clear, but in the meanwhile the water had become alive with strange life; the lily roots were matted into a sub-aqueous jungle where things crawled from branch to branch; and when I had swum through them twice, I was cold, scratched, and almost on the side of the sceptics. If they had said merely that one *should* not swim in this Indian pool, they would have had my hearty agreement.

Disentangled from the trailing stems, and again clad, I continued my visit down the marble walks to the shrine itself. Its spectre glimmered against the black sky, an apparition in the dimness—no night can be so deep but the luminous whiteness of the mausoleum triumphs over it. Although the season was midwinter, the chill in the air only refreshed and intensified the luxuriance of the grass and the perfume of the flowers. Showers of snowy clematis could be seen even through the fragrant dark. The whole garden, the sky, the black velvet night, all flowed together to honour and to bless the ghostly presence of the Taj.

Here and there about the dais groups of Indian visitors strolled. Along with them, I moved through the marble doors, again to pay homage to the Empress Arjemand. During the years since last I'd made a pilgrimage to her grave, my ideas of what true beauty is had doubtless changed. Yet on this second pilgrimage her tomb seemed even more beautiful, if possible, than before: even more the expression of a love that passed all understanding, and the creation of genius that drew its inspiration from the gods.

Outside, the night wind blew from across the Jumna. In the darkness, I wandered over the pallid marble flagstones to the river-edge of the dais. There, listening to the music of this wind and this river, I made my New Year's resolution: Henceforth the Taj was to be my temple; here would I return as often as possible to seek refuge from the malice and the ugliness of life . . . but never again would I go swimming in the lily pond!

CHAPTER XXVI

THE GODDESS MOTHER OF THE WORLD

THE tallest mountain on earth, outside the Himalayas, is Aconcagua, in the Andes—23,080 feet, climbed the early part of the present century under the most appalling difficulties. I had once seen it from Santiago, Chile, blocking out the sky, and soaring higher in the heavens than imagination dared to follow—God's supreme effort in all the Americas.

But here before us, as we watched from the Flying Carpet eighteen thousand feet above Nepal, stretched a chain of super-giants containing nearly *one hundred and fifty mountains higher than Aconcagua!* One hundred peaks reach 24,000 feet. Another twenty climb to 26,000. Six soar past 27,000. Kinchinjunga, 28,146; Godwin-Austen, 28,250; and Everest, the spectacular summit of the world, 29,145.

To me, Mt. Everest is the most dramatic name in all geography. Mt. Everest—the monster mountain, the all-highest, the Goddess Mother of the World. Protected by her Himalayan barricades she stands, fascinating—and forbidden; irresistible—and unattained; a gleaming and perpetual challenge, and the last reserve held by Nature against the onslaughts of exploration. The two poles have become familiar. Every inch of ocean has been surveyed. The desert and the jungle have been forced to divulge their deepest secrets. But Everest, with defences greater than any of these, is still inviolate.

That is why the Flying Carpet, drawn by the terrible beauty of the Goddess, went to her—a gold-and-scarlet moth lured by the beckoning flame of ice.

And what a staggering sight it was! Alp piled on Alp—the Matterhorn on top Mont Blanc.

Nor was Everest alone in her majesty. She was the

dominating feature, but close beside her clustered a group of sister goddesses, not one of which measured less than five miles high: and on either side, as far as we could see, other peaks appeared, almost as great.

A jagged wall of ice, these colossal mountains sweep from east to west. At a hundred miles an hour, through the freezing January skies, the Flying Carpet was speeding straight north toward the heart of them. We were still forty miles away, but from our elevation above the clouds we could command already the great centre section of the bewildering panorama, and count two score of the mighty sentinels.

Among the forest of these peaks it was hard at first to distinguish the Goddess Mother from her neighbours. We could not at this distance determine which of two mountains was the higher; which of all the mountains was the highest. But we were presently able to dismiss any uncertainty, for we saw that an overtowering mountain *did* stand exactly where Everest was indicated on the map. Also this mountain's southern face, unlike the others, fell sheer 14,000 feet, exactly as described in the reports of the English climbing expeditions—"the greatest sheer drop on earth."

And then we had a third—and final—proof. I had studied Captain John Noel's splendid book, *The Story of Everest*, which records the three attempts to conquer the mountain. In this book I had marked the following paragraph: "Inseparable from Everest is her 'streamer' drifting in heaving clouds from her ridges, twisted and torn from the westward—for some unknown reason ever from the westward." And there, floating from the pinnacle of the mountain-of-the-precipice, as if fixed to a giant flag-pole on the summit, a long thin pennant of clouds streamed out for miles to the east, "twisted and torn from the westward." And no other mountain carried such a flag.

There could be no mistake. *This* was the great peak, and toward it we were roaring at top speed, forcing the Flying Carpet to climb to its last desperate inch of altitude.

I had been in India shortly after the first assault on Mt. Everest. The attempt to reach the earth's highest point had caught public imagination. Everest . . . the Mysterious Mountain sacred to the Tibetans, who worshipped it and peopled it with guardian monsters and demons—a mountain whose summit reached nearly a mile higher than any human being had ever climbed. Everywhere people had watched the bulletins issued by the climbers, but I believe no one could have been more intensely interested than I in the progress of the expedition. Here was the one last great exploration adventure left in the world—last because most difficult, and being the most difficult, the most alluring.

Right up until 1921 the twenty thousand square miles around Mt. Everest were still a blank on the map.* The mountain rises on the border-line between Nepal and Tibet, and both countries have inflexibly forbidden foreigners, on pain of death, to cross their frontiers. Even the triangulations in 1852, that established Everest as the highest mountain (and brought about the naming of the peak in honour of India's Surveyor-General under whom the surveying had been started), had to be carried out not in Nepal, but from Indian territory a hundred miles away. Nor did surveyors get any closer for nearly seventy years. In fact, before the first Everest expedition, no white man had even *seen* the mountain at close range.

When in 1920 the Royal Geographical Society decided to back an Everest venture, the Nepalese, as usual, refused to give the climbing party a right of way through their country. But the Dalai Lama at Lhasa proved more obliging, despite the fact that Chomo Lungma (the Tibetan name for Mt. Everest) was venerated by his people as a holy mountain. Consequently it was from Tibet, the northern side, that the English climbers made their first attack.

It took this party all the brief climbing season (a few weeks between the winter thaw and the early summer monsoons) just to *find* this Chomo Lungma. There were no roads, no guides, no information. The jumble of uncharted giants conspired to block them and confuse them. The weather at the breathless altitudes where

* The following historical information relative to the three. Everest expeditions has all been taken from Captain Noel's book, *The Story of Everest*, published by Little, Brown and Company. On each expedition Captain Noel acted as the official photographer and historian. His book proved an invaluable guide during the Flying Carpet's Himalayan flight. To its author I am greatly indebted.

they pitched their camps—18,000—19,000—20,000 feet —made life one long frozen struggle for mere existence. The temperature fell to zero and below. The blizzard wind, sometimes blowing a hundred miles an hour, did its part to fight them back. But with it all, before this "good" weather ended, the climbers had explored the mountain's approaches, examined its glaciers and opened its doors. That there was a way up, the expedition definitely determined; and Mallory, one of the party's younger leaders, reached 23,000 feet—as high as the summit of Aconcagua—before the monsoon storms drove them down. The next year a second party went back to resume the struggle, accompanied again by the indefatigable Mallory.

Even though a possible route to the top had been found, a number of problems remained. For example, there was the wind. From 23,000 feet it had been observed that the entire dome of the mountain was lashed ceaselessly, day and night, with a raging blizzard which caught up the snow in wild vortices and flung it a thousand feet into the air. Could any camp stand against this hurricane? Would not a climber be hurled, along with the snow, right off the mountain?

But even more serious was the problem of air-deficiency. Could human beings breathe, much less climb, at 29,000 feet? The case of the Duke of Abruzzi's party, the best-equipped in Himalayan history up to that time, which collapsed on another mountain at 24,600 after breaking all climbing records, did not augur well for the Everest group which had to continue still another mile higher than the "dead line."

To lessen this major difficulty, oxygen tanks were brought along. But they were experimental and very heavy, and useful at best for no more than an hour and a half. They also leaked. The climbers feared they would be more of a burden than a blessing.

In the face of all these dangers and discouragements one moral factor gave the climbers hope—the steady upcurve of altitude records during the past half-century. Forty years before, 21,000 feet had been considered the utmost limit of human endurance. Twenty years before, the dead line had been advanced to 23,000 feet. Ten years before, the Duke of Abruzzi had pushed the curve up to 24,600, to the astonishment of the world . . . but now, in 1922, from an advance camp at *25,000 feet* on Everest, Mallory and Somervell and Norton were seen climbing upward five hundred feet above. By this relentless conquest of new heights the 26,000-foot mark was bound to fall sooner or later—and 27,000—and 28,000—and 29,145.

Mallory, Somervell and Norton were already approaching 26,000 feet. They passed 26,000! But they were enduring the most terrible torture—gasping desperately for air, vomiting, frost-bitten, semi-delirious . . . advancing at the utmost speed—two hundred feet an hour—up to 26,800! They could go no farther.

But the 27,000 mark fell within the week. The first trio of climbers were utterly prostrate from their supreme effort, so Finch and Bruce took up the fight—this time with the oxygen tanks. They reached 26,800, where the other party had turned back. Every added foot of altitude now made a new world's record—26,900—27,000—27,100 . . . up and up they crawled. The weather was clear, the hour early. Was this going to be the day? Only 2,000 feet more to go. Nothing was going to stop these two supermen now . . . nothing—except an oxygen tank that broke down. Bruce's oxygen suddenly ceased to flow. He collapsed in the snow. A soldering iron would have conquered Everest that afternoon. As it was, Finch and Bruce were just able to stagger down into their camp before the night fell—down from 27,100.

And then came the terrible avalanche. Seven porters, preparing to elevate still higher the high-altitude camp, were swept into an ice crevasse, and dashed to pieces.

This catastrophe put an end to the expedition's endeavours. Chomo Lungma remained defiant and unconquered.

Nineteen-twenty-four. Once more the Royal Geographical Society sent a party to attack the mountain. The possibility of human survival on Everest's upper slopes had been proved. Men could become acclimated, if given sufficient time and protection, even to 27,000 feet. All they needed now to attain the pinnacle were improved oxygen tanks.

Norton, Somervell and, for a third time, Mallory—a trio of veterans—led this new assault. With them came a novice at mountain climbing, young Irvine, only twenty-two years old, an undergraduate at Oxford.

Back on the old camping grounds the climbers organised themselves as never before. This was to be for them the supreme effort—now or never. They were prepared to make superhuman efforts.

Their efforts *were* superhuman. Norton and Somervell, distrusting the oxygen tanks and refusing to use them, carried their tent to 26,000 feet and slept there. And next morning, achieving what is probably the greatest single day's endurance feat in all history, they drove themselves to 28,000 . . . with the top three hundred and eighty yards beyond. There Somervell could go no farther. He sank down before the shrieking wind. Norton fought on alone, but in an hour he had climbed only eighty feet—and the afternoon sunlight was fading fast. Somehow they managed to get back to their camp. Their mark was 28,080, and without oxygen.

Meanwhile Mallory and Irvine were girding themselves to attack *with* oxygen. First of all they lifted their tent to 27,000 feet, and prepared to make their dash for the top next morning.

The morning broke reasonably fair. All eyes from the lower camp were turned toward the supreme ridge. Through the telescope two tiny specks were seen climbing an inch at a time upward from their tiny tent. Painfully but steadily—28,000—28,080—past the Norton-Somervell mark—28,500—going strong. The other climbers could still watch the sensational battle. Was there ever a more dramatic suspense in exploration history! The indomitability of man! These two specks were suffering the tortures of hell, but the siren-summit drew then on . . . only two hundred yards more to go!

And then a mist drifted across Mt. Everest's pinnacle, and the two climbers faded out of sight.

Forever.

What happened, that they never came back? No one knows. Did they reach the top, to perish of exhaustion there, struck down by the fury of Chomo Lungma's guardian demons? Did they collapse while descending, and freeze? Did their oxygen tanks, as had happened so often before, fail them, and let them die for lack of air to breathe? Were they blown over the 14,000-foot precipice by the raging hurricanes? The rescue parties struggling up to their tent learned nothing. We only know that Chomo Lungma, the jealous Goddess, slew her victims behind her veil of mist and left no traces of her revengeful work.

When the mist had lifted, the summit of Mt. Everest shone forth in glory once again—towering and frozen, merciless and beautiful, still unconquerable, still the most defiant thing on earth, still the inviolate stronghold of the gods . . . .

Yet still calling to the world of adventure-hearted men.

This is the epic record Captain Noel gives in his book. It must always be the first chapter to any story of the mountain that will ever again be told. To this chapter, the Flying Carpet has added a footnote.

But let me explain how.

CHAPTER XXVII

THE MOTH AND THE FLAME OF ICE

WHILE in Agra, Elly and Moye and I received an unexpected telegram. It came from the Flying Club in Calcutta, inviting us to that city in order to take part in a flying meet being held shortly in honour of the Maharajah of Nepal. This was a miraculous answer to all my prayers, for if the interest of the Maharajah could be aroused by the Flying Carpet's antics, he might grant us permission to fly across Nepal to Mt. Everest; and Everest, now that we were in India, had become our major goal. Only one other airplane, that of Sir Alan Cobham, had ever approached the Great Mountain, because the Nepalese native officials, who control the southern route, emphatically refuse to give pilots permission to cross the borders; and any flight from the northern side involves first surmounting the entire Himalayan range before even reaching Tibet.

And now, awaiting us in Calcutta, by the grace of God, was the one and only person who had the power to lower the Nepalese barriers and open for us the aerial gates to Everest.

Elly was just as eager as we were to visit the mountain. Even though her little ship had only a twelve-thousand-foot ceiling she would be able, provided she could gain permission from the Rajah, to have a good look at Everest from that height. We counted on the girl's aerobatics interesting him more than ours. But all three of us planned to put on the greatest flying show in our power. Mt. Everest was at stake.

We reached Calcutta just in time. On the morning of the meet the whole official colony of Bengal gathered at the field to honour the Maharajah. He arrived—a grand old man of nearly eighty years, looking most impressive in his frock coat and long white beard. The royal pavilion had been raised before the hangar, and under its crested canopy, in the place of honour, the Maharajah sat, surrounded by members of his family and his court. So strict had been the isolation in which he had always chosen to live, that he had never seen an airplane fly before!

The Flying Carpet was polished till its gold and scarlet colours glittered in the sun. I begged Stephens, when our turn came, to go the limit, risk anything, to astonish Nepal. Excepting Elly's agile Klemm, the other airplanes entered in the meet were mostly training ships of small power, modest performance and subdued colours. In this show-off competition, we had an enormous advantage—just through a more powerful engine and a more spectacular plane.

Calcutta probably never saw such a stunting exhibition as Stephens put on. With the very first wide-open dive at the royal tent, the Maharajah was on his feet, white beard flowing in the wind, hat in hand, looking up in amazement at the wild-flying Carpet. He was wondering, no doubt, how the airplane ever held together—and so was I. Moye had stunted with me before but never like this. After exhausting our bag of tricks, as one last stroke we shot past the tent upside down and, hanging on our safety-belts, waved at the grand old King. Elly was startling him with gyrations hardly less intricate than Moye's. In fact, her whip-stall, three hundred feet off the ground, was a stunt we did not dare to do so close to earth.

Both planes landed to find the Maharajah as excited as a small boy. . . . What astonishing things people were doing in the world outside his little hermit country! Now, now, was the time to broach the subject of Everest. We made Elly act as spokesman—for who would bar her from any country!

Beside the Maharajah, acting as interpreter, stood his oldest son, the Crown Prince, whose grey moustache indicated that he himself must be no younger than forty-five. Through him Elly made our appeal, and at the same time invited him to go joy-riding over Calcutta with her aboard the Klemm.

He turned to his regal old father, and they spoke in Nepalese. Then with a sad and disappointed face he turned back to her: "Papa say I can't go."

"And Mt. Everest . . .?"—holding our breath.

The Prince smiled: "Can do!"

The next day Elly's plane and ours headed for the Himalayas. The first night out was spent in Siliguri, just at the foot of the mountains. The following dawn, stripped of every possible ounce of weight and carrying as few gallons of fuel as we dared, we sailed up into the sky, and after climbing the foothills, struck out for Darjeeling.

This celebrated little town, sixty-five hundred feet high, seemed to be sleeping on its ridge-top, half-blanketed in mist. To wake it up and to give the tourists watching the sunrise from Tiger Hill something to talk about, we did a few loops and slow-rolls. In the background, appallingly immense, loomed Kinchinjunga, thrusting its ice peaks five and a half miles into the clear cold blue—a mountain normally clothed in purest white, but now turned gold and purple by the sunrise glow. The early morning light fell full upon the shining flukes and spires, the castles of snow, the cascades of ice. From ten thousand feet we could see this glorious peak, which is only one thousand feet lower than Mt. Everest itself, stretching out its whole vast length before us.

We had previously arranged with Elly, because of the great inequality in our climbing-power, to part company over Darjeeling and approach Everest separately. We now waved good-bye and good luck to her, and started to climb.

The cold dug beneath our fur-lined flying suits as we reached fifteen thousand feet and turned westward across the borders of Nepal. For an hour we sped down the Himalayan range until we were a hundred miles west of Darjeeling and about seventy miles south of Everest. Then we turned at right angles and flew straight north. In wave upon wave of hills, rising higher and higher, Nepal climbed toward the supreme peaks. A few scattered villages appeared below on the river banks, and though we could not observe their inhabitants, we knew that they were probably looking up in bewilderment at the airplane.

Thinner and thinner the vegetation grew as the foothill ridges of Mt. Everest ascended the stairs—and thinner grew the air as we climbed above them. But the stairs were climbing faster than the Flying Carpet. Though we pushed up to seventeen thousand feet, the ridges still pursued us. Through a tremendous effort (and a light load) we struggled to eighteen thousand—two thousand feet higher than the Carpet had ever been before. The engine was being forced to its utmost revolutions, but even so we were just hanging on by our very teeth. This— eighteen thousand—was our absolute ceiling. Not one more inch could we gain. Would eighteen thousand be enough to take us around Everest, which was the most we had ever hoped to do?

The Great Mountain loomed ahead, forty miles away now—one peak from the titanic wall of peaks. Kinchin-junga still dominated the east. Westward of Everest, the Himalayan sentinels soared and fell and soared again in a vast phalanx of snow and clouds. We were beholding the most stupendous panorama the eyes of man are privi-leged to see, a panorama of the highest and the mightiest monuments on this planet, the great white beacons for which the inhabitants of Mars look when they turn their telescopes upon the Earth . . . and we were beholding this sublime picture from a vantage-point which only one other man had ever shared—from the sky above Nepal.

I had seen the famous mountain peaks of the Alps. But Alps! They seemed now like toy mountains compared to these overtowering giants. Before me one precipice on Everest's southern slope measured as high as the top of the Matterhorn measures from the sea. At sixteen thousand feet, in this same Flying Carpet, we had flown well above the summit of Mont Blanc: now at eighteen thousand we were about to bump into the foothills of the Himalayas.

Mt. Everest continued to approach, but with every mile our flying problems multiplied. The thin cold air seemed to give us no support at all, and the ridges below were licking up at us closer and closer with each succeeding wave.

At twenty-five miles distant, every detail of the Everest group appeared brilliantly clear. The mighty Makalu, 27,850, shaped in the form of an armchair, paid but small homage to her Majesty. Cho-Oyu, 26,750, would have bedazzled the world with its frozen spires had it been in any other company but this.

And then Everest itself, indescribably magnificent, taun-ting the heavens with its gleaming crown. Her precipice, her clinging glacier shield, her royal streamer forever flying eastward from the throne, her court of gods and demons, her hypnotic, deadly beauty . . . what incomparable glory crowns this Goddess Mother of all mountains!

Where on this huge mass did Mallory and Irvine lie? On the point of that last high tower? On the slope a thousand feet below? At the bottom of that appalling cliff? Wherever they are, they have not died in a lost cause. Already other men have taken up the fight, determined to conquer the mountain and all her demon train. Chomo Lungma is doomed. The spirit of Mallory will see to that.

Despite our heavy flying clothes, Stephens and I were suffering from cold. Remember, we were flying in January, over three and a half miles high, and had reached the belt continually harried by the freezing blasts from Everest's glacier fields. Our Carpet struggled forward against these winds. Our hands grew numb as we manœuvred the plane. Respiration became increasingly laboured. But however sharp our own discomfort, I realised it was a bed of roses compared to the torments endured, not for a moment as was our distress, but for days and weeks, by the Everest climbing parties. If we were miserable at eighteen thousand feet, think what they must have suffered having to *live* at twenty-five thousand, and endure not only the everlasting below-zero cold and the hundred-mile-an-hour blizzards, but also the tortures inflicted on lungs and heart by the least exertion in this oxygen-less air.

The buttresses of Everest were now reaching up so dangerously close to us, we saw we had no chance whatsoever of making a flight around the mountain. Even the passes at the base, passes we had hoped to cross in order to reach the Tibetan side, rose another mile above us. We decided that no airplane with less than a twenty-five-thousand-foot ceiling could possibly encircle Everest; and to fly *over* it one would need, in the face of the fearful winds, a safety margin of five thousand feet, or a ceiling of thirty-four thousand. Obviously, with our inadequate power, we must rest content with a visit to the southern slope.

Just how close could we go? Twenty miles had been reduced to fifteen. But now the rocky slopes were only five hundred feet below, and directly ahead of us they rose abruptly. Pilot Stephens did not dare go nearer. This was the time for a photograph. Hoping to record the vision before us, I unslung my camera, unstrapped my safety-belt and leaned over the cockpit's edge to focus on the mountain. But I promptly realised there was no hope of a picture. The straining, vibrating engine, pushed to the limit, was almost shaking the camera out of my hands. Any photograph could only be a blur.

And Moye could not cut the motor. It would have meant a sudden dizzy drop of probably a thousand feet—with the ridges now not half that distance below us. We had reached the absolute limit of any possible advance —another brief moment and we would have collided with the mountain-side. While there was yet margin enough, we turned about and headed away, lamenting for the first time the Flying Carpet's inability to rise as high as our desire.

As we retreated, I looked back for one last time at Everest's summit, untrodden and unflown, another eleven thousand feet above us. I *must* have some sort of photograph to record this unique view. But I had to wait until we had retreated twenty miles, where we cleared the rocks below by four thousand feet. Again I aimed my camera. Moye cut the motor, and naturally, as we expected, we took a headlong dive through the thin air like so much solid rock. The fall, before we straightened out, almost lifted me, freed of my belt, bodily out of the cockpit. As for the picture, it recorded the mountain, though a very badly shaken mountain photographed by a badly shaken photographer. But however imperfect, it is the only aerial view of Everest ever made, and definitely shows the streamer and precipice which identify the peak.

Thus Mt. Everest repelled one more attack—or rather, two more, for Elly's little plane had been driven back at a lower altitude than ours.* But these two attacks were only the latest and the least—not the last. Other climbers and other fliers the mountain must yet reckon with. The more defeats men suffer at her hands, the more new volunteers will enlist to fight against her.

Some day, some flier with a super-powerful plane, and oxygen tanks, will launch an attack at thirty-four thousand feet and conquer the Goddess Mountain from above. Stephens and I like to hope that we ourselves may be able

* Sir Alan Cobham reached eighteen thousand feet. Owing to rising clouds he had to turn about when thirty miles away.

to return with a greater Flying Carpet and accomplish this. It would be a great adventure to fly over the mountain and all around it, and photograph every angle of its summit with special cameras. Perhaps such photographs will serve the next party of determined climbers when they follow the guiding spirits of Mallory and Irvine up the terrible trail to the pinnacle—the pinnacle of that cursed, divinely beautiful Himalaya.

Why must men match themselves with such a cruel opponent? One man will say—Because it is monstrous, merciless, demanding the utmost of one's energy and effort. Another will say—Because with the summit attained, everything else on Earth will be below. And yet a third— Because that streaming and defiant flag flying from Mt. Everest's citadel is the greatest challenge in the realm of exploration.

But Mallory himself gave the best reason of all.

To the literal-minded his reply seems puzzlingly abrupt and inadequate. But to the questing spirits, to those who understand, it is eloquent and altogether sufficient—an answer that reveals, moreover, the impulse in the souls of such men as Mallory.

"Why do you wish to climb Mt. Everest?" an unimaginative person asked of him.

"Because it's *there!*" he said.

CHAPTER XXVIII

CONCENTRATED TROUBLE

In some book I once read, all descriptions of scenery and weather were omitted from the text, but inserted at the end, in a sort of postscript, to be taken or left alone according to the taste of the reader. This impressed me as highly considerate on the part of the author, and I resolved to follow his good example. But when it came to the actual writing of my own books, I weakened, for these manifestations of Nature gave me my best chance to use the large stock of elaborate adjectives acquired during a most expensive college course. However, I *am* going to follow that system in regard to the mechanical difficulties encountered (but not hitherto recorded) with the Flying Carpet. I've kept them out of all the previous chapters, to touch upon—and dismiss—at this point.

This "point" is Singapore.

The Flying Carpet, still accompanied by Elly's Klemm, had travelled from Mt. Everest back to Calcutta, and on around the marshy coast of the Bay of Bengal. After a visit to the gilded temples of Rangoon, we sailed down the Burma shores till we saw "the old Moulmein Pagoda, looking lazy at the sea." Here we turned inland and headed for Bangkok, across two hundred and fifty miles of sharp ridges and deep canyons, all smothered beneath a dense and unrelieved blanket of steaming jungle.*

In Bangkok, the King and Queen of Siam gave Elly a party, but Moye and I could not wait to attend it, as our pontoons had arrived in Singapore and we were impatient to get them attached.

As we flew southward down the coast of the Gulf of Siam, the thousand miles of Malay Peninsula looked

* See first paragraph, line nine !

beautiful and colourful enough. However, I had painful memories of this country. I had once attempted to tramp across the narrowest part of it during the flood season. The distance was only forty miles, but it took three days and two nights to fight my way through the morasses of roots and water. Now, when we crossed my old trail at right angles, I could discern the Bay of Bengal on the other side of the peninsula. It was hard to believe that such a narrow strip of land could once have seemed so endlessly broad to me, afoot.

Another five hundred miles, following the beach below, took us into Singapore.

And now for the promised difficulties!

We had our share of them from the very first. On the third day's flight eastward from California, our engine had stopped dead just as we were taking off from the Oklahoma City airport. It required the most skilful piloting on Moye's part to get us back—with only two hundred feet of altitude and no speed—into the field. The Flying Carpet's career almost ended then and there.

Motor trouble hounded us all the way to New York. Here we were held up three weeks while our engine was being doctored.

Then, loading the plane aboard the *Majestic*, the stevedores allowed the fuselage to swing against a ventilator and several huge holes were the result. Disembarking in Europe, the fabric was ripped completely off one wing. And all these damages had to be repaired before we could "merely speak the magic name of Timbuctoo to be transported there"!

In Paris, our aileron pushrods, which had always vibrated more than they should, began to oscillate dangerously. For four long weeks the combined force of technicians at Le Bourget airport could not locate the cause. Then an American aeronautical engineer, called all the way from Finland for the purpose, found that in assembling the airplane in California, the riggers had installed the pushrods upside down—an error by no means as obvious as it sounds. Once found, the trouble was remedied in five minutes. Even so, I began to wonder if my new "province" was going to be all the workshops of the world, as well as "the clouds and the continents."

Landing in Colomb Bechar in the sand-storm, we tore the cushion tyre off our tail wheel, and rather than wait for a new one to be shipped from London, we wrapped the rim in heavy cord and flew on across the Sahara. When the roaring Fire Bird frightened the storks in Timbuctoo, it still bore this bandaged tail.

In Venice the motor began to falter again, and from there to Bagdad we sputtered along, never knowing at what inconsiderate moment it would die away entirely. We seemed to have a jinx motor, as though our Magic Carpet had the wrong spell cast upon it. Four separate exorcisms, even with Moye's adept direction, failed to banish the trouble. Then, after three hundred hours of its temperamental behaviour, we threatened to throw the blasted motor into the Tigris—and immediately it reformed of its own accord and ran superlatively well thenceforth.

So we could forget the engine. But we were by no means clear of trouble. In Teheran the snow and frost of the hangarless landing field damaged our fabric to such an extent that Moye had to hasten to Bushire for repairs. Exposure to Persian winter weather may improve oriental rugs, but it doesn't improve Flying Carpets.

In Karachi, we found that all our Karachi-to-Singapore flying maps, which had been sent out from London, had been received before our arrival—and returned! We used chiefly our imagination to fly by, for the next three thousand miles.

In Agra, while we were flying upside down to salute the Taj, a section of the main fuel tank worked loose and dumped forty gallons of gasoline into my lap. We managed to land without catching fire: but lost a week waiting for the tank to be repaired.

These troubles, however, were nothing compared to what awaited us in Singapore. Our pontoons arrived there without the support struts, which we had been told could be made "easily" in Singapore. But it took the engineers and local mechanics from January until April to finish the work. The delay was maddening, and the struts and their installation cost as much as the pontoons themselves.

Three things helped make life endurable through these twelve impatient weeks of waiting. One was the courtesy and hospitality of the Royal Air Force, whose airbase we were using in Singapore. Another was the support of the Shell Oil Company. Back in America, we had made arrangements to have them supply us with fuel wherever we needed it, and to have them accept signed receipts to be collected in New York, instead of our making complicated payments in local currencies. In Colomb Béchar—at the isolated Saharan tank—in Timbuctoo—in Lisbon—in Galilee—in Maan, near Petra—in Persia—in Siliguri, where we fuelled for Everest—in Burma and Malay—in short, everywhere we went, the Shell company had supplies for us. The problem of fuel proved to be no problem at all. We could always be sure of finding not only oil and gasoline, but also friendly assistance, even in the outposts where Shell stations are almost the only link with civilisation. The company's officials were particularly obliging in Singapore, doing their best to lighten the tedium of our delay.

But the third, and pleasantest, distraction from our mechanical trouble was Elly. Following us on from Bangkok, she was persuaded to wait with us through a whole month of our tribulations. She kept insisting that she should fly on to Australia right away, but we wouldn't let her. We'd put *What Good Am I Without You?* on the phonograph, and she'd weaken and stay another day.

But at length she really did decide to go, and all our efforts to hold her were in vain. Our own route, fixed for Borneo and the Philippines, must now diverge from hers. We would not fly with Elly Beinhorn again.

We escorted her to the flying field to send her and her "husband" on their way. For Moye and me, it was a blue moment when she said good-bye. Elly had become an essential part of our adventure. We three had enjoyed a comradeship in which we thought and acted as one. To lose her upset everything. She had spoiled us, scolded us, lifted us at one bound up to the gay and gallant level of life in which she moved. And then, when we had learned to depend on her to take care of us completely—she left us flat!

Her little Klemm took off and circled overhead. Elly waved—and disappeared into the tropical sky.

Shortly after, we received a note from Batavia:

My dear Papas:
　Batavia was easy—only six hours—but it seemed a such long time with no Flying Carpet to keep me com-

pany. The world became very big and very empty again, after I left Singapore. *What Good Am I*—without my two Papas? And what will you do without Elly? Who will keep Moye from talking about aviation, and who will make Dick wear his sun-helmet? I'm sure you both go to the dogs. But I'll play *St. Louis Blues* for you on my phonograph each day, and you must play *Falling In Love Again* for me, and love me very much.

I kiss   both on your sunburned noses—and will always stay your good child—

ELLY.

CHAPTER XXIX

THE QUEEN OF BORNEO

BEHIND us across the jade waters of the South China Sea,
Singapore was rapidly disappearing. Before us stretched
a myriad jungled islets, the tattered fringe of the Eastern
continent, pierced by the arrow of the Equator. The
Flying Carpet was on its way again.

But what a changed Flying Carpet! Its undercarriage,
with the fat balloon tyres which had rolled us across a
hundred flying fields, had been removed, and two twenty-
foot silvery pontoons attached (at long last!) in their place.
The dry land where it had paused between flights for
nearly forty thousand miles it must now disown, and
henceforth rest, like the albatross, upon the waves.

This Floating-Flying Carpet, proud of its new sea-going
power, had cast about for new sea-tracks to travel—for
destinations as lost in the sea as Timbuctoo had been in the
Sahara. We decided, first of all, to call upon the White
Queen of Borneo.

But has Borneo a white queen? Isn't it a savage
aboriginal island, inhabited only by head-hunting wild
men and orang-outans? Speaking largely, that is true.
But over these head-hunters, and over these jungles where
the big apes live, there rule a white King and Queen as
cultivated, as urbane, as any in the world—with a history
as romantic and remarkable.

In the year 1803, there was born in India, of English
parents, a baby boy, James Brooke, who was destined to
live a life unique in modern annals. From childhood
he had one all-consuming ideal—he wanted to make
a country of his own. And with his imagination, his
powerful personality, and his zest for fighting—qualities
which became apparent as he grew—he seemed well
equipped to achieve his ambition, rash as it was.

At thirty-two, James Brooke was able, on inheriting a small fortune, to buy a sailing ship, the *Royalist*, in which to pursue his idea. He set out from England to take his vessel to strange unexplored regions of the globe, to see what no Englishman had ever seen before, to fight pirates, to dethrone kings—and to raise a new throne, somewhere, for James Brooke to sit upon.

The East, at that period, was still the most adventurous part of the world, so he drifted eastward. In Singapore he heard that the northern coast of Borneo offered endless opportunities for exploration and adventure; that its Malay rulers were at war with the inhabitants, and that the whole island was harassed by pirates and slave-traders, who prevented any development of its rich resources.

To James Brooke this promised just the exciting element he was seeking. He set his course for Borneo. Reaching it, and finding a beautiful nameless river debouching past a Gibraltar-like promontory into the sea, he steered his auspiciously named ship some twenty miles up-stream. There he came to a thatched village, which its handful of Malay and Dyak inhabitants called Kuching.

But Kuching, when he arrived, was not the peaceful place its peaceful setting indicated. The town was in ruins; its people in rebellion against the oppression of their overlord, the Sultan of Brunei, who lived farther up the coast. Brooke, just to stretch his legs, went ashore with gun and cutlass, and practically single-handed, through moral suasion and physical force, established order in the distracted land. The citizens of Kuching, impressed with Brooke's air of power, insisted that he become their King and govern them as a state completely independent of Brunei. This was the opportunity he had dreamed about. He not only accepted, but forced the Sultan to recognise him, and to cede him seven thousand square miles of land along the river.

So James Brooke had a country of his own.

The next thing he did was to give his country a name—Sarawak. Then he began to organise it and develop it. He built himself a palace—for he felt he was there to stay; chose a council of state, created an army, designed a national flag, and composed a Constitution which gave him and his heirs absolute ownership for ever. His subjects numbered about two thousand partly civilised Malay townsmen, and twenty thousand head-hunting

Dyaks living in communal long-houses in the jungle.

But from the first, Brooke had to face the most powerful opposition. England looked upon him as a menace to her interests in the Indies, if not as an actual pirate, and withheld support. The Sultan of Brunei conspired constantly to recapture Sarawak from this alien interloper. The Moro slave-dealers swooped down to loot his new "capital." The Dyaks proved unruly subjects, warring continually for each other's head, and for Brooke's, too, when he tried to interfere. One rebellion brought about the murder of all his native officials. In another, his palace was burned to the ground, and he himself escaped only by swimming the river. Still a third started a conflagration that wiped Kuching completely off the map.

But Rajah Brooke, as this resourceful one-man government was called between revolutions, never relaxed from his original purpose of making—and holding—a country of his own. He rebuilt Kuching. He drove out the pirates and overcame every rebellion. And he actually managed to become leader of a British punitive expedition against Brunei, where he captured the capital, drove the Sultan into the jungle, and put an end to any threat of danger from this neighbouring country.

In 1864—twenty-four years after his landing in Sarawak —Rajah Brooke's greatest desire was granted: England recognised his government, and sent a consul to Kuching.

Four years later, worn out by the cares and battles of his extraordinary career, he died, and was succeeded— having no sons of his own, since he had never married—by his nephew, Charles Brooke. A Brooke Dynasty was thus begun.

The new Rajah proved to be no less energetic than his predecessor. He began to expand his boundaries by accepting the governing responsibilities of adjoining states. Brunei became only an isolated port, its territory having been annexed by Sarawak. At last, finding himself king of half a million people and fifty-five thousand square miles (a country larger in area than England itself), Rajah Charles Brooke made a treaty with Queen Victoria which guaranteed Sarawak's independence. Only in foreign affairs was England to be consulted, in exchange for her protection against foreign aggression.

Secure and well governed, this new state grew out of its savage infancy. Agriculture was promoted, slavery abolished and head-hunting discouraged. Several other adventurous Englishmen came out to explore and govern the wild interior. In 1917, when Rajah Charles Brooke died and his son Vyner became Rajah in turn, Sarawak was a going concern.

Vyner Brooke had been educated at Winchester and Cambridge. But the moment he became of age his father brought him to Borneo and made him the government's agent in the loneliest and most savage part of the backwoods. Vyner Brooke learned his Rajahship from the bottom rung. He fought cholera plagues among the Dyaks; he quelled local rebellions; he learned the dialects; he explored every inch of his father's territory. At forty-three, as thoroughly prepared for his office as any king who ever ruled, he ascended the throne.

And with him ascended Her Highness, the Ranee Sylvia, daughter of Lord Esher.

This royal couple, in their turn, have ever since ruled Sarawak with the same wisdom and benevolence that marked the reigns of the two previous Rajahs. Audience with them awaits any poorest, nakedest subject of the realm who seeks the palace at Kuching. The Dyak chiefs, leaving their smoked human heads in their long-houses, and dressed largely in beads and tattoo, paddle down to the capital and march into the palace. There, squatting on the floor and chewing the inevitable betel-nut, they gravely place their difficulties before the Great White *Tuan* and are as gravely listened to and counselled.

Despite the intimate and paternal form of Sarawak's government, it is taken quite seriously in Europe. Young Englishmen are always ready to accept the Rajah's appeal to enter the service of his proud, romantic little nation. Fully seventy-five English-born 'state officers are now scattered about the country, maintaining order, and offering protection to the childlike race of jungle-dwellers who inhabit it.

It is not strange, therefore, that the White Rajah and the Ranee, with their unique position, have become celebrated throughout the Far East. But their position explains only part of their distinction. They have become famous, too, for their charm, their hospitality, their democratic manners, and, in recent years, for their strikingly beautiful daughters—the three white Princesses of this land of head-hunters.

With such enlightened rulers, Sarawak has made great progress since the World War—but progress without that distressing capital "P," for the rulers are determined not to exploit the country nor to change it from what it still remains: the native land of their primitive subjects. What changes they have wrought are not such as to spoil the little kingdom's character. Rubber has been planted along the coast, and an oil refinery operates, to supply all the Far East with gasoline. Otherwise, there is little encroachment upon the native colour of the land, except in Kuching itself. There, a moving-picture house equipped for sound (and such sound! mostly Chinese) has been given to the citizens by the Princesses—who are themselves its best customers. A radio station talks over the local news with Singapore. A race track and grand-stand ornament the park.

And one day, during the running of the Grand Prix, a few months before the publication of this book, the radio excitedly called up Singapore to tell how an airplane—a gold-and-scarlet airplane equipped with huge shining pontoons—had come roaring in from over the sea, found the race track, wheeled above the royal box, and lit upon the river before the palace. It was the biggest news in months.

Having landed, Moye and I found a buoy to which we secured the ship. Then, completely exhausted from the most trying day since our encounter with the sand-storm on the Sahara, we stretched out on our pontoons and waited for a boat—any boat—to pick us up.

While waiting, I was unable to dismiss from my mind the painful things that had happened since that morning.

Back in Singapore, having little confidence in the new and untried support-struts of our pontoons, we had not been willing to risk the four-hundred-mile open water flight to Kuching. We thought it wiser, until our new equipment had been proved, to court the shore as much as possible, and approach Sarawak *via* the six-hundred-mile chain of islands that swings south from Singapore to Sumatra, and from there west to Borneo. Our first day's destination, a land-locked harbour on the coast of Sumatra, we reached safely. The next day, still experimenting with anchors and ropes and all the unfamiliar features of water-flying, we struck westward along the Equator, still following the chain. It was a brilliant day—the sea, dazzlingly blue, beat upon the little isles in rings of foam. Dense forests of palms hid every foot of land. One quiet cove, isolated, lonely, indescribably beautiful, so lured us that we landed on its surface, anchored, swam to the sandy beach, and bathed in the sun for half the day.

Our goal that afternoon was Pontianak, a small seaport on the west coast of Dutch Borneo. We found it, strewn along a river, and came down, to the great astonishment of the community. Ours was the first airplane that had ever been there. In an instant a hundred dugouts and row-boats came out to welcome the Flying Carpet.

But next morning, as we prepared to fly on to Sarawak, misfortune fell upon us.

The river at Pontianak is greatly affected by the tides. During the ebb and flow, the current races by at violent speed. Unfortunately, at the moment of our departure, this current was at its height, flowing seaward. By the time I'd pulled the anchor up and cranked the engine, we were already rushing down-stream. Moye, in order to hold us against the flow, had to accelerate the engine. With the propeller whirling two feet away from me, I stood on the pontoon and tried to coil up the new and stubborn anchor rope, and unshackle the anchor. But an especially fierce blast from the propeller caused me to lose my balance; and as I clutched wildly at a strut to keep from going overboard, a blade of the prop caught a flying loop of the rope—and I still had most of it wrapped around my arm. In a flash, the rope and the anchor and I were all jerked toward the prop. Moye, hearing the banging and the clatter and my cry, instantly cut the engine and looked around to see what was happening.

He saw the rope ripped into shreds; he saw the propeller bent into a bow-knot; he saw the water pouring into a big hole in the pontoon where the anchor, before it was hurled overboard, had been whipped against it; and he saw me, with all the skin raked off my arm and hand, lashed to the motor cylinders by the same strands of hemp which had fouled the crankshaft—my head not an inch from the prop . . . and the Flying Carpet rushing helplessly down-stream, right in the path of an oncoming freighter.

Moye, true to form, kept a cool head. Diving out fo his cockpit with a knife, he slashed the rope which, bound around my shoulders, was sawing me in half. He didn't stop to analyse the miracles that had saved me from the propeller—the freighter was upon us—the left pontoon was sinking dangerously low. He waved frantically at the steamer—it veered to one side and we scraped past. A half-dozen launches, seeing our distress, came hurrying to our aid. One threw us a towline, and we were dragged into a side canal.

Fortunately, our pontoon had four compartments, and only one was flooded. The crankshaft did not seem to be bent. The propeller, however, looked hopeless. But Moye, taking blocks of wood and a blunt-headed hammer, beat the prop out—believe it or not!—more or less straight again. And a local machine-shop fitted a makeshift patch over the hole in the pontoon—all in five hours.

Then, when that was done, Moye looked after me. My arm and hand had been savagely skinned by the rope, and were swollen to twice their normal size. But except for that (and my very shaky knees) I was all right.

So, rather than give ourselves a chance to think about my narrow escape, we got back in the Flying Carpet and started off again for Sarawak, three hours beyond, with a crankshaft that might or might not be bent, and with a propeller that was only as smooth and straight as an iron mallet could make it.

But there was no further help to be had in Pontianak. We might as well try to fly on toward Kuching.

Somewhat to our surprise, the Carpet flew! Borneo unrolled beneath us again. We followed the completely wild and uninhabited coastline around the north-west corner of the island, found Kuching, and landed in the river.

As I have said, it had been a trying day.

But we had no time to brood over our troubles. Hardly were we ashore when Ranee Sylvia sent us a summons to appear at the palace that evening for the annual Grand Prix Ball.

And Moye and I, dressed in our flying togs (I with my arm in bandages), accepted.

It was a memorable party.

Practically every European in the entire country—over two hundred—had collected at the capital for race week, and they were all on hand. But the Rajah himself was not there. He had gone to England with his oldest daughter just the week before, leaving the Ranee and her two younger daughters to receive the *haut monde* of Sarawak at this, the climax of the social season.

Half-encircled by a bank of orchids, the Ranee, in white and wearing a magnificent diamond necklace, greeted her guests, assisted by the Princess Elizabeth, age eighteen, and the Princess Valerie, sixteen. Every woman present was jewelled and smartly gowned in the latest (minus eight weeks!) Paris mode; and every man resplendent in military or civil service uniform . . . scarlet jackets, medals, ribbons. A Filipino orchestra played for the hundred couples dancing in the great banquet hall, from the walls of which gazed the portraits of Sarawak's Rajahs, past and present. It was as beautiful and graceful a picture of social life as I've ever seen . . . and outside, the head-hunters, dressed in gee-strings, watched from the lawn.

Each with a Princess on his arm, Moye and I, wearing the flying clothes Elly Beinhorn had patched together for us in Persia, led the Grand March!

So this was Borneo!

On our arrival, we had been presented to the Ranee. She was slim, vivacious, keenly alive.

"What a surprise you gave us this afternoon!" she said. "When you flew over our heads at the race track the *most* important race of the week was being run. The Rajah's horse was leading . . . but I didn't know whether to watch the finish or look at the airplane. It was excruciating."

"I hope' your horse won, just the same," I said, trying to be gallant.

"He didn't—but nobody seemed to care in the excitement. I've never seen the natives so agitated. We weren't expecting you—an American airplane, unannounced, swooping out of nowhere down on top of us, out here in Sarawak—really, it seemed almost supernatural."

"We couldn't have asked for a more royal welcome," said Moye, looking about.

"Yes, it is fortunate that you came to-day. We don't dress up like this often. You might have found Kuching dull at any other season than race week. . . . But how did you come?—where did you start from?—it's all too amazing!"

"We started in Hollywood, Ranee Sylvia. But we came here from Singapore. We're on our way to Manila."

"I suppose you left Singapore just this afternoon?"

"No," Moye answered ruefully. "We left three days ago. We had a little trouble along the way that delayed us. We almost lost the ship this morning, and Mr. Halliburton's head."

"How dreadful! Did you come down among my head-hunters?"

I explained briefly what had happened. "It was very embarrassing," I said. "I'm still a bit shaky. The champagne helps greatly, though. Now, if I could only dance with you, I'd be completely revived."

"You may. I always like to dance with Americans."

I was fortunate, because the Ranee was decidedly the best dancer at her party. We waltzed beneath a beautiful full-length portrait of the first Rajah Brooke.

"What would he think," I asked, "—seeing the present Ranee of Sarawak at the swankiest palace party of the year, dancing with a man in corduroy trousers—and patched corduroy, at that?"

"I'm sure he'd be delighted," she answered, "—especially as you are an American. He always felt friendly toward your country. It was the very first to recognise Sarawak, you know—long before England. And your plane, by the way, has the same colours as our flag."

What a charming person my dance-partner was. Her friendliness gave me an inspiration:

"Ranee," I said suddenly (she was *Sylvia Ranee of Sarawak*, but "Ranee" to her guests!) "—would you, as a great favour to Stephens and me, go riding with us aboard the Flying Carpet? In spite of the accident, it seems to be running well enough."

"Of course I would," she said, with enthusiasm. "I was afraid you weren't going to ask me. No other woman has ever flown before in Borneo—I'll be the first."

"We promise not to do any dangerous stunts—looping-the-loop and all that."

"Then I don't want to go," she said, laughing.

Our invitation to the Ranee and her immediate acceptance seemed to me to be a purely personal affair, but it almost caused a civil war in Kuching. The government was horrified—the Ranee trusting her life to a couple of perfectly strange foreigners who had just landed in their midst, unbidden, unexplained, unintroduced. Perhaps we were kidnappers—"Kidnappers in Airplane Steal White Queen of Borneo—Rajah Hurries Home—Army Called Out—Head-hunters throughout Sarawak are instructed not to take head of any Englishwoman found wandering in the jungle. . . ." The idea of such headlines in the Sarawak *Gazette* only raised the Ranee's enthusiasm for this unheard-of adventure.

Presently the proposed flight was on every tongue—Malay, Chinese, Dyak and English. Some of the younger government secretaries were heartily in favour—if we'd flown here from Timbuctoo we must be safe enough! The Minister of Public Works and the Chancellor of the Exchequer were also pro-flight. But the Secretary of State and *all* the wives (who hadn't been invited) were vehemently anti-flight. What would happen in the Rajah's absence, they asked, if the Ranee were injured? The Rajah would hold the Secretary of State and the Minister of Health responsible. And if she were killed, the government would be without a ruler for several weeks. There might be a *coup d'état*, even a revolution. The Secretary of State threatened to radio the Rajah to radio back to his wife and forbid her to take this foolish risk. In fact, the Secretary did just that.

"Now we've got to hurry, and have our flight before the Rajah's cable comes," the Ranee confided in me. "I *do* want to fly!"

And so we hurried. The Ranee, the pro-flight Chamberlain, and the Princesses Elizabeth and Valerie, with two Dyak chiefs as escorts, and Moye and I, set off on the royal yacht, down-stream to where the Flying Carpet was anchored. The Ranee, provided with helmet and goggles, climbed into the front cockpit. I raised the anchor, cranked the engine, and climbed in beside her. Moye, in the rear cockpit, soon rocked us off the water, and in a moment we were far up in the sky.

Straightway we flew back over the palace and the town. Shops and offices were emptied and all business suspended, as the entire population rushed out into the streets to gaze up at their Ranee overhead in the flying boat.

Sarawak looked extraordinarily beautiful from the air. Smoky-blue jungle hiding every foot of ground . . . and the broad river winding down from the mountains, past the neat little whitewashed, palm-shaded town, and flowing out into the China Sea—the river up which James Brooke had sailed in his *Royalist* over ninety years before, to make a country of his own.

We landed safely beside the yacht, and delivered our passenger back on deck—unkidnapped. She was elated over her flight, but had some trepidations about facing the Secretary of State. The Rajah's cable came just in time to save the situation—it insisted that the Ranee must by no means miss this opportunity of riding aboard the Flying Carpet and seeing Sarawak from the air!

Next day, loaded down with little presents from the royal family, and armed with letters of safe-passage, we set sail for the interior to call upon the head-hunters. Before turning inland, however, we circled over the palace grounds. As we did so, the Ranee and the two Princesses ran out on to the lawn, and waved good-bye with big white scarfs. We returned them all the salutes an airplane is capable of giving, and ended with a dive straight toward the waving figures. At the right moment, I dropped overboard the helmet which the Ranee had worn, and then we rose again and left the town behind. Looking back, I could see the Ranee picking up the helmet and reading what we had inked upon it:

LONG LIVE THE QUEEN!

From The Flying Carpet and
Its Crew.

CHAPTER XXX

WILD MEN

MY FIRST encounter with Wild Men of Borneo came some years before this visit to their native island. It happened in Berlin, where I was visiting a circus sideshow. The Wild Men were on exhibition—dark brown, almost black, skin: clothed only in a loin-cloth, and decorated with red paint on their faces and wild-boars' tusks around their necks and ankles. They were in an iron cage, before which a large crowd, fascinated by such ferocious and dangerous savages, stood and stared. As curious as any one, I pressed close to get a good look at the exhibits, and as I did so I overheard this Bornean conversation:

"Sho' is hot," one savage said to the other.

"Sho' is!"

They were perfectly good Mississippi negroes, making an easy living by this great impersonation.

My faith in Wild Men was considerably shaken by such disillusioning experience. I wondered if, when we landed at the Dyak long-house we were headed for, the chief was going to greet me with "Good mornin', suh! Ain't that airyplane *sump'm!*"

Our objective was marked clearly on a huge chart I had before me in the cockpit. The chart had been given to us by the Ranee, after the officials who best knew the interior had indicated on it the long-house chosen for us to visit, on the Rejang River at a point two hundred miles from the sea—a long-house ruled by one of the greatest Dyak chiefs in Sarawak.

There were other reasons, too, why this house had been recommended: Besides being one of the greatest Dyak communities, it was also one of the most remote from civilisation—very near the heart of the island. And yet, the Rejang River and its tributaries connected it directly with the sea. We could follow this river as a guiding thread and come down in smooth water at almost any point. If anything went wrong with the flying mechanics of our plane, we would be able to float the entire two hundred miles back to the coast.

The Headman of the district, Chief Koh, made this particular long-house his capital. He was a great favourite with the Rajah and the Ranee, despite the fact that he had been to Kuching only once in his life. The Ranee had urged us to visit him in order not only to meet the native ruler best able to show us Dyak life in its richest and most unspoiled form, but also to present ourselves as good-will ambassadors bearing a gift from the Throne.

From Kuching, with our pontoons and propeller properly mended, we had sailed up the coast a hundred miles, come to the estuary of the Rejang, and turned up this enormous river—a river pouring into the China Sea a volume of water as great as the Mississippi.

For another hundred miles this vast yellow flood twisted and turned as if trying to shake us loose: but we made every effort not to be shaken, for on either side stretched jungle as dense and as hostile as any in the world. The banks were the home of countless giant crocodiles. The pythons waited in the trees above the waterside for the wild pigs to come to drink; and the orang-outans, big as men, ruled as undisputed kings throughout this kingdom of swamps and trees.

At rare intervals we noticed long-houses beside the river, and an occasional government post ornamented by a log fort.

During the second hundred miles, the river narrowed greatly and ran more swiftly as we approached the highlands. We watched carefully for every fork and landmark, to keep our exact position clear on the chart.

Guided by that chart, we came at length to the post called Kapit, and according to instructions from the Ranee, landed there to make the acquaintance of the district Resident, a young Englishman. Official letters requested him to follow us to Chief Koh's long-house, to act as escort and interpreter. It was agreed we should depart next morning, and that as soon as he saw we had escaped the dangerous floating logs and were on our way, he would follow as quickly as possible in his motor-dugout, arriving at the long-house perhaps six hours later than we.

Starting off again, at the appointed time, we flew for another twenty minutes across jungle penetrable only *via* the river. This river-route would take the Resident and his servants, in the most modern conveyance in Central Borneo, twenty times as long as it was taking us.

Amid such a sea of tree-tops, the clearing on the river bank around our particular long-house destination marked it before we got there. Just above the clearing we selected a broad smooth patch of water where two rivers joined —an ideal place to alight.

But first we would announce ourselves by diving wide-open at the long-house!

In all the history of Borneo, there was probably never such excitement, such consternation, as prevailed inside that house. Its three hundred Dyak inmates rushed out upon the front veranda-like platform that extended the entire length of the building, and darted about in complete panic, supposing no doubt that the shrieking demoniac bird had come to devour them. Some leaped to the ground and fled into the jungle. Others seized their babies and hid underneath the house. There was pandemonium.

We had hoped that our arrival might bring these jungle people some entertainment, and were sorry that our first appearance had frightened them half to death instead.

So, desisting, we landed on the river and anchored in shallow water.

Not a soul appeared.

How were we going to get ashore? The river was too full of crocodiles to risk swimming: and anyway, there were no banks to swim to—just a border of half-drowned branches of trees. Taxying around to the long-house in the hope of attracting a boat seemed unwise, for we did not know what hidden rocks the water might conceal. There seemed nothing to do but wait six hours for our friend the English Resident to overtake us.

Then, just as we were resigning ourselves to spending half a day on our pontoons, a dugout appeared around the bend, manned by an extraordinarily fine-looking young Dyak. He wore only the usual red cotton cloth, wrapped tightly about his loins. His trim muscular body, shining in the sun and extravagantly tattooed on arms and legs, made a perfect picture of natural grace and strength. Thick, straight, jet-black hair hung in

227

bangs across his forehead and down his back to his waist. From each ear dangled a heavy gold ring, suspended from long slits in his ear-lobes. And around his wrists were dozens of black grass bracelets.

Paddling at full speed, he came toward us, shouting and smiling. He drew alongside our pontoons and shook our hands, talking excitedly in Dyak and trying desperately, with gesticulations, to make us understand that we were welcome. He explained—and we understood quite clearly enough—that everybody else had fled to the jungle, but that he had been not only to Kuching, but even to "Singapura," and had seen a "be-loon" (balloon, meaning an airplane) fly there. *He* knew what we were, but nobody had given him time to explain.

Moye and I embarked in his dugout, paddled to the long-house and climbed the ladder from the water's edge up to the front platform. Peering timidly around corners at the extreme end of the house, a handful of Dyaks reappeared. Our escort shouted at them to come and meet us—we were only *Tuans* like the Resident, come in a be-loon to visit them.

Little by little, like wild forest animals, the Dyaks began to gather closer, shyly at first, but with increasing courage and increasing numbers, until presently three hundred brown bodies were swarming toward us from the jungle, from the branches, from the hillside above. It finally became a race to reach us—and the naked little children, agile as squirrels, got there first.

We looked about curiously at our new friends. They were all full-blooded Dyaks—surprisingly small, but surprisingly beautiful. The men were dressed uniformly in red loin-cloths and narrow aprons, heavy earrings, anklets and wristlets of twisted grass. The women were dressed as simply—bare from the waist up, with their hips wrapped in a single cotton cloth. A few of them wore high corsets made of rattan hoops wrapped in copper wire, fitting snugly around their waists. They wore their hair pulled back and tied in a knot. All the men, on the other hand, allowed theirs to fall freely down their backs. It not infrequently reached their knees. Everybody was adorned with the same tattoo, always dark blue in colour, we had noticed on the young man in the dugout.

What agreeable faces! True, all the noses had flat

bridges, and the eyes had a slight Mongolian slant, but in their glance were quick intelligence and appealing kindliness.

But what gave them all such a surprised expression? . . . It was their eyebrows and eyelashes—there *weren't* any. Every eyelash and eyebrow had been pulled out. Only the littlest girls were still unplucked.

We could not help observing their teeth as they crowded around us, now talking and laughing. Each mouth was black from betel-nut: each tooth had been filed down almost to the gums. Only the black stumps remained, or in some cases, among what was obviously the better class, to these stumps were fixed bright brass teeth. (Any dog can have white teeth, but only rich people can have beautiful brass ones!) It seems hard to believe that these disfigurements would not completely wreck their appearance. But despite all their efforts to mar themselves, they still remained strikingly handsome. Such physiques did not need eyebrows or teeth to compel admiration.

From out of the dense ring around us, an especially fine figure of a man, probably fifty years old, emerged to greet us. Grey hair—deep chest—powerful arms and legs—and a face that was as noble and as full of character as any face I've ever seen. It had firmness about the mouth, but good humour in the wide-set eyes. This Dyak would have commanded attention and respect any place in the world.

He was Chief Koh. The young man who had first come to welcome us was his son, Jugah.

Into their hands we now put ourselves and, followed by a small mob, were shown about the long-house.

A Bornean long-house is a community dwelling, always erected lengthwise along a river bank. The rear half is given over to a long row of cubicles, one for each family, all of which open upon the front half, which consists of one long, unpartitioned public gallery that extends from end to end of the building and forms a sort of covered Main Street. In the case of Chief Koh's house, this gallery was thirty feet wide and fully six hundred feet long. Here the children play, the mats are woven, the rice is winnowed, the drums and the blow-pipes and the spears are kept; all community life takes place here. And from the rafters of this gallery the smoked human heads, trophies of the tribe's prowess in war, hang in hundreds.

We noticed that our entire house was lifted some twenty feet off the ground on poles. The space below the house was used for the pig-pens and chicken coops, and as a general receptacle for all the refuse. Our long-house was not a model of sanitation, but that did not keep it from being an amazing structure nevertheless, considering its colossal size and the skilled craftsmanship that had taken the reeds and trees from the jungle, and with the crudest of implements—without bricks or stone, without saws or nails—fashioned a co-operative apartment that sheltered three hundred people and contained all the requirements of their village life.

That afternoon, the Resident overtook us. He spoke Dyak like a native, and proved fully informed about this interesting and attractive race.

At sunset, Moye and I, having learned that the depth of the water permitted, taxied the Flying Carpet up to the crude dock before the long-house. This gave the entire population of the place all the chance they wanted to inspect the monster.

Old Chief Koh stood on the bank and gazed with consuming curiosity at the winged demon. He turned to the Resident and asked several earnest questions relative to our plane.

"Is it a bird?" he inquired. Everything that flies in the air must be a bird. "Does it lay eggs?"

"Yes," I said, through the interpreter, when he told me about Koh's questions. "It is a magic bird. But it will fly only for a special magic-maker, and only when it is roaring. If allowed, the bird will hurl itself to the ground in order to destroy any one riding upon it. Yes—this bird can lay eggs, too—iron eggs. They are always laid while flying, and wherever they fall, they explode with a terrible roar and demolish everything in sight. When you wish to destroy your enemy's long-house, you just make this bird fly overhead and lay an egg, which falls down on the roof and blows it up."

Chief Koh listened with open mouth, but Jugah wouldn't believe a word of it. He knew it wasn't a bird at all. It was a be-loon.

Chief Koh's intense interest in our magic vehicle was not without an ulterior motive. He took the Resident aside, and asked him if it might be possible for us to fly over the long-house of the mountain Dyaks, fifty miles

230

farther inland, with whom he'd been having no end of trouble—and lay an egg on the rival chief. The Resident was horrified. After all these years of pacification, old Koh's foremost thought was still the destruction of his neighbours. The Resident excused us by pointing out that the exploding eggs would smash the enemies' heads to bits, and make them useless as trophies.

Koh's request, however, gave the Resident what he thought was a much better idea—What a grand spectacle it would be for all the tribesmen if their chief could be persuaded to go for a ride! . . . but not immediately—not until he could collect his sub-chiefs and their retainers to watch.

Moye and I naturally responded to the idea. We'd play it up, prepare the stage, make his flight an event that would go down in Dyak history, make it an impressive honour bestowed in the name of the Rajah's government at Kuching.

The Resident announced this plan to Koh and explained that it would give him prestige beyond calculation. It would also bring to the tribe as much glory as a successful head-hunting war. But Koh was dubious. This seemed like invading the realm of the gods and the demons. To give him courage, Moye led him on to the pontoons, and into the front cockpit, and tried to explain that it really wasn't dangerous at all.

Moved chiefly by his pride, he finally agreed to fly.

And that very night, he instructed messengers to go into the tributary rivers, carrying the fantastic story of the magic bird to all the other tribal long-houses and their subsidiary chiefs. These chiefs must be summoned to appear three days hence, in the morning, to meet the *Tuans* who had come there riding through the air on the magic bird that laid iron eggs, and to behold their great *Penghulu* carried up into the clouds and brought home again by this same monster. It was to be a *very* great event. They must wear all their best feather head-dresses, and all their silver jewellery, and bring their swords and shields, and come in the war-boats with as many followers as possible.

From the dock where the Flying Carpet was tied, a dozen dugouts, each manned by two paddlers, pushed off to spread the news throughout Chief Koh's territory.

CHAPTER XXXI

HEAD-HUNTERS AT HOME

SOCIAL activity began to seethe that night. Rice wine was brought out by the jugful, and all the men, crouched on their heels in an arc about the three white *Tuans*, got pleasantly drunk. In ceremony after ceremony, we had to take part. Seated beside Koh and Jugah in the long gallery, lighted only by the line of open cooking fires, we were fed an official dinner. Five piled-up plates of rice were placed before us, and a tray of eggs, fish, onions and so forth. Each of us had to garnish his own rice with these various dressings, and in a rigidly conventional routine. We watched Koh prepare his plate, and then followed his example. Before we were allowed to eat it, five young, unmarried (but highly marriageable!) girls came and kneeled before us, one girl for each, with large gourds of rice wine. We had to drink it down as they held the gourds to our lips with their own hands. Then a live squawking rooster was passed to us by its legs, and we had to wave the flapping fowl over our bowl of rice and over our maiden and ask the gods to give us the good fortune always to have a full dinner pail and a full love-life.

All round, the men and boys sat and watched, drinking gourd after gourd of rice wine and making comic innuendos (judging from the boisterous laughter) about the virgins and ourselves. The women and girls collected at a distance, but missed nothing.

This memorable scene had one other feature that I'll never forget—the dogs. There were several dogs to each Dyak, and *such* dogs!—ratlike, mangy, starved. At the smell of food they broke through the circle like hungry flies, and snatched food from our very hands. A blow sent them yelping, but in a moment they had sneaked back again. We had to eat our rice with one hand—

literally—and beat off the swarms of these scaly, hairless little beasts with the other. The wretched animals never seemed to be fed and certainly were not loved—not even wanted. But to destroy one was considered extremely bad form. So they were allowed to multiply and starve, accepted as a curse like the mosquitoes.

Our eating ceremony began before Chief Koh's apartment, and was conducted by his womenfolk. The moment it was over, we were moved down the long gallery to the dining space belonging to the next family of importance, and exactly the same meal as before was brought out, with the same wine-bibbing and rooster-waving. To our consternation, we learned that we must go through this ceremony *twenty* times, and to omit a single gesture would be unpardonable rudeness. The rice began to swell before our eyes, and to resist being swallowed. The wine (about twenty per cent alcohol) began to intoxicate us. Only by pretending to eat, and by making our lovely virgins drink not only their half the loving-cup but ours too, were we able to finish up this gastronomic endurance test in a conscious condition.

Our sleeping quarters were in a large partitioned corner of the chief's apartment. A bit wobbly, Moye and the Resident and I were each led by two maidens, holding our hands, across the rickety cane floor into this guest room. These floors were never made for two-hundred-pounders like Moye to walk upon. His foot found a weak spot, and with a crashing and splintering of bamboo, he plunged through the hole his foot had made. Only the clutch of his two pretty escorts saved him from tumbling straight into the pig-pens below.

As I undressed for bed—three pallets of mats and cotton quilts had been prepared side by side for the three *Tuans*—I looked up through the dim light shed by the Resident's kerosene lamp, and to my horror I saw several dozen human heads suspended from the low rafters by rattan cords, and grinning down at us—or was it the effects of the rice wine? I tried to hide under the cotton spread, but these gruesome gaping heads kept leering down at me through all protection.

"Is Koh at peace with the world?" I asked the Resident, visioning a night attack from some enemy tribe eager to add white men's heads to their collection.

"Quite," the Resident assured me. "Koh is at peace—or at least too strong to be attacked. Anyway, Rajah Brooke has almost succeeded in stamping out the practice of head-hunting in Sarawak—if that's what is worrying you. Heads are still taken in the wild mountain districts along the Dutch Borneo border: but even there the custom is rapidly coming to an end. There are probably very few, if any, heads up there above us taken within the last five years.

"Head-hunting is still practised by the Sarawak Army soldiers, though. When they slay an enemy in authorised warfare, no power on earth can stop them from decapitating their victim. The soldiers all carry, along with their rifles, a short sword—hoping for the best. If the do take a head in this manner, they return with it to their native long-house and are welcomed like conquering heroes. There is a feast and dancing, and much drinking of rice wine, and many invitations from the maidens.

"But every adult in this house can remember the old days. Dyaks have always been the most pugnacious tribe on the island, and the most incorrigible hunters—and any slim excuse for a war was sufficient. If there was no excuse, they made raids anyway—just the collector's instinct! No Dyak girl would look at a boy until he had at least one head to present to her.

"Life was cheap then. Every Dyak had to be constantly on guard. The fighting men slept with their swords and shields beside them. It's a true and familiar story that the man with the scaly skin disease—you've seen several people in this house afflicted with it—was considered highly useful as a watch-dog, because he itched and scratched all night, and couldn't sleep. The disease actually had a monetary value. The lucky owner could *sell* the infection to others who wanted to keep awake.

"Attacks on enemy long-houses were usually made just at early dawn. Bundles of shavings were always thrust under the house first and set on fire. As you can see, the long-houses are perfect tinder-boxes. A fire once started underneath will consume the entire house in fifteen minutes. While the inhabitants were fleeing down the ladders, trying to escape from being burned to death, the attackers pounced upon them and didn't spare man or woman. A head is a head, and its sex of no consequence when it has been dried and smoked, and hangs from a ceiling at home.

"Naturally, there would be reprisals upon the houses of the attackers. So it became perpetual motion. It's a wonder the Dyak race ever survived this organised slaughter of one another. Now that the Rajah has just about pacified this country, the Dyaks are multiplying rapidly. Their numbers have doubled in twenty years."

"Do you suppose these heads up there are community trophies, or the proof of Chief Koh's private prowess?" I asked.

"They are all his own. He was made a chief in his early manhood because of his ability as a war-leader, and his ruthlessness in taking heads. He boasts of having taken over fifty. There must be that many here—though you can't tell how many are of women. A few may even have been chopped from orang-outans or corpses, just to add to the impressiveness of his collection."

That night was weird and restless for all three of us. Our ribbed-cane mattress—the floor—began to leave its cross-marks. The innumerable dogs yelped interminably, fighting for possession of the dying ashes in the cooking fires, ashes they slept in. The pigs grunted down below. Old men, in the long room outside, scratched and talked. The cocks began their canticle long before daylight—and the hideous heads hanging above kept peering into our very souls. Only the overdose of rice wine made sleep possible.

But next day was occupied with new interests and we soon forgot our uncomfortable night.

At sun-up the entire population of the long-house trooped down to the river and bathed. However careless they may have been about the state of their dwelling, personally they were scrupulously, almost fanatically, cleanly. Two, even three, baths a day are the custom. They bathed in families and in groups, as completely unconscious of their nudity as the monkeys and the parrots that watched in the trees above.

We were seeing and learning new things every minute. Jugah, travelled, liberated, keenly intelligent, quick thinking and quick acting, was always by our side, anticipating, though he spoke not one word of any language that we spoke, our every wish.

He took us into his own apartment, next to Koh's. There we met his wife and their two strikingly beautiful little children—a boy about three and a girl a year older.

Perfectly formed, clean, lovable, they would have taken prizes in baby shows anywhere.

It was obvious that Jugah was passionately fond of his children. And in this respect he was typical of all Dyaks. Children are the strongest interest in their lives. They can never have enough. Barrenness on the part of a wife is the commonest ground for divorce. Dyaks will buy children, steal children, do anything to get them. The occasional Chinese one sees among the people are the result of Chinese traders selling their own unwanted babies to baby-crazy Dyaks.

Jugah led his tribe in introducing the smartest and latest modes of dress and entertainment. On his return from "Singapura" (where the Resident had arranged for him to work for a season on a rubber plantation, by way of "education") he had acquired vast tone with his new mechanical purchases and his new wardrobe. He showed us his special treasures: three cheap alarm clocks—though he had not the faintest idea how to tell time by them, or even knew what "time" meant. But the alarm part, all three going at once, brought joy to his soul.

And then he showed us his treasured store-clothes. He had one pair of high-button, bright yellow shoes, into which he thrust his tough prehensile feet. On his head went a Homburg hat, so big it fell over his ears. His suit, sold to him by some Arab trader, was a nauseating green shade and made to fit a man twice Jugah's size. Dressed in all his glory, the young Dyak, elated as a child in fancy-dress, paraded around the room to show off his elegance, and asked me to take his picture.

I could not suppress my despair at seeing such a beautiful young animal hidden under this clownish garb. I begged him to take it off and put on his own colourful, barbaric adornments—his shell necklaces, his embroidered loin-cloth, his silver girdle with the carved buckles, his glorious head-dress stuck with feathers two feet long: and to seize his spear and his shield covered with the hair of dead enemies: to dress like the noble young prince he was: and *then* I'd photograph him to his heart's content. He obliged me, however disappointed he may have been at my low taste.

Mrs. Jugah was as grandly arrayed as her husband. Her party dress was the usual corset, but wrapped in silver wire, and a short knee-length skirt made entirely of beads and bells. There was a sweet soft tintinnabulation when she moved. Mrs. Jugah also possessed the most elaborate tattoo in the long-house. Every inch of her lovely brown body was decorated with graceful and really beautiful designs, all done in dark blue ink. It had taken years of pain and patience to acquire her decorations. Every Dyak in our long-house was tattooed from head to foot: but Mrs. Jugah's undoubtedly cost the most.

Her brass teeth also were something marvellous. At twelve or thirteen, she had deliberately lain down, as is the custom for all girls of that age, and allowed a Chinese pedlar to draw his heavy iron file across her teeth until they were ground off to the gums. The girls undergoing this operation squirm and suffer, not because of the pain, which doesn't seem to bother them at all, but because their position is so *immodest* !

Mrs. Jugah had gone all the way to Sibu, one hundred and fifty miles down-stream, for *her* teeth, and they were worth the journey, for upon the brass background were enamelled in red and green colour the suits of a deck of cards—hearts, clubs, diamonds and spades.

While Jugah was leading the hunting and the fishing and the dancing (alas, there was little fighting unless you joined the army), and with his wife lending the social gaiety to their long-house, his father was handling the departments of Government and Justice. In his hands rested the administration of all moral and social affairs. But in Dyak-land, so simple, so natural, are their moral and social codes, and so faithfully are these codes followed, that Koh really did not have a great deal to do.

Nowhere is the relationship between the sexes so uncomplicated as in Borneo. The Resident, who had lived several years in the company of these people, and had learned to understand and to love them, explained that for Dyaks completely free love is not only accepted, but encouraged. The moment an adolescent boy feels the attraction of girls, he "goes looking for tobacco" and loses no time in solving the sex-mysteries. Eligible maidens sleep in the loft above their parents' quarters— Jugah had shown us these special apartments and, with a few sly comments and gestures, the ladder connecting the loft with the outside world. The girl receives whom she likes when she likes. The language of love is simple enough. For all her suitors she rolls cigarettes. Tied in one manner, the cigarette means: "Let's talk about books." Tied in another manner, it means: "I'm so glad you came—I'm cold and lonely." Consequently in this utterly natural society there is no such thing as prostitution or repression.

There is such a thing, however, as maternity. But maternity is not unwelcomed, for a girl who has proved her ability to bear a child has all the more reason to expect a permanent child-loving husband and a "home" of her own. If there is any uncertainty about the father, she names the man she suspects (or desires), and the betrothal is announced. But if the boy rebels and refuses to marry her, he need only pay a fine equalling five dollars in our money to the girl's family, and the case is dropped. For a few babies by various previous lovers in no way interfere with the girl's ultimate marriage eligibility.

Such a standard of fines is the punishment of every deviation from a social rule. If a married man goes "hunting for tobacco" and is caught, he must pay a one-dollar fine. If he wishes to divorce his wife, because he's tired of her, the fine is three dollars and a half. But if he is found guilty of their crime of crimes—incest with his aunt—the fine is the maximum—ten dollars, a whole life's savings.

Incest is supposed to bring unfailingly a curse upon the entire tribe. When the rice crop fails, when a plague of cholera comes upon them, when a flood washes away their property, in short, when any dire event happens, the chief begins to look for an incestuous cause. And so prohibited is incest, and consequently so alluring, that he usually finds what he's looking for. The guilty party is denounced, the fine is paid, the plague departs, and everybody is happy.

Their rule against incest is most frequently broken by a father or his son with an adopted daughter, and by a son with his father's second or third or fourth wife's sisters. These sisters are all considered "aunts" and in many cases may be the same age as, or younger than, the guilty boy. In a natural, free-loving society, this last offence seems pardonable enough, as there is no blood relationship. But for some strange reason the knowledge of one's "aunt" is a disastrous, unspeakable sin—yet not so unspeakable that ten dollars paid to the chief doesn't wash everybody clean.

On the second afternoon of our visit, Jugah gave us each a blowpipe and a quiver of darts, such as the Dyaks use in their hunting, and we went out to look for game along the twilit jungle trails leading from the long-house. The power and accuracy of these pipes amazed us. Fifteen feet long, straight, light, hollowed true, they are effective at two hundred feet. The slightest puff sends the dart shooting forth almost faster than the eye can follow. Jugah was a wonderful marksman. He got a wild pig on the run, and brought down half a dozen wood pigeons from the tree-tops. The darts were all dipped in poison, which, while almost instantly fatal to birds and small animals when introduced through a wound, seemed in no way injurious to their flesh. We ate the birds and felt no harmful effects.

Our own first efforts with the blowpipes were completely unsuccessful. We missed everything and used up all our darts. But following Jugah's example, we made little bullets of mud, and found those could be fired through the pipe with the same deadly force as the darts. Jugah killed almost as many pigeons with these tiny mud pellets as with the poisoned arrows.

As entertaining, and even more curious, was our *tuba* fishing. With fish providing for the Dyaks, along with rice, the chief staff of life, they cannot be condemned for the unsportsmanlike way their fish are caught. Tuba is a poison made from the root of a tree; and when it is poured into a stream, all the fish die of suffocation. In preparation for the hundreds of guests due next day, Jugah organised a first-class tuba expedition, and we went along.

He chose a stream that had not been poisoned in several months. A platform sloping into the water was first built across the hundred-foot mouth of the stream. This was to catch the fish when, in their death struggles, they came leaping down-river. Then three canoe-loads of us went half a mile farther up, and with rocks beat to a pulp a hundred pounds of tuba root. The juice, when mixed with water, instantly turns to a milk-white colour. This fatal fluid we poured into the stream, and with nets and spears stood by in our canoes to capture the fish when they came to the surface.

As they began to rise, there were wild shouts of delight from the boatmen. Jugah and his friends had fished this way a hundred times, but from the hullabaloo they made, one would have thought this was a pursuit as new to them as to us.

With paddles flashing and the canoes darting back and forth, we made after the big fellows. Nets were whipped about, spears jabbed into the water. With almost every stroke, a struggling fish was swept into our boats. More shouts on the platform down-stream indicated that they too were busy. The biggest catch of all was there. Fish weighing three and four pounds were splashing about, landing on the platform, and being clubbed by the Dyaks who, brandishing their heavy sticks, were simply dancing with excitement. It was more of a harvest than a hunt, but it was interesting while it lasted.

We returned home with our three dugouts loaded down. This was our contribution to the great feast that would come to-morrow.

CHAPTER XXXII

CHIEF KOH AND THE BE-LOON

MEANWHILE, during my own adventures and observations, Chief Koh was busy indeed. He was expecting several hundred, perhaps even a thousand, visitors for our Bornean flying-meet. For two days basket-loads of rice were made ready; a dozen pigs were killed; and the fish we had caught were cleaned and stored; and rice wine, jars upon jars of it, waited in readiness.

However apprehensive Koh may have been over his forthcoming travels aboard the demon bird, he did not dare express his apprehension now. But the night before, he began imbibing considerably more rice wine than usual; and next morning, when the war-boats big and small began to pour in, old Koh had reached a state wherein he was willing to ride on any bird that flew. And if he had to perish in the clutches of this roaring monster—whoopee!—he would die like a man!

Larger and larger grew the visiting company. Each moment brought new boats and new crews. Soon there was a numerous fleet of dugouts tied along the bank, and a dense group of Dyaks gaping at the Flying Carpet still tied to the dock.

American Indians in all their war-paint and regalia were never arrayed like these dressed-up Borneans. The jungle had been combed for the brightest, longest feathers to be stuck in their huge head-dresses; their bronze chests were half-hidden by yards of necklaces. Many wore a small shoulder-cape made of white monkey fur. Each brave carried his five-foot shield, a sword in its sheath of silver, and a long slim spear. There were high spirits, loud laughter, ardent speculation about the magic bird and what it would do, and why. Jugah went about still explaining that it was a be-loon; but this explained nothing, for nobody knew what *that* was.

At last the great hour arrived. Koh stood at the top of the ladder, drunk as a native lord can get, but still looking, with his noble face, like a brown-skinned Olympian. The most striking thing was the extreme simplicity of his dress. While his guests and his family were ablaze with jewellery and fur and feathers, Chief Koh had *removed* every adornment, even to his earrings. About his loins and down his thighs hung a simple black cotton cloth. Otherwise he was undraped and undecorated.

I wondered if he knew that this simplicity gave him a hundred times the distinction of his barbarically dressed fellows. Did he know that when he descended the steps to meet, as he believed, his destiny, a thousand eyes looked upon him with awe?

We strapped the helmet and goggles over his head, and placed him in the front cockpit. His subjects pressed close about, not even daring to speak now—the situation was too deadly serious, too fraught with magic and with potential disaster for them all.

I cranked the engine. The bird roared. I fastened the safety-belt across Koh and myself, and we glided away from the dock, on around the bend to where the Flying Carpet had first landed. Behind, like the tail of a scarlet comet, a hundred dugouts of all sizes paddled after us. We reached the broad water, motioned to the gallery to keep back, opened the throttle, raced down the river and rose into the air.

I watched Chief Koh. His eyes were very big and exceedingly anxious; he trembled, but seeing my own composure, he relaxed and even looked overboard, grinning, at the flotilla below.

Moye kept us in sight of the canoes. Presently, taking careful aim, he zoomed straight down, within thirty feet of them, and then sky-rocketed a thousand feet back into the sky. The boats scattered like so many water-bugs, but when they saw that the magic bird was only playing a game and not dashing their chief to his death, they waved their spears and feather helmets in wild acclamation.

We flew low over Koh's long-house. We roared up the river at a hundred and twenty miles an hour, just skimming the waves. We raced past the other neighbouring long-houses, to give their inhabitants, too, the thrill of beholding Koh's triumph. For twenty minutes the magic bird carried the chief back and forth, up and down, above the heads of his tribesmen.

When he landed, he was no longer a mere Dyak chief-of-chiefs. He had become almost a deity.

That night our long-house gallery swarmed with five hundred visitors, all ready, *eager*, to pay obeisance anew to the great Koh, who had flown through the air.

Koh himself, bursting with pride, received all this homage solemnly. He had achieved the pinnacle. He, Koh, had done what no other Dyak had ever done since the beginning of his race. But there would be enough broadcasting throughout Borneo of this momentous event, without his having to talk about it.

So he merely sat there quiet and aloof, presiding over the feast, as louder and louder his people sang his praises.

When the time seemed ripe, the Resident asked to have the floor. He translated to the audience of warriors the message of good-will Moye and I had brought to Koh from the Ranee. The Resident eulogised the chief as a conspicuous example of bravery and wisdom; and told how the Great White *Tuan* in Kuching loved him and trusted him to continue leading his people into paths of peace, and dignity, and honour. The Ranee's gift to Koh, which we had brought with us in the Flying Carpet, was then presented—O rarest and loveliest gift in the world!—a hunting rifle!

But Koh was not to be outdone in generosity. With striking eloquence, he launched forth in counterpraise of the Rajah and the Ranee, and swore eternal allegiance to their rule. He had kind things to say for Moye and me, and to demonstrate his appreciation for the distinction we had brought to him, he made us a gift such perhaps as no other foreigner ever received in the history of Borneo—*twelve human heads!*

And still the rice wine flowed, flowed in a steady, inexhaustible stream. The orchestra of gongs and drums and native bagpipes began to resound through the long-house. The rice and fish and pork were brought out, piled mountain high on wicker trays. There was no limit to the food, no bottom to the wine jars.

Happier and happier grew the guests. They crowded around Koh, around Jugah, around the Resident and Moye and me, pressing cups of wine upon us, giving us their bracelets, their necklaces, as presents; offering us their wives and daughters if we'd only come visit *their* longhouses. Jugah, dressed in all his gorgeous belts and feathers, cleared a space and, brandishing sword and shield, danced with superlative grace a wild, leaping, shouting war dance that would have done honour to a Nijinsky. Encouraged by the son of the chief, and animated by the wine, a dozen other young warriors seized their spears and did their best to out-dance the prancing Jugah. Twelve were soon twenty; one orchestra had grown to four; the shouting and singing became almost deafening, echoing and re-echoing out into the dense jungle surrounding us. . . . And down upon this riotous scene looked the rows and rows of black and grinning human heads, mocking this effort to clutch at life, this vainglorious disdain of death; waiting for those who danced to cease their dancing and come to join the grim society of the skulls.

It was a wild, boisterous, abandoned evening—but it was not without its beauty, too. Whoever calls these people savage does not know the Dyaks. Except for the smoked heads, which are after all merely their war monuments, every expression of their nature is intensely appealing. Gentler, more lovable people are not to be found. Clean-hearted, untroubled, artistic, moral in their way, following the simple life Nature intended man to follow— perhaps, heads or no heads, they are wiser, perhaps far more nearly arrived at the ultimate goodness of life, than ourselves.

Those who know the Dyaks hope fervently that they will never change, that the blight of our Western age will never spread to their home in the heart of Borneo. Fortunately, the foremost of their friends is the Rajah of Sarawak himself, who has sworn that as long as he is a power in the land, his children of the jungle will always be allowed to remain natural, simple, beautiful, as they were when his great ancestor first came to Borneo to make a country of his own.

CHAPTER XXXIII

THE FLYING CARPET COMES THROUGH

WHEN Moye and I flew back down-river from Chief Koh's long-house, we had aboard our Flying Carpet one of the strangest cargoes ever carried by an airplane—Koh's gift of human heads.

These heads had created a problem from the very start. In the first place, they were surprisingly heavy—some twelve pounds apiece, or a total of nearly one hundred and fifty pounds. Since leaving America we had been chronically over-loaded with necessary baggage and extra fuel-tanks. And when we had added our extra-large pontoons, this overload had become a serious, indeed a dangerous, problem. True, we had carried third persons several times since the Flying Carpet became a flying-boat, but each time we had first removed the two hundred pounds of books, clothes and spare parts that we always had carried with us. This unburdening of the plane was imperative for safety's sake.

Consequently, when I calmly added another hundred and fifty pounds at the long-house, where we planned to subtract nothing from our load, Moye politely but firmly refused to fly. He also argued that besides being heavy, the heads took up all our baggage space; that they smelled to heaven of stale Dyak and old smoke; and that such passengers would certainly prove to be a jinx.

But on the other hand, we couldn't leave the heads behind. To have done that, since Koh had presented them so formally, would have been a most unpardonable rudeness. Moreover, to injure Koh's sensibilities after we had helped to promote the *entente cordiale* between him and the government, would have been exceedingly poor diplomacy. Anyway, I wanted those heads to put in my what-not back home, as a souvenir of the Flying

Carpet's reception in Borneo. As to the jinx, I didn't believe in hoodoos—yet.

I finally got around Moye's most serious objection by cutting down the baggage load. Thirty pounds of books, my entire cockpit library, were given to the Resident. I next gave half my flying clothes to the delighted Jugah—and half of Moye's when he wasn't looking. That reduced us by twenty pounds more. And then came a stroke of genius—the phonograph. It was no longer much pleasure to us, since most of the music had been played off the records. But its dreadful stridency thrilled Mrs. Koh no end, when we carried it to her, playing full tilt, as a sort of thanks-for-the-week-end gift. That saved twenty-five pounds more. Thus by seventy-five pounds, our load was lightened.

That still wasn't enough. So I began reducing the heads. Two of them were orang-outan skulls which any child would have known were not human heads at all. The most Neanderthaloid man never had a forehead like that. Koh had perhaps insisted to everybody for so long that these two trophies were gained in desperate combat, that he had come to believe it himself; or else he hoped we wouldn't know the difference. They could go out. The Resident wanted them as curios, so without Koh's knowledge we reduced the twelve to ten. One of the ten was crumbling to pieces. It had been cloven half in two by a kris, and only rattan held it together. So we discarded that one also.

Nine were left. But with our suitcases still to go into the baggage compartment, we had no space to carry even nine. This difficulty was solved, too. Dumping the heads into the front cockpit, I sat on them.

As they became warm, the third problem rose to my attention insistently. That offensive odour had to be conquered. Groping among my shaving things in the flap-pocket, I found a bottle of Listerine and sprinkled them with that.

The jinx question, however, baffled me. I could only hope that it was one of Moye's foolish pilot-superstitions, and that by sitting on the heads I'd keep their baleful influence properly suppressed.

Moye still mistrusted my cargo: if changing one's helmet, and carrying crucifixes or flowers, brought bad luck, *think* what nine human heads were going to do!

He was quite genuinely surprised when we reached Sibu, the little Malay-Chinese town a hundred and fifty miles down the Rejang River, entirely without mishap. But sure enough, right away next day, we began to have trouble— the Flying Carpet, with every tank filled for the first time since Singapore, refused to rise from the water. We charged up and down, rocking and lunging, trying to break the clutch of the waveless river upon our pontoons which, with the plane overloaded, sank too deep to permit a take-off.

It was the heads—not their weight, but their evil power. Moye glared at them and at me. I agreed to throw one— just one—overboard, and did so, choosing the heaviest. But it soon became evident that tossing all of them overboard wouldn't lighten us enough to balance our heavy load of fuel. Before we could finally rise from the river, we had to dump our gas, send it ahead to the coast, fly there with only a few gallons, refuel again and take off in the open sea, where the salt water buoyed us up and the waves helped bounce us off.

Our next stop was Brunei, up the coast, a most curious and interesting town, built entirely on stilts above the water of a bottle-neck bay. This bay was the chief stronghold of the China Sea pirates until the time when James Brooke himself drove them out. Here also the Sultan who played such a large part in the history of the first White Rajah, had lived and ruled. His descendant reigns there to-day, over a remnant of the Sultanate from which Brooke wrested Sarawak.

Brunei offers an unexpected sidelight on Borneo, for it claimed distinction as a seat of Malay commerce and culture as far back as the tenth century. But now only a cluster of thatch houses remain, and the commerce and culture are long since forgotten.

I'm sure Moye watched for trouble again when we took off, headed for Sandakan, the capital of British North Borneo. Anyway, we got it. While taxying up the bay, though we both were watching carefully, we hit a log which was so far submerged as to be almost invisible. The result was another terrific dent in our already badly wounded left pontoon.

Overboard went another head. That seemed to be the easiest way to appease Moye, who insisted that I, sitting on my nest of skulls, was only hatching trouble for him.

With only seven heads now, we flew on again.

Moye's superstition had begun to prove contagious. If anything had happened at Sandakan, I too should have been inclined to suspect that my death-heads were exerting an evil influence, and have fed them to the sharks. But for once, we avoided trouble.

Just the calm before the storm . . . !

Having left Borneo behind, and crossed a hundred miles of open sea, we reached one of the southernmost islands of the Philippines—Sulu. Here, with our Carpet anchored in the open harbour, we visited the Sultan—"the wretched Sultan of Sulu." He was a nice old man—and proud of his distinction as the only Sultan ruling under the American flag. We were so taken with his island we might have spent a week there, had disaster not threatened us again.

A freak typhoon, three months ahead of season, came screaming out of the Pacific straight at Sulu. The American radio station there got the warning, and the island steeled itself for the onslaught. Moye and I flung our baggage and my seven heads into the Flying Carpet, and fled at top speed to the protection of the breakwater at Zamboanga, a hundred and fifty miles north on the island of Mindanao.

That night the typhoon struck Sulu with appalling, unpredecented fury. The Sultan's palace was torn to bits; the shores of the harbour where we'd anchored our Carpet were strewn with the wreckage of two score native boats that had sought refuge there—and alas, with the bodies of their crews. Under the torn and twisted wreckage of the town, sixty people were found dead—several, we learned to our distress, whom we had known.

Even at Zamboanga, on the outer edge of the vortex, the wind was terrifying and destructive. Tied stoutly to a buoy in the comparative shelter of the breakwater, the Carpet rode out the storm—and we with it, to be on hand in case it broke its moorings. At the height of the gale I climbed down to see how the pontoon-patch was holding, and instantly Moye, reaching into my cockpit, began throwing overboard those hoodoo-heads. Before I could leap to the rescue of my treasures, three had gone to the bottom of the harbour.

Surely, with only four heads left, we might hope to reach Manila without further incident. And so we would have, had we not suffered a brain storm on hearing about a fantastic lake in the heart of Mindanao, where crocodiles were so abundant that though thirteen thousand had been killed for their skins in recent months, the waters were still alive with the sinister beasts. This lake, called Buluan, had other interesting features. In places, it was said to be completely covered over with a layer of small floating snails. Its banks were bottomless ooze composed of the rotted shells of these snails. Naturally, with such an inexhaustible food supply, water birds flocked there in hundreds of thousands. Wild ducks, particularly, collected in such numbers that shooting them was too easy to be called sport. Crocodiles—snails —ducks—all eating one another in rotation. This sounded like a place worth visiting.

We said good-bye to Zamboanga, and flying eastward for two hours along coast and river, came to the teeming lake, where we dodged the ducks and landed on the snails, surrounded by the crocodiles.

One look at the lake revealed that the tall tales we had heard about the acres of floating snails were true. In fact, near the shore, the stagnant odour of these molluscs, both living and dead, made my smoked heads seem like hyacinths.

For several days Moye and I, stopping with the local constabulary, shot ducks by day and harpooned crocodiles by night. Shooting the big brutes was useless, for they always got away. But in the darkness, a torch revealed their glittering eyes, and a harpoon thrust behind the ugly heads kept our quarry from escaping. We sometimes got a twelve-footer, when it took the combined strength of our boat's crew to pull him close enough to end his struggles.

With the great creatures lashing about in the reeds, and the countless water birds rising up in shrill alarm, it was the most exciting form of hunting in which I've ever taken part. Nor was it mere wanton slaughter, for the marketing of crocodile skins was the local population's chief means of livelihood.

Tired of crocodiles, we turned again toward Manila. But again the heads—according to Moye—did their best to prevent our reaching it. I did not want to admit that I shared his typical flier's-superstition, but misadventures had been coming with such regularity since acquiring the heads, that it seemed illogical to attribute them all to chance.

This time we encountered one of the strangest dangers of all. In Morocco we had flown through a sand-storm; in Timbuctoo, through storks; through terrific winds and fog over the Alps; through snow and hail in Persia; and in Zamboanga, through the backlash of a typhoon. There was only one thing left for us to fly through with our Flying Carpet—and this we met while leaving Mindanao for the north.

Locusts! One large section of the island was being devoured by swarms of these devastating insects, and it was our luck to stir up and bang into a vast barrage of them just as we were taking off from the Buluan River, where we had stopped for fuel. Their myriad bodies struck like hail against every surface of the plane as the propeller tore through their dense formation. Fortunately we avoided learning what might be the result of a prolonged flight in this locust-fog, for Moye, retreating and climbing hurriedly, soon lifted us above the living cloud, which actually hid the earth for at least a mile.

But that night when we came down in the harbour of Cebú, Moye, with this defeat by the bug-battalions in mind, resumed his complaint against Koh's grisly presents. "Why *will* you keep all those horrors, Dick? I tell you, they're going to make a flying hearse out of us yet!"

And so I let him give away two more.

Perhaps because of this capitulation, nothing alarming happened at Cebú. We paused only long enough to pay our respects at the grave of Magellan, whose death there in 1521, during a battle with the natives, ended his command of the first ship to circumnavigate the globe.

Cebú was only one day's flight from Manila. Perfect flying weather prevailed, and our route lay over beautiful and well-sheltered waters. Surely, following such a course on such a brilliant day, we need fear no further calamities—particularly since just two heads remained.

And the flight *would* have been perfect—this five hundred miles of island-dotted sea—if we only had gone on straight to our destination.

But some malign influence urged us to deviate from our course, and in consequence I suffered a personal misfortune which convinced me, finally, that Moye might after all be right in attributing evil powers to my precious, baneful souvenirs. I had to hold something responsible, beyond my own foolhardiness, when I nearly lost my skin!

As we came to the island of Luzon, and had only fifty miles more to reach Manila, we noticed on one side a large and extraordinarily beautiful lake, some twenty miles wide. On our flying map, it was called Lake Taal. In the centre of this lake rose the jagged stump of a volcano, about five miles in diameter. We had learned in Cebú that this is the most famous and most dreaded of all volcanoes in the Philippines. In 1911 it had exploded through a new crater, and killed over fourteen hundred people. After the eruption, water entered the crater through a new earthquake crack, forming a lake a half-mile wide, from the centre of which rose a single huge lava cone. This cone is thus an island in a lake in an island in a lake in an island in the ocean.

When we saw this curious pair of concentric lakes, the temptation to land and explore them was too great to be resisted. The lava-tower in the inner crater made it inadvisable to alight there, so we came down near a native village on the shore of the larger lake. We soon found a guide who rowed us across to the volcano and guided us up to the brink and down to the water inside. The water, of a dark brown colour, looked unpleasant and tasted worse. Our guide also volunteered the fact that it was "not nice to swim in." But I was so warm from the climbing, I disregarded this mild warning, took off my clothes, and swam out around the lava centrepiece.

The water proved unusually buoyant; but this, unfortunately, was not its only distinction. As I swam back, my eyes and skin began to burn, faintly at first but with increasing severity, until by the time I had reached shore again I felt as if I'd been set on fire. It was as though the whole temper of the fiery volcano had been distilled into this pool. Its virulent effect had an explanation simple enough, though I had not thought of it in time. The lake was floored with chemicals cast up from the bowels of the earth, chemicals that had saturated its waters to an incredible degree with caustic poisons. Their irritant action on bare skin had been criminally understated by our native guide.

Still suffering fearfully, I hurried to the outer lake to wash away the corrosives. But not until next day had I cooled off enough to fly again.

"See?" said Moye, when I finished rubbing coconut oil into my burns, back in the village.

"See what?"

"See what the heads——"

"Oh, to hell with the heads. Throw them in the lake. No—give 'em to that guide. The curse may be transferable."

It may have been only the strong tail wind, but as we continued on to Manila, it seemed to both Moye and me as if a sinister spell had been lifted, and that now our guardian angels, who obviously had been routed by the gaze of those evil, hollow skulls, would come back and fly wing-to-wing with the plane until our journey was over.

And it must have been so, for the remaining miles to our destination were reassuringly uneventful.

Nor could we have hoped for a better welcome than we received in Manila. Every day for over two weeks we had reason to congratulate ourselves on having chosen this hospitable and romantic city as the terminus of the Carpet's Far Eastern flight.

When the S.S. *President McKinley*, San Francisco bound, steamed out of Manila Bay that May afternoon, Moye and I and our airplane were aboard her. We watched the sky-line of the city disappear behind . . . and four weeks later, saw the Golden Gate opening ahead.

Rid of the pontoons and equipped with wheels again, the Flying Carpet soared high into the sky of California, turned toward the south and arrived at last above the familiar hills. Like a homing pigeon, the plane spiralled down to the airport from which, one morning some forty thousand miles before, we had set out to see the world.

And now our travels in the air were ended. Moye and I wheeled the old Carpet into a hangar, where bright, impertinently new planes elbowed it for space; and there, for the first time, we realised how much it showed the marks of battle with the elements in a hundred lands. The scarlet was flaked away; the gold was tarnished. Scarred, weather-beaten, very worldly-wise, the Flying Carpet had returned, a veteran of many conflicts and adventures. But each patch it bore seemed to us like a medal honourably won by the old campaigner, for proved valour and fidelity.

Honourably won! Through desert and jungle, Africa and Arabia, Himalaya and the islands of the sea . . . these brave and sturdy wings, these willing and fleet wings, had brought us safely home.

Now they could rest.